A Bibliography of
State Bibliographies,
1970-1982

A Bibliography of
State Bibliographies,
1970-1982

David W. Parish

1985
Libraries Unlimited, Inc. — Littleton, Colorado

Z1223.5

A1
P36
1985

LIBRARIES UNLIMITED, INC.
P.O. Box 263
Littleton, Colorado 80160-0263

Library of Congress Cataloging in Publication Data

Parish, David W.
    A bibliography of state bibliographies, 1970-1982.

    Includes index.
    1. United States--Government publications (State
governments)--Bibliography. 2. Bibliography--
Bibliography--United States--States. 3. United States
--Bibliography. I. Title.
Z1223.5.A1P36   1985   [J83]   015.73'053   85-130
ISBN 0-87287-466-4

Libraries Unlimited books are bound with Type II nonwoven material that meets
and exceeds National Association of State Textbook Administrators' Type II
nonwoven material specifications Class A through E.

*On completion of this fourth reference work
published by Libraries Unlimited, it is time to thank
my wife Ava, son David Andrew, and Milne Library
Director Richard C. Quick for their understanding
over a period of fourteen years. Also, appreciation
is extended to my secretary, Betty A. Blanchard.*

TABLE OF CONTENTS

INTRODUCTION

The United States Government is generally regarded as the world's largest publisher with over 20,000 titles produced annually. Less well known is that state governments also are prodigious publishers. The 1981 *Monthly Checklist of State Publications*, for example, listed 29,466 separate titles. While compiling both editions of *State Government Reference Publications: An Annotated Bibliography*, I realized that many useful bibliographies had been and were being produced by state government agencies, but that no attempt had been made to describe them comprehensively. This work is a first attempt to bring together and make accessible this rich store of information.

Over one thousand titles are listed and annotated. Most have been published between 1970 and 1982, although some important pre-1970 imprints are also included. The Library of Congress definition of a state document as applied in the *Monthly Checklist of State Publications* has been used here. Therefore, bibliographies originating in state colleges and universities were included if listed in the *Monthly Checklist*. Titles from state university presses have been excluded with the following two exceptions: Joint state-federal bibliographical works have been included if the state government body had been largely responsible for publication and distribution; university press publication checklists have been included if important enough to serve as useful bibliographic tools. Puerto Rico and the Virgin Islands are represented, along with all U.S. states, except New Hampshire and Rhode Island.

This work is arranged alphabetically by state and within state alphabetically by subject. Thirty-nine broad subjects (listed on p. xiii) are used to group the bibliographies. Within subject, the arrangement is alphabetical by title. Bibliographic information provided for each item typically includes sponsoring agency, title, personal author if applicable, place, date, pagination, price if known, LC card number if available, and series statement if applicable. Items known to be out of print are so marked. Concise annotations describe the content of each bibliography.

A comprehensive acquisition guide and an agency address list are given in the appendix. Addresses of all agencies or sources of documents noted in each bibliographic entry are provided so that publications can be procured. Sources of state documents including a list of state depository libraries are also provided to facilitate interlibrary loans.

Title and subject indexes complete this guide.

LIST OF SUBJECT HEADINGS

Agriculture

Animal Husbandry

Archaeology/Anthropology

Area Studies

Arid Lands

Arts

Disabled

Drug Use and Abuse

Economy/Economics

Education and Training

Employment

Energy

Environment

Equal Opportunity

General

Geography

Geology

Health

History

Land Use

Language and Linguistics

Laws and Legislation

Libraries

Minority Groups

Native People

Natural Resources

Oceanography

Personalities

Planning

Politics and Government

Recreation/Tourism

Safety

Social Conditions

Space Exploration

Technology

Transportation

Wetlands

Wildlife

Women

EDUCATION AND TRAINING

    1.   Alabama. State Department of Education. **Alabama State Adopted Textbook List, 1982-83.** Montgomery, 1982. 171pp. Free.

The textbooks are arranged by subject areas and are also listed alphabetically by publisher. Each text is noted as being either basic or supplementary. The over eighteen hundred texts provide a current bibliography of teaching materials in all curricular areas for all grade levels.

GEOLOGY

    2.   Alabama. Geological Survey. **Alabama Coastal Region Ecological Characterization: Coastal Bibliography.** (By Patrick E. O'Neil, Maurice F. Mettee, and Elizabeth J. McCullough) Tuscaloosa, 1982. 404pp. $5.00. Information Series No. 60.

This bibliography with over one thousand citations is a major guide to the most important titles on the Alabama coastal areas.

    3.   Alabama. Geological Survey. **Bibliography of Alabama Geology, 1935-1958.** (By E. L. Hastings) Tuscaloosa, 1960. 138pp. $1.75. Bulletin No. 67.

This landmark bibliography includes over nine hundred reports on all aspects of geology, many published by the Survey.

    4.   Alabama. Geological Survey. **Hydrology of Limestone Terranes, Progress of Knowledge about Hydrology of Carbonate Terranes ... with an Annotated Bibliography of Carbonate Rocks.** (By William M. Warren and James D. Moore) Tuscaloosa, 1975. 168pp. $2.25. Bulletin No. 94E.

Almost eight hundred citations on all aspects of carbonate rocks are included.

    5.   Alabama. Geological Survey. **Index and List of the Publications of the Geological Survey of Alabama and the State Oil and Gas Board.** Tuscaloosa, 1983. 49*l*. Free.

This list has over one thousand biennial reports, bulletins, circulars, information series titles, monographs, oil and gas reports, and maps. There is an excellent subject index that increases the bibliography's value as a reference tool.

6. Alabama. Marine Resources Laboratory. **A Selected Bibliography of Alabama Estuaries.** (By Johnie H. Crance) Dauphin Island, 1969. 21pp. Free. LC card No. 71-2350. Marine Resource Bulletin No. 2.

"The purpose of this bibliography is to provide references to published and unpublished information germane to Alabama estuaries." There are 275 citations arranged alphabetically by author followed by a chronological arrangement.

HISTORY

7. Alabama. University, Library. **Confederate Imprints in the University of Alabama Library.** (Compiled by Sara Elizabeth Mason) University, 1961. 156*l*. Out-of-Print. LC card No. 62-62614.

Over one thousand official publications issued by the central government of the Confederate States of America are described. A listing by each state of the Confederacy is also included. This historic work was completed in collaboration with Lucile Crutcher and Sarah A. Verner.

NATURAL RESOURCES

8. Alabama. Geological Survey. **Bibliography of the Mineral Resources of Alabama, Exclusive of Coal, Iron, and Petroleum.** (By Oscar E. Gilbert, Jr.) Tuscaloosa, 1980. 53pp. $1.75. Geological Circular No. 93.

Over four hundred citations on the mineral resources of Alabama are included.

9. Alabama. Geological Survey. **Ground-water Investigations in Alabama with a Selected Bibliography.** (By W. J. Powell and P. E. LaMoreaux) Tuscaloosa, 1960. 4pp. $1.75. LC card No. 6558-191 rev. Information Series No. 15.

This is considered a classic bibliography on ground water in Alabama, aquifers, and problem areas.

PLANNING

10. Alabama. Development Office. **A Selected Bibliography of Alabama Local Planning and Development Documents since 1973.** (By Mark Worsham) Montgomery, 1976. 1 vol. $1.00. LC card No. 74-193647.

"The purpose of this bibliography is to present on a current basis the comprehensive views of local planning for select urban and rural communities in Alabama." It acts as a supplement to the *Selected List for 1939-1973*. Over two hundred studies are included.

GENERAL

11.   Alaska. Historical Commission. **Alaska: An Introductory Reading List.**
      (By Stephen W. Haycox) Anchorage, 1979. 14pp. $3.00.
Compiled by a university teacher of Alaskan history, this annotated bibliography is
organized into sections on anthropology and history, the discovery of Alaska,
Russian America, the transfer of Alaska to the United States, the early period of
Alaska, the turn of the century, and contemporary Alaska.

12.   Alaska. Agricultural College and School of Mines. **A Bibliography of
      Alaskan Literature, 1724-1924.** Fairbanks, 1928. 635pp. Out-of-Print.
      Miscellaneous Publication No. 1.
Histories, accounts of travel and voyages, newspapers, and periodical articles
in the English, Russian, German, French, and Spanish languages comprise this
bibliography of Alaskan literature.

13.   Alaska. University, College. Institute of Social, Economic, and Govern-
      ment Research. **Comprehensive Publications List.** College, 1983. 69pp.
      Free.
This is a publication list of studies done by the institute, offering approximately
twelve hundred citations arranged into twenty-four subject categories. Topics
include Alaska natives, demography, energy, forestry, international studies, public
finance, recreation, and social services. A wealth of studies on Alaska and Arctic
regions are represented.

14.   Alaska. University, Anchorage. Arctic Environmental Information and
      Data Center. **Current Research Profile for Alaska, 1979.** Anchorage,
      1980. 420pp. Free.
A total of 1,674 research projects on Alaska in the natural and social sciences,
with related publications, are included. Information provided includes the name
and address of the researcher, a one-paragraph review of the project, and descriptive key words. There are both subject and regional indexes.

ARCHAEOLOGY/ANTHROPOLOGY

15.   Alaska. Division of Parks. **Alaskan Archaeology: A Bibliography.** (By
        Karen Wood Workman) Anchorage, 1972- . Irregular. Price on application.
This document was prepared for use by the Division of Parks, in response to their
"need to know the history of archaeological work in Alaska." There are over twelve
hundred citations—including periodical articles, anthropological papers from the
University of Alaska, manuscripts, and Smithsonian reports—arranged alphabetically by author, with each author's work then arranged chronologically.

DRUG USE AND ABUSE

16.   Alaska. Historical Commission. **Alaska Alcohol History.** (By Thayne I.
        Andersen) Anchorage, 1981. 25pp. $1.00.
This annotated bibliography lists Alaskan materials that relate to the history of
alcohol use and abuse in that state. Alcoholism in Alaska is a serious social problem
that has been widely researched.

ECONOMY/ECONOMICS

17.   Alaska. University, Anchorage. Arctic Environmental Information and
        Data Center. **Alaska Subsistence Bibliography.** (By Patricia O'Brien
        McMillan) Anchorage, 1982. 216pp. Price on application. LC card No.
        83-622263.
This bibliography is based on the subsistence database of the Alaska Division of
Subsistence. It was prepared in cooperation with the Alaska Native Rights Protec-
tion Branch. It has over seven hundred citations and is designated Phase I.

18.   Alaska. Joint Federal-State Land Use Planning Commission for Alaska.
        Bibliography on Alaskan Subsistence. (By Terry A. Tuten and John M.
        Eckhart) Juneau, 1977. 63pp. Out-of-Print.
This is an excellent bibliography specializing on the economic aspects of subsistence and survival in Alaska. It is designated to be used with the subsistence bibliographies issued by the Department of Fish and Game, listed below.

19.   Alaska. Department of Fish and Game. **Regional Subsistence Bibliography:**
        Volume I, North Slope Alaska. Juneau, 1982. 1 vol. Free. Technical Paper
        No. 1.
"The first in a series of regional subsistence bibliographic publications, this bibliography includes a wide range of topics dealing with subsistence activities, economics,
and culture of Alaska's North Slope." There are 665 works, each with a brief
abstract and indexed by key word.

20.   Alaska. Department of Fish and Game. **Regional Subsistence Bibliography: Volume II, Interior Alaska**. Juneau, 1982. 1 vol. Free. Technical Paper No. 2.

This bibliography presents references on a wide range of topics concerning various aspects of subsistence in Alaska's interior region. The document references 473 works; each citation includes a brief abstract and is indexed by key word and author.

21.   Alaska. Department of Fish and Game. Division of Subsistence. **Regional Subsistence Bibliography: Volume III, Northwest Alaska**. (By David B. Andersen) Juneau, 1984. 147pp. Free.

This is the third in a series of regional bibliographies on subsistence in Alaska. These publications are an outgrowth of a computerized literature database compiled by the division. There are 434 citations included on all aspects of the lives of Alaska residents living in the Northwest boundary area between Cape Thompson and Unalakleet. Most citations have ample annotations.

ENVIRONMENT

22.   Alaska. University, Anchorage. Arctic Environmental Information and Data Center. **Comprehensive Bibliography and Index of Environmental Information along the Three Alternative Gas Pipeline Routes**. Anchorage, 1979. 1 vol. with supplement included. $11.75, paperback; $3.00, microfiche.

This is an important pipeline bibliography, originally compiled for the U.S. Department of Energy, including three hundred citations about the route.

23.   Alaska. University, Fairbanks. Alaska Sea Grant Program. **Literature Search Survey of Spray Icing on Small Fishing Vessels**. (By Robert F. Carlsob, John P. Zarling, and Charlotte I. Hok) Fairbanks, 1982. 44pp. $5.00. Alaska Sea Grant Report No. 82-5.

"Vessel icing is one of the most dangerous phenomena a fisherman can encounter." The objectives of this bibliography were to "determine state-of-the-art methods for dealing with ice accretion." There are 198 citations; many with annotations.

24.   Alaska. University, Anchorage. Arctic Environmental Information and Data Center. **Prince William Sound: An Annotated Bibliography and Index**. Anchorage, 1979. 180pp. $4.00, microfiche.

Over six hundred citations on the ecology and geology of Prince William Sound in the Arctic region are covered in this specialized bibliography.

GEOLOGY

25.   Alaska. Division of Geological Survey. **Bibliography of Alaskan Geology, 1831-1918**. (By C. E. Fritts and M. E. Brown) College, 1971. 88p. $1.00. Special Report No. 21.

This report serves not only a bibliography of over six hundred citations, but as a record of early exploration in Alaska, as well.

26. Alaska. Division of Geological Survey. **Bibliography of Alaskan Geology, 1919-1949.** (Compiled by Crawford E. Fritts and Mildred E. Brown) College, 1971? 92pp. $3.00. Special Report No. 22.

Over four hundred reports, open-file materials, and maps are included in this major record of Alaskan geology.

27. Alaska. Division of Geological Survey. **Bibliography of Alaskan Geology, 1950-1959.** (Compiled by Crawford E. Fritts and Mildred E. Brown) College, 1971. 83pp. $1.00. LC card No. 72-610110. Special Report No. 23.

This bibliography cites over five hundred geologic reports from all geographic areas of Alaska.

28. Alaska. Division of Mines and Geology. **Geological Literature on the Cook Inlet Region and Vicinity, Alaska.** (By J. C. Maher and W. M. Trollman) College, 1979? 82pp. $1.50. LC card No. NUC70-72009.

This bibliography, completed cooperatively with the U.S. Geological Survey, contains over 250 citations on the Cook Inlet region.

29. Alaska. Division of Geological and Geophysical Surveys. **Geological Literature on the Copper River Basin and Middle Tanana River Basins.** (By K. S. Emmel and P. L. Coonrod) College, 1982. 11pp. $5.00. Special Report No. 30.

Approximately one hundred geological citations are included on these Alaskan areas.

30. Alaska. Division of Geological and Geophysical Surveys. **Geological Literature on the North Slope of Alaska.** (By K. S. Emmel) College, 1982. 127pp. $5.00. Special Report No. 29.

An important bibliography on the North Slope oil development area, containing over seven hundred citations.

31. Alaska. Division of Geological and Geophysical Surveys. **List of DGGS Reports by Region and Quadrangle.** College, 1983. 46pp. Free. Information Circular No. 27.

This document is a compilation by region and quadrangle location of all reports published by the division. There are over five hundred reports divided into Alaska generally, northern, western, eastern, southwestern, south-central, and southeastern Alaska, the Peninsula, Kodiak, and reports by quadrangle.

32. Alaska. Division of Geological and Geophysical Surveys. **List of Informal Reports Issued by the Alaska Division of Geological and Geophysical Surveys.** College, 1983. 38pp. Free.

In January 1983, DGGS began publishing a new category of report, the report of investigations. The two hundred reports listed in this publication are either reports of investigation or open-file reports. Price and date of release are listed.

HEALTH

33.　Alaska. University, Fairbanks. Rasmuson Library. **Arctic Regions Psychology: A Bibliography**. Fairbanks, 1971. 9*l*. Out-of-Print.

Approximately one hundred citations, taken mainly from *Psychological Abstracts* (1927-1970) and the *Arctic Bibliography* (v. 1-14), present an overview of psychology, alcohol habits, alcoholism, suicide, and mental depression in the Arctic regions of the world.

HISTORY

34.　Alaska. Historical Commission. **An Annotated Bibliography for the Nenana River Valley**. (By Jean A. Murray) Anchorage, 1982. 32pp. Price on application.

This is primarily a bibliography of historical sources; writings on the region between Nenana and Cantwell are recorded with some 150 citations.

35.　Alaska. State Library. **Education in Russian Alaska**. (By J. Lincoln Starr) Juneau, 1972. 50pp. Free. Historic Monograph No. 2.

This bibliographic survey of education in Alaska before 1867 includes chapters on mission schools, secular education, religious seminaries, and a summary analysis. It contains 211 citations in English and thirty-nine primary Russian sources. A separate supplement includes a glossary and highlights of educational history in Russian Alaska.

36.　Alaska. Historical Commission. **Filipino-Alaska: A Heritage**. (By Sue Ellen Liljeblad) Anchorage, 1980. 25pp. $2.50.

This bibliography presents over one hundred citations on the history of Filipinos in Alaska, focusing on their role in the canneries and labor unions.

37.　Alaska. Historical Commission. **Focus on Interior History**. (By Jonathon McCauley Nielson) Anchorage, 1980. 49pp. Price on application.

This is a useful bibliography for historical or ecological research; its three hundred citations place Alaska's past in regional perspective.

38.　Alaska. Historical Commission. **History of Transportation and Communication in Alaska**. (By Caedmon Liburd) Anchorage, 1980. 14pp. $1.40.

Over one hundred citations offer a history of land and water transportation and Alaskan mail and electronic communications.

39.　Alaska. Historical Commission. **An Interpretive Survey of Alaska's Military History 1867-1979**. (By Jon M. Nielson) Anchorage, 1980. 25pp. $2.50 plus postage.

This is a bibliography of Alaska's military history from its purchase by the United States to the present. There are over one hundred citations; the World War II period is particularly well covered.

40. Alaska. Historical Commission. **Missionaries in Alaska: A Historical Survey to 1920.** (By Michael D. Waggoner) Anchorage, 1980. 12pp. Price on application.

The history of Christian missionary activity in Alaska since the beginning of settlement is recorded in one hundred citations.

41. Alaska. Historical Commission. **Publications and Research Reports Supported by the Alaska Historical Commission, 1973-1983.** Anchorage, 1982. 20*l*. Free.

This is a bibliographic price list with over two hundred historical publications on all aspects of Alaskan life; information on acquisition is included.

NATIVE PEOPLE

42. Alaska. University, College. Institute of Social, Economic, and Government Research. **Alaska Eskimos: A Selected Annotated Bibliography.** (By Arthur E. Hippler and John R. Wood) College, 1977. 333pp. $15.00. ISER Report No. 45.

This is a major bibliography containing over one thousand citations on all aspects of Eskimo culture.

43. Alaska. University, College. Institute of Social, Economic, and Government Research. **Alaska Native Land Claims Bibliography.** (By Victor Fischer) College, 1978. 12pp. Free.

Over one hundred citations on all aspects of the Native Claims Law are presented in this bibliography, which was used at the Seventh Libraries Colloquy sponsored by the Centre d'Etudes Arctiques.

44. Alaska. University, College. Institute of Social, Economic, and Government Research. **Aleut Bibliography.** (By Dorothy Jones and John R. Wood) College, 1975. 193pp. $15.00. ISER Report No. 44.

The economic and social aspects of Aleut life in Alaska are covered in over six hundred citations.

45. Alaska. State Library. **Bibliography of Alaska Native Organizations and Selected References on Alaska Native Land Claims.** Juneau, 1971. 7*l*. Free.

This bibliography has approximately one hundred citations in the categories of native organizations, specific organizations, legal history of the Tlingit, and federal documents pertaining to native land claims.

46. Alaska. Department of Education. Bilingual-Bicultural Program. **Bibliography of Educational Publications for Alaska Native Languages.** (Compiled by Jane McGary) Juneau, 1978. 168pp. Free.

This bibliography of printed school materials useful for Alaska natives "attempts to collect in one document all materials printed from 1968-78." The annotations are descriptive rather than evaluative. There are fourteen Indian language divisions and six for Eskimo-Aleut. Each section is divided into general, reference, and educational categories. A supplemental list of 1978-79 materials is appended.

47. Alaska. University, Fairbanks. Center for Cross-Cultural Studies. **Bibliography of Publications**. Fairbanks, 1980. 11*l*. Free.
Fifty-eight titles on Native Alaskan schools, crosscultural teaching, and specific tribes are included in this bibliography. Many of the works cited deal with the problems of rural students attending urban high schools. Full bibliographic information and cost are provided.

48. Alaska. University, College. Institute of Social, Economic, and Government Research. **Eskimo Acculturation: A Selected Annotated Bibliography of Alaskan and Other Eskimo Acculturation Studies.** (By Arthur E. Hippler) College, 1970. 209pp. $5.00. LC card No. 70-634618. Research Report No. 28.
Over one thousand citations on Eskimo culture and adjustment to modern life are included in this important bibliography for sociologists and anthropologists. It was updated by the author in 1978.

49. Alaska. University, Fairbanks. Department of English. **Selected Bibliography of Alaska Native Literature in English Translations and Versions.** (By John W. Bernet) Fairbanks, 1977. 3*l*. Free.
Here is an unusual bibliography of both texts and tales found in monographs and journals since 1902. These sources would be useful for teachers needing supplemental materials on Eskimo culture.

50. Alaska. University, College. Institute of Social, Economic, and Government Research. **Subarctic Athabascans: A Selected Annotated Bibliography.** (By Arthur E. Hippler and John R. Wood) College, 1974. 331pp. $15.00. LC card No. 74-620010. ISER Report No. 39.
This report provides a comprehensive bibliography on all aspects of Athabascan life.

NATURAL RESOURCES

51. Alaska. University, Fairbanks. Institute of Water Resources. **Alaska Water Resources: Selected Abstracts, 1974.** (Compiled by Charles Hartman and Sheila Finch) Fairbanks, 1977. 60pp. Free.
This bibliography of Alaskan water research is arranged into ten broad subjects and sixty subcategories. Title, author(s), availability, and a lengthy digest for each is included.

52. Alaska. University, Fairbanks. Institute of Water Resources. **Cold Climate Water/Wastewater Transportation and Treatment: A Bibliography.** (By Timothy Tilsworth and others) Fairbanks, 1977. 135pp. Free. IWR Report No. 72.
This bibliography contains fourteen hundred citations, including published and unpublished papers, on cold climate water and wastewater transportation and treatment systems. Both state and federal titles are listed. Arrangement is alphabetical by author with a minimum of bibiliographical data supplied.

53.   Alaska. University, Fairbanks. Alaska Sea Grant Program. **Marine Mineral Bibliography for Alaska.** (By Joan S. Zenan and P. H. Brommelsick) Fairbanks, 1976. 20pp. $5.00. LC card No. 77-621110. Sea Grant Report No. 76-10.

This document presents over one hundred citations on ocean mining and mineral deposits in Alaska.

OCEANOGRAPHY

54.   Alaska. University, Fairbanks. Alaska Sea Grant Program. **Bibliography of Marine Teaching Materials.** (By R. S. Lee and F. F. Wright) Fairbanks, 1976. 40pp. Free. Marine Science Curriculum Aid No. 1.

This bibliography of marine teaching materials offers over one hundred useful teaching sources for elementary and secondary school levels.

PLANNING

55.   Alaska. Department of Community and Regional Affairs. Division of Community Planning. **Bibliography of Planning Reports, 1973-1977.** Juneau, 1978. 7pp. Free.

This is a complete listing of reports authored by the department on even the smallest communities of Alaska. It is also available on loan from the Alaska State Library.

WILDLIFE

56.   Alaska. Department of Fish and Game. **Abstracts: Annual Performance Reports for Federal Aid in Fish Restoration and Anadromous Fish Studies.** Juneau, 1982. 22pp. Free.

A review of twenty-eight well-annotated reports on Alaska fisheries with the emphasis on trout, salmon, and general sport fishing in popular rivers and streams.

57.   Alaska. University, Fairbanks. Institute of Arctic Biology. **Bibliography of Fishes of the Beaufort Sea and Adjacent Regions.** (By William E. Pfeifer) Fairbanks, 1977. 76pp. Price on application. A Biological Paper of the Institute, No. 17.

This paper is very important as a guide to over four hundred citations on the Beaufort Sea.

58.   Alaska. Department of Fish and Game. **Bibliography of Selected References to the Tanner Crab Genus *Chionoecetes*.** (By William E. Donaldson and David M. Hicks) Kodiak, 1978. 24pp. Free. Fish and Game Informational Leaflet No. 174.

One hundred citations are included in this comprehensive, specialized bibliography on the tanner crab.

59. Alaska. Department of Fish and Game. **Bibliography of the Parasites, Diseases, and Disorders of Several Important Wild Ruminants of the Northern Hemisphere.** (By Kenneth Neiland and Clarice Dukeminier) Juneau, 1972. 172pp. Free. LC card No. 73-620633. Wildlife Technical Bulletin No. 3.

This is a unique bibliography on big game fauna disorders, including those of the reindeer, caribou, moose, sheep, mountain goat, and deer. There is a section for each type of fauna, subdivided by protozoa, helminths, arthropods, and bacterial and viral pathogens. Over two thousand briefly annotated citations are included.

60. Alaska. University, Fairbanks. Marine Advisory Division. **A Guide to Marine Prey of Juvenile Salmon.** (By Judy MacDonald Paul) Fairbanks, 1982. 58pp. Free. Sea Grant Advisory Bulletin No. 12.

This is a bibliographic guide to literature, mainly journal articles, on approximately twenty salmon predators.

61. Alaska. University, Fairbanks. Alaska Sea Grant Program. **Life History of the Snow Crab,** *Chionoecetes opilio:* **A Literature Review.** (By Albert E. Adams) Fairbanks, 1978. 141pp. $7.00. Sea Grant Report No. 78-13.

This is a major bibliography on the snow crab, offering over four hundred citations and a thorough index.

62. Alaska. Cooperative Wildlife Research Unit. **Sandhill Crane Bibliography, 1950-1974.** (By D. Ilgenfritz) Fairbanks, 1974. 1 vol. Free.

Over five hundred citations are included in this bibliography on the habits of the sandhill crane.

ARID LANDS

63. Arizona. University, Tucson. Office of Arid Land Studies. **Arid Land Abstracts**. Tucson, 1972- . Irregular. Free.
Each edition of these abstracts includes approximately two hundred entries in the following categories: environmental engineering, fauna, geography, land use, range movement, surface materials, vegetation, water resources, weather and climate, and bibliographies. Author and subject indexes are provided.

64. Arizona. University, Tucson. Office of Arid Land Studies. **Arid Land Abstracts: Desert Animals**. Tucson, 1974. 120pp. Free. Arid Land Abstracts No. 5.
Included in this collection of abstracts are citations for 212 books, periodical articles, and state documents relating to desert fauna. Many foreign studies have been included. Most entries are amply annotated. Arrangement is alphabetical by author followed by year of publication. Both subject and author indexes are included.

65. Arizona. State University, Tempe. Laboratory of Climatology. State Climatologist. **Bibliography of Precipitation and Runoff in the Arid Region of North America**. Tempe, 1978. 1 vol. $5.00. Bibliographic Series No. 5.
This is an excellent bibliography of over five hundred citations covering all aspects of arid land runoff.

66. Arizona. University, Tucson. Office of Arid Land Studies. **Sonoran Desert: A Retrospective Bibliography**. Tucson, 1976. 1 vol. Free.
This bibliography presents 777 abstracts on the Sonoran Desert—"the second richest world desert"—arranged into sections on the environment, fauna, geomorphology, geography, surface materials, vegetation, water, and weather. There are author and key-word-in-context indexes.

ENERGY

67. Arizona. State University, Tempe. Laboratory of Climatology. **Bibliography of Solar Energy Instrumentation Measurement Network Design.** (By S. Brazel) Tempe, 1976. 1 vol. $5.00. Bibliographic Series No. 1.

Over one hundred highly technical solar energy studies are included.

ENVIRONMENT

68. Arizona. State University, Tempe. Laboratory of Climatology. State Climatologist. **Drought: A Selected Bibliography.** (By A. Hasemeirer) Tempe, 1977. 1 vol. $5.00. Bibliographic Series No. 3.

Over 150 citations on the problem of drought in the Southwestern United States and how it can be overcome are included in this compilation.

NATURAL RESOURCES

69. Arizona. Water Commission. **Bibliography of U.S. Geological Survey Water-Resources Reports for Arizona, May 1965 through June 1971.** Phoenix, 1972. 60pp. Free. LC card No. 73-620597. Bulletin No. 2.

This bulletin, prepared cooperatively by the U.S. Geological Survey and the Arizona Water Commission, lists over 150 water resources reports for all parts of Arizona.

70. Arizona. University, Tucson. Institute of Government Research. **Natural Resources in the Governmental Process.** Tucson, 1970. 99pp. $3.00.

This bibliography provides an extensive classified collection of monographs and journal articles in the field of governmental policy related to natural areas. Citations are arranged by resource and by river basin developmental areas with particular emphasis on water resource development.

PLANNING

71. Arizona. Department of Economic Planning and Development. **Annotated List of Publications, 1968-1972.** Phoenix, 1972. 1 vol. Free.

This is a bibliography containing seventy-five Arizona planning studies grouped into five categories: statewide and general information, community planning, working papers, economic research, and reports under preparation. Ample annotations are provided.

WILDLIFE

72.   Arizona. Department of Game and Fish. **Wildlife Research in Arizona, 1976-1977**. Phoenix, 1977. 32pp. Free.

This short bibliography of bird and mammal research presents the state of the art. Project title, objectives, a summary of progress, and investigators are cited.

DISABLED

73.   Arkansas. Rehabilitation Research and Training Center. **Rural Rehabilita-
      tion: A State of the Art.** (By Leland Michael and Mary Jo Schneider)
      Hot Springs, 1982. 100pp. $2.00.
This is the first of two reports of the center's Rehabilitation Service Needs of the
Rural Disabled project. This first report is designed to familiarize the reader with
existing literature pertaining to the characteristics and problems of the rural
disabled.

EDUCATION AND TRAINING

74.   Arkansas. Rehabilitation Research and Training Center. **Selected
      Abstracts: Case Weighting Systems in Vocational Rehabilitation.** (By
      Paul Cooper, Jim Harper, and Linda Vest) Hot Springs, 1978. 111pp.
      One free copy.
Over three hundred documents, representing the "most relevant and useful publications relating to case weighting systems" have been assembled for this bibliography.
Included are professional journals, federal studies, and working papers from vocational agencies, which are organized into sections on weighted systems, case difficulty, evaluation of counselor performance, design methodology, and related
literature.

75.   Arkansas. Rehabilitation Research and Training Center. **Studies of Clinical
      Judgement 1960-1970: An Annotated Bibliography.** (By Brian Bolton et
      al.) Hot Springs, 1972. 33pp. Free.
This document was prepared for the dual purposes of providing an overview of
research on clinical judgement during the decade of the 1960s and for providing
a basis for a synthesis of findings for rehabilitation counselors. Most of the 170
annotated entries were obtained from *Psychological Abstracts.* The following
subject headings are used: clinical, personality, social, developmental, industrial,
counseling, abnormal, therapy, and guidance.

ENERGY

76. Arkansas. Industrial Development Commission. Energy Office. **Energy Bibliography**. Little Rock, 1980- . 1 vol. Free.

These short bibliographies are designed as source documents for the layman, emphasizing conservation and power resources. They are coauthored with the National Center for Appropriate Technology and the National Solar Heating and Cooling Information Center.

LAND USE

77. Arkansas. Division of Community Affairs. **Land Use Terms and Source Materials**. Little Rock, 1973. 18*l*. Free.

One of a group of background papers being used by the state's Department of Planning, this publication lists materials available at the department for reference. The bibliography includes over 250 books and documents on general land use and land use specific to the state of Arkansas.

NATURAL RESOURCES

78. Arkansas. Geological Commission. **Bibliography and Selected Abstracts of Reports on Water Resources and Related Subjects for Arkansas through 1975**. (By R. T. Sniegocki) Little Rock, 1976. 237pp. Free. Water Resources Summary No. 10.

Over two hundred citations are included in this important bibliography, with sections on the nature of water, water supply, quantity, management, planning, resource data, engineering work, and manpower. Most of the works cited have comprehensive annotations; there is a subject index.

AGRICULTURE

79. California. Biological Control Services Program. **Bibliography of the Mediterranean Fruit Fly**, *Ceratitis capitata.* (By Venita Kent-Basham) Sacramento, 1980. 150pp. Free.
This 649-citation bibliography, based on Agricola data, was prepared at the time California was threatened by this fly. It has been updated (see below).

80. California. Biological Control Services Program. **Current Research on the Mediterranean Fruit Fly (*Ceratitis capitata*) as of December 22, 1980.** Sacramento, 1980. 37*l*. Free.
This is an updated bibliography on the Kent-Basham bibliography of 1980. It includes an additional forty-two citations based on several database searches.

81. California. Giannini Foundation of Agricultural Economics. **Economic Research of Interest to Agriculture, 1976-1978.** Berkeley, 1979. 52pp. Free.
"This bibliography represents the research activities of the Agricultural Economics Group of the Foundation." The approximately eight hundred reports are listed in part I by economic classification and in part II by commodity classification. Part III includes only those items which pertain explicitly to particular farm products.

82. California. Giannini Foundation of Agricultural Economics. Library. **Economic Research of Interest to Agriculture, 1979-1981.** (By Grace Dote) Berkeley, 1982. 64pp. Price on application.
This bibliography of holdings found in the Giannini Foundation library offers two hundred agriculturally related reports on California and on the United States in general. Those of an economic classification are included in part I, while part II is organized by commodity classification. Some important subjects emphasized in part I include marketing, economic theory, pricing, and supplies.

83. California. State Library. **Land, Agriculture, and the Family Farm.** (By E. Barbara Taylor) Sacramento, 1977. 17pp. Free. Agricultural Research Library Special Bibliography No. 1.
A useful bibliography for researchers as well as farmers, this collection of 150 items is divided into sections on general agriculture, agriculture in California, research,

land, urbanization, regulations, and alternatives. A supplement was issued in December 1977, and a second supplement in 1979 (see below).

84.   California. State Library. **Land, Agriculture, and the Family Farm, Supplement.** Sacramento, 1979. 3*l.* Free.

This bibliography on the American farm family of the late 1970s supplements a 1977 title. It consists mostly of government publications. Arrangement is by author.

85.   California. Prune Board. **Prune Research Abstracts, 1982.** San Francisco, 1982. 15*l.* Free.

A unique bibliography of over fifty citations on the economic aspects of prunes.

86.   California. Giannini Foundation of Agricultural Economics. **Research of Interest to Agriculture, 1970-1972.** Berkeley, 1973. 35pp. Free.

A representative bibliography of almost 350 major works found at the foundation. Part I includes titles in fifteen various economic categories. Part II is divided by eight commodity classifications.

ARCHAEOLOGY/ANTHROPOLOGY

87.   California. University, Berkeley. Department of Anthropology. **A Bibliography of California Archaeology.** (Compiled by Robert F. Geizer and Albert Elsasser) Berkeley, 1970. 78pp. Price on application.

This selective bibliography assists in locating resources on California regional archaeology. There are over sixteen hundred citations on physical, ethnographic, and biological backgrounds. Special features include sections on Indian flint clippings and early man.

88.   California. University, Berkeley. Department of Anthropology. **Bibliographical History of California Anthropological Research 1850-1917.** (By Elizabeth Wuertele) Berkeley, 1975. 116pp. Price on application. Contribution No. 26.

This is a bibliographic record of California anthropology since statehood (1850). Some three hundred citations are divided first by ten-year periods and then according to general surveys, archaeology, and ethnology. There are author, subject, and tribal indexes.

89.   California. Department of Parks and Recreation. **Selected Bibliography of Maidu Ethnography and Archaeology.** (By Norman L. Wilson and Arlean Towne) Sacramento, 1979. 78pp. Free.

This in-depth bibliography on the Maidu Indians of California includes over three hundred citations, both historic and current.

AREA STUDIES

90. California. University, San Diego. Library. **Bibliography on European Integration: List of the Books, Documents, and Periodicals.** (By Andrew Szabo and Walter H. Posner) San Diego, 1967. 62pp. Price on application. LC card No. 68-64202.

First published in 1965 under the title *Bibliography on the Economics and Political Integration of Europe*, this is an excellent bibliography on the European Common Market and European politics of the 1960s. There are approximately 250 citations.

91. California. State University, Los Angeles. Latin American Studies Center. **Black Latin America: A Bibliography.** Los Angeles, 1977. 74pp. $4.50. Latin American Bibliography No. 5.

This bibliography, part of the center's Latin American Bibliography Series, presents 1,274 sources on blacks in Latin America.

92. California. State University, Los Angeles. Latin American Studies Center. **Central America: A Bibliography.** Los Angeles, 1980. 112pp. $4.75. Latin American Bibliography No. 2.

This is a timely bibliography of Central America, citing 1,756 sources.

93. California. State University, Los Angeles. Latin American Studies Center. **Chile: A Bibliography.** (By Robert Oppenheimer) Los Angeles, 1977. 91pp. $4.50. Latin American Bibliography No. 6.

An excellent bibliography presenting 1,303 entries on current social and political events in Chile.

94. California. State University, Los Angeles. Latin American Studies Center. **Latin America and Japan: A Bibliography.** Los Angeles, 1975. 19pp. $3.50. Latin American Bibliography No. 1.

This specialized bibliography offers almost two hundred citations on the relationship between Latin America and Japan.

95. California. State University, Los Angeles. Latin American Studies Center. **Military and Politics in Latin America: A Bibliography.** (By Herbert Gooch) Los Angeles, 1979. 76pp. $4.75. Latin American Bibliography No. 7.

A current bibliography of 939 citations on the strong influence of the military in Latin America.

ARTS

96. California. State University, Los Angeles. Latin American Studies Center. **Latin American Women Writers in English Translation: A Bibliography.** (By Graciela N. V. Corvalan) Los Angeles, 1980. 109pp. $4.50. Latin American Bibliography No. 9.

This noncritical bibliography includes 282 citations. Writings from colonial times to the present of over four hundred women are listed. A special section of bibliographies on these writers is appended.

97.　California. State University, Sacramento. Library. **Non-Western Music: A Selected Bibliography of Materials.** (By Sheila J. Marsh) Sacramento, 1982. 45pp. Free. Library Bibliography No. 10.

This bibliography of Asian, African, Near Eastern, and Oceania music, including catalogs in the library collection, is a useful reference for music libraries.

98.　California. State University, Los Angeles. Latin American Studies Center. **Selected Bibliography of Contemporary Spanish-American Writers.** (By Stella Lozano) Los Angeles, 1979. 127pp. $4.50. Latin American Bibliography No. 8.

This collection offers materials on forty-seven individual authors, including their critical essays, dissertations, and critical books. An index of critics is included.

DISABLED

99.　California. Advisory Council on Vocational Education and Technical Training. **Barriers and Bridges: An Overview of Vocational Services Available for Handicapped Californians.** (By Linda Philips) Sacramento, 1977. 149pp. $3.00.

This bibliography includes a lengthy listing of publications and services of use to the vocationally handicapped.

100.　California. Southwestern Region Deaf-Blind Center. **A Bibliography of Resources for Sex-Education of Deaf-Blind.** (By Margo Dronek) Sacramento, 1977. 9pp. Free.

This work, completed in cooperation with the California Department of Education, contains over fifty useful citations on sex education for the general handicapped population.

101.　California. State Department of Education. **Bibliography: Proceedings and Publications of Regional Deaf-Blind Centers, 1970-1977.** Sacramento, 1978. 28pp. Free.

There are over 250 citations in this valuable reference work. It represents an "update of information submitted by nine regional deaf-blind centers." In the first section, each region is identified and its publications listed. The second section includes a listing of all publications alphabetized by author.

102.　California. State Department of Education. **State-of-the-Art: Perspectives on Serving Deaf-Blind Children.** (Edited by Edgar L. Lowell and Carole C. Rouin) Sacramento, 1977. 338pp. Free.

Authored cooperatively with the Southwestern Region Deaf-Blind Center, the scope of this important work includes education, European practices, primary and secondary prevention, infant stimulation, and ten other categories.

DRUG USE AND ABUSE

103. California. University, Berkeley. School of Public Health. Social Research Group. **Alcohol Use among Native Americans: A Selective Annotated Bibliography.** (By Pamela B. Street, Ronald C. Wood, and Rita C. Chowenhill) Berkeley, 1976. 115pp. Price on application.

This compilation of six hundred items emphasizes anthropological sources. Arrangement is alphabetical by author. The annotations are very thorough but there is no index.

104. California. University, Berkeley. School of Public Health. Social Research Group. **Alcohol Use among the Spanish-Speaking: A Selective Annotated Bibliography.** (By Beatrice R. Treiman et al.) Berkeley, 1976. 47pp. Free.

Authored in response to need by the state's Office of Alcoholism, the material in this collection deals with drinking patterns, behavior, general problems, treatment, and related issues concerning the Spanish-speaking population, with particular emphasis on California. There are sixty-eight thoroughly abstracted citations including journal articles, proceedings, and books.

105. California. Youth Authority. **Antecedents of Drug Abuse: A Review of the Literature.** (By D. Faye Widmann) Sacramento, 1973. 103pp. Free. Community-Centered Drug Program Research Report No. 1.

The citations included in this collection are intended to explore the validity of various attributed antecedents to drug use and abuse. The material is divided into sixty-six sections, with emphasis on specific drugs such as marijuana, heroin, stimulants, barbiturates, and solvents.

106. California. Office of Alcoholism. **Women and Alcohol.** Sacramento, 1977. 1 vol. $2.00. For sale by the Department of General Services, P.O. Box 1015, North Highlands, Calif., 95660.

This is a bibliography of current sources useful for drug and alcohol collections. Titles on all aspects of women and their excessive use of alcohol are included.

107. California. Office of Alcoholism. **Youth and Alcohol: A Selective Annotated Bibliography.** (By Beatrice R. Treiman and Doris Sami) Sacramento, 1977. 252pp. $2.50.

This is an excellent bibliography on all aspects of the youth alcohol problem, with over five hundred annotated citations.

ECONOMY/ECONOMICS

108.   California. Department of Consumer Affairs. **Consumer Resource Guide:**
         A Selected Bibliography. Sacramento, 1978. 69pp. $1.50.
This bibliography offers over one thousand entries drawn from books, pamphlets,
audiovisuals, and teaching resources. The arrangement is by subject. Prices and
ordering information are included, as well as a directory of publishers.

109.   California. Department of Consumer Affairs. **Food Co-op Bibliography**
         and Guide. Sacramento, 1978. 1 vol. Free.
"A comprehensive listing of information on consumer cooperative history, legal,
organizational structures, training programs, conferences, periodicals, technical
assistance material, and those from state and national associations."

EDUCATION AND TRAINING

110.   California. State Department of Education. **Bibliography of Audiovisual**
         Instructional Materials for Teaching of Spanish. Sacramento, 1975. 1 vol.
         $1.00.
This is an excellent bibliography, useful for foreign language instruction and in-
service education.

111.   California. State Department of Education. **Bibliography of Instructional**
         Materials for Teaching of German. Sacramento, 1975. 1 vol. $1.00.
This is a useful bibliography of texts and background materials for teaching German
in secondary schools. It is recommended for California teachers.

112.   California. State Department of Education. **Bibliography of Instructional**
         Materials for Teaching of Portuguese. Sacramento, 1976. 1 vol. $1.00.
This bibliography is a guide to over one hundred sources for teaching Portuguese
in the secondary classroom.

113.   California. State Department of Education. Bilingual Education Unit.
         Bibliography of Spanish Materials for Children. Sacramento, 1971. 1 vol.
         Free.
This bibliography lists pictorial and printed Spanish-language books for students in
K-6.

114.   California. State Department of Education. **Bibliography Relative to**
         Teaching and Learning English as a Second Language. Sacramento, 1967.
         13pp. Free.
Included in this bibliography are seventy-two significant citations recommended for
a special library. Each is briefly annotated and they are divided into five chapters:
application, linguistics, language and related disciplines, periodicals, and textbooks.

115.   California. State Department of Education. **Catalog of Instructional Materials in Bilingual/Bicultural and ESL.** Sacramento, 1983. 1 vol. $1.85.
Designed for teachers and social workers, this list includes over one hundred current curriculum guides and manuals with emphasis on Spanish-Americans.

116.   California. State Department of Education. **Catalog of Instructional Materials in Literature.** Sacramento, 1980. 1 vol. $1.85.
This title is designed to be used as an instructional materials selection guide as well as a bibliography of current textbooks.

117.   California. State Department of Education. Vocational and Continuing Education Division. **Resources in Health Careers Programs for Teachers of Disadvantaged Students.** (By Barbara Nemko) Sacramento, 1983. 1 vol. $6.00.
This title is a bibliography of vocational education textbooks, audiovisual materials, and general books appropriate for presenting over twenty specialized health careers to disadvantaged high school students.

118.   California. State Department of Education. Vocational Education Section. Research Coordinating Unit. **Selected Bibliography: Evaluation in Vocational Education.** Sacramento, 1970. 9*l.* Free.
This is a functional bibliography of over one hundred titles on the effectiveness of vocational education.

119.   California. State Department of Education. **Sources of Information in Career Education: An Annotated Bibliography.** Sacramento, 1975. 1 vol. $1.00.
Useful for both elementary and secondary grades, this bibliography includes over two hundred citations on seventy-five occupations.

EMPLOYMENT

120.   California. University, Berkeley. Institute of Transportation Studies. **Flexible Work Hours and Transportation: An Annotated Bibliography.** (By Daniel C. Krummes) Berkeley, 1981. 17pp. $3.25. LC card No. 82-620501. UCB-ITS-LR-81-3.
As flextime experimental work schedules become more popular, this bibliography of approximately fifty titles will increase in value for managers and planners.

121.   California. University, Berkeley. Institute of Governmental Studies. **Strikes by Public Employees and Professional Personnel: A Bibliography.** (By Dorothy C. Tompkins) Berkeley, 1967. 92pp. Price on application. LC card No. 67-65515.
This older bibliography of 442 citations maintains its usefulness. Citations are provided for each state. There are sections on strikes by public employees in localities, and by federal employees, firemen, the police, probation workers, and other public employees. A special section lists citations on professional personnel. There is a joint subject-author index.

ENERGY

122. California. University, Berkeley. Institute of Governmental Studies. **Power from the Earth: Geothermal Energy.** (By Dorothy C. Tompkins) Berkeley, 1972. 34pp. $2.50. Public Policy Bibliography No. 3.

Over one hundred citations on all aspects of geothermal energy are presented in this bibliography.

123. California. Solar Business Office. **Sources of Information on Solar Energy.** Sacramento, 1979. 2pp. Free.

This document serves as a basic bibliography and information source for the beginning solar energy researcher.

ENVIRONMENT

124. California. University, Santa Cruz. Coastal Marine Laboratory. **Annotated Species List of the Benthic Algae and Invertebrates in the Kelp Forest Community at Point Cabrillo, Pacific Grove, California.** (By John S. Pearse and Lloyd F. Lowry) Santa Cruz, 1974. 1 vol. Free. Technical Report No. 1.

This report presents approximately four hundred studies (some are annotated), arranged into the following categories: area descriptions, phaeophyta, rhodophyta, porifera, *cnidaria, polychaeta, polyplacophora, gastropoda, decapoda, bryozoa, echinodermata,* and *ascidiacea.*

125. California. Air Resources Board. Research Division. **Extramural Research Report.** Sacramento, 1982. 77*l.* Free.

This bibliography of over 250 reports on air pollution completed between 1970 and 1982 lists abstracts of recently completed studies, titles of funded reports by the board between 1970 and 1982, and studies in progress in 1982. Many are on health effects of pollution in Southern California.

126. California. Department of Conservation. Division of Mines and Geology. **Preliminary Bibliography: Lake Tahoe Basin, California-Nevada.** (By R. A. Matthews and Charles Schwarz) Sacramento, 1969. 102pp. Free.

The purpose of this bibliography is to provide a ready-reference for regional and local planning agencies in the basin. There are sections on history, legal controls, physical and biological characteristics, planning, and water quality; arrangement is alphabetical by title within each section. Almost one thousand sources have been cited. The bibliography was completed as a cooperative report with the Pacific Southwest Forest and Range Experiment Station.

127. California. State Library. **Hazardous Waste Bibliography.** Sacramento, 1979. 4pp. Free. Agricultural Research Library Special Bibliography No. 2.

Twenty-six references on hazardous waste, gleaned from popular scientific magazines and government documents comprise this brief bibliography.

128.   California. State Library. Government Publication Section. **Pollution: A Checklist of California State Agency Publications 1960-1970.** (Compiled by Lorna Flesher) Sacramento, 1970. 21pp. Free. Publication Section No. 6.

Over 160 titles in environmental pollution, consisting of the most important state titles deposited in the California State Library are cited herein. Earth, air and water pollution are covered. Arrangement is alphabetical by author. Basic bibliographic information is provided.

129.   California. University, Berkeley. Institute of Governmental Studies. **Strip Mining for Coal: Bibliography.** (By Dorothy C. Tompkins) Berkeley, 1971. 86pp. $5.00. Public Policy Bibliography No. 4.

Three hundred citations on the economic and environmental effects of coal mining comprise this bibliography.

130.   California. University, Davis. Institute of Governmental Affairs. **Public Policy Making and Environmental Quality: An Annotated Interdisciplinary Bibliography.** Davis, 1971. 176pp. Price on application.

This is an annotated, classified bibliography of monographs, articles, and documents useful for policy making. The references are arranged according to environmental problems.

EQUAL OPPORTUNITY

131.   California. San Jose State University. Library. **Affirmative Action and Equal Opportunity: A Bibliography.** (By Kathryn S. Forrest and Wendy Chang) San Jose, 1977. 19pp. Free.

Separate sections of bibliographies, books, pamphlets, articles, and speeches are included in this bibliography. The 285 citations are then arranged primarily by year and then author.

GEOLOGY

132.   California. University, San Diego. Malcome A. Love Library. **Geology of Baja California: A Bibliography.** (By John Ambriano) San Diego, 1972. 105pp. Price on application.

This bibliography is intended as a comprehensive guide to the literature on Baja, California geology found in the Love Library. It includes over five hundred citations arranged by author.

133.   California. Resources Agency. Department of Conservation. Division of Mines and Geology. **Index to Graduate Theses and Dissertations on California Geology, 1962 through 1972.** (By Gary C. Taylor) Sacramento, 1974. 89pp. Free. Special Report No. 115.

This is the fourth supplement to the original *Index to Graduate Theses on California Geology* (below). A total of 853 studies are listed with author and title. Part I indexes theses regarding specific areas of the state.

134.   California. Resources Agency. Department of Conservation. Division of Mines and Geology. **Index to Graduate Theses on California Geology to December 31, 1961**. Sacramento, 1963. 39pp. Free. Special Report No. 74.

This bibliography cites over one thousand studies on seventeen categories of California geology. Arrangement is by author and specific geographic area.

135.   California. Division of Mines and Geology. **List of Available Publications**. Sacramento, 1972. 33pp. Free.

Although basically a publication list, this reference acts as a useful bibliography to some three hundred geologic reports. Categories include: bulletins, special reports, maps, and the *California Geologic Atlas*. Entries are briefly annotated and availability information is provided.

136.   California. Division of Mines and Geology. **Some Sources of Information on California Earthquakes and Faults**. Sacramento, 1970. 4pp. Free. CDMG Note No. 10.

Thirty-one books, documents, and maps relating to this ongoing California problem are cited, to aid in research. All sources include bibliographic descriptions and annotations.

HEALTH

137.   California. Health and Welfare Agency. Center for Health Statistics. **Data Matters**. Sacramento, 1983. 25pp. Free.

This catalog contains a brief statement describing each of over ninety reports produced by the center within the past five years. Publications are divided according to ten categories including many on medical and mental health services. The length and cost of each report is provided.

138.   California. State Library. **Morbidity and Mortality Statistics: Bibliography**. (Compiled by Eileen Heaser) Sacramento, 1974. 28pp. Free. Bibliographic Series No. 16.

This bibliography of over one hundred well-annotated citations was "compiled in order to aid the user in locating morbidity and mortality statistics." Emphasis is on the health and social sciences, and the material is organized into the categories of: Sacramento county, California, other states, national, and international.

139.   California. University, Los Angeles. Brain Information Service. **Sleep Bibliography, 1969-70**. Los Angeles, 1970. 2 vols. Price on application.

This comprehensive bibliography on sleep was part of the NINDS (National Institute of Neurological Disease Studies) Neurological Information Network.

LAWS AND LEGISLATION

140. California. State Board of Correction. **Administration of Criminal Justice, 1949-1956: A Selected Bibliography.** (By Dorothy Campbell Tompkins) Berkeley, 1956. 351pp. Price on application.
This is a systematic and exhaustive listing of over six thousand citations on crime commissions, conferences, statistics, prosecution, and treatment of offenders. This was an updating of three previous Tompkins bibliographies of 1934, 1935, and 1949.

141. California. State Library. Law Library. **Bibliography on Prisons.** (By Betty Anne McCarthy) Sacramento, 1970. 4pp. Free.
Approximately seventy citations, arranged alphabetically by author, are presented in this bibliography on prisons. Many of the citations are taken from law reviews.

142. California. University, Berkeley. Institute of Governmental Studies. **The Confession Issue—From McNabb to Miranda.** (Compiled by Dorothy C. Tompkins) Berkeley, 1968. 100pp. Price on application. LC card No. 68-64269.
This bibliography documents over eight hundred citations on confessions as court evidence. The entries are divided into: *McNabb* v. *U.S.; Mallory* v. *U.S.; Escobedo* v. *Illinois; Miranda* v. *Arizona;* other decisions; and materials related to various aspects of confessions. There is a table of cases and an excellent subject-author index.

143. California. Youth Authority. Parole Services Branch. **Correctional Volunteer Program Information Service and Resource Library Catalog.** (By Lynda Lea Thorpe) Sacramento, 1978? 111pp. Free.
This bibliographic catalog offers information on over five hundred sources related to the administration of criminal justice and volunteer correctional workers.

144. California. University, Berkeley. Institute of Governmental Studies. **Court Organization and Administration: A Bibliography.** (By Dorothy C. Tompkins) Berkeley, 1971. 200pp. $8.00.
An important bibliography of over six hundred items on court organization and administration, including sections on reorganization, types of court plans, and judges. It is indexed.

145. California. University, Berkeley. Institute of Governmental Studies. **Furlough from Prison.** (By Dorothy C. Tompkins) Berkeley, 1974. 61pp. $5.00. Public Policy Bibliography No. 5.
This important reference work was authored during a time when many innovative correctional plans were being tried. Over three hundred annotated citations are included.

146. California. University, Berkeley. Institute of Governmental Studies. **Sentencing the Offender: A Bibliography.** (By Dorothy C. Tompkins) Berkeley, 1971. 102pp. $3.50. LC card No. 75-634804. Monograph No. 67.

This is an important bibliography of over four hundred citations dealing with experimental sentencing projects.

147.   California. Youth Authority. **Status of Current Research in the California Youth Authority.** Sacramento, 1960- . Annual. Free.
This is a bibliography of studies on youth sponsored by the authority, both completed and underway. The Youth Authority assesses the effectiveness of correctional treatment activities, parole, and staff training. Each annual bibliography describes twenty-five to thirty projects with background and objectives.

148.   California. State Library. **Taxation: Selected Material in the California State Library.** Sacramento, 1980. 4pp. Free. Agricultural Research Library Special Bibliography No. 4.
This brief document serves as a current reading list on both the philosophy and methods of taxation. The thirty-five citations are mostly governmental publications, and include books, periodical articles, and government documents.

LIBRARIES

149.   California. State Library. Law Library. **California County Law Library Basic List.** Sacramento, 1975. 40pp. Free.
This list, comprising over 17,900 volumes, was compiled for use by average-size law libraries. Categories include United States, California, tax reporting, periodicals, publishers, and law book dealers.

150.   California. State Library. **Library Organization and Operation: Selected Materials in the California State Library.** (By Michael J. Hardin) Sacramento, 1981. 9pp. Free. Agricultural Research Library Special Bibliography No. 5.
This bibliography on library organization and operation contains approximately eighty citations, most with annotations, divided into the following categories: audio-visual materials, cataloging, government publications, library planning, administration, reference services, and weeding.

MENTAL HEALTH

151.   California. University, Los Angeles. Brain Information Service. **Cerebral Dominance, Laterality, and Handedness: Reference Bibliography.** Los Angeles, 1975. 53pp. Out-of-Print. Reference Bibliography No. 79A.
This bibliography of over five hundred citations is divided into human and animal studies. Human studies are then subdivided by language and speech functions, motor, and sensormotor categories. Many foreign-language studies are included.

MINORITY GROUPS

152. California. State College, San Fernando Valley. Library. **Black Experience in the United States.** (By Dennis Bakewell) Northridge, 1970. 162pp. Price on application. LC card No. 74-136287.
This lengthy bibliography of over one thousand items includes the majority of the San Fernando campus library holdings arranged under forty subjects. There are extensive sections on American history, and a separate section on juvenile works. An extensive author index is included.

153. California. University, Los Angeles. Chicano Studies Center. **The Chicano: A Comprehensive Bibliographic Study.** (By Roberto Cabello-Argandóna) Los Angeles, 1975. 308pp. $7.95.
This is an important Chicano bibliography, several hundred citations of all types are included.

154. California. University, Los Angeles. Chicano Studies Center. **Selected Bibliography for Chicano Studies.** (By Juan Gomez-Quinones) Los Angeles, 1975. 56pp. Price on application.
"This selected bibliography of articles and books gives critical attention to Chicano studies materials and emphasizes recent writings in the field." The almost five hundred titles are divided into twenty-five sections. There is emphasis on history, public health, general society, and Mexican writings. Basic bibliographic information is provided.

155. California. University, Berkeley. Institute of Governmental Services. **Selected List of References on Minority Group Employment in the Public Service.** (By Dorothy C. Tompkins) Berkeley, 1964. 34*l*. Out-of-Print. LC card No. NUC 68-39271.
This is a classic bibliography of approximately 150 citations on employment of black Americans.

NATURAL RESOURCES

156. California. Department of Water Resources. **Abstracts of DWR Publications, 1922-1969.** Sacramento, 1970. 208pp. Free. Bulletin No. 170/69.
This bibliography serves as a historic record of water research at the department since William Hall was appointed its first engineer in 1878. There are over five hundred reports with in-depth abstracts. An excellent subject index is included.

157. California. University, Davis. Water Resources Center. **Annotated Bibliography on the Design of Water Resource Systems.** (By Hani Asfur and William Yeh) Davis, 1971. 85pp. Free. LC card No. NUC 72-85010. Water Resources Center Publication Contribution No. 134.
This collection presents 225 abstracts in six subject divisions according to single purpose or multipurpose facility systems. An appendix includes reports by individual authors.

158. California. University, Davis. Water Resources Center. **California Water Resources Center Chronicle of Research 1957-1980.** Davis, 1980. 148pp. Free. Report No. 48.

This bibliography lists over three thousand titles sponsored by the center. Projects are grouped according to research categories. Brief abstracts are provided and there is an index to researchers.

159. California. University, Davis. Water Resources Center. **Inventory of Water Research in the University of California.** (By Robert W. Hinks and J. Herbert Snyder) Davis, 1980. 130pp. Free. Report No. 50.

This is the first comprehensive attempt to identify and catalog all of the water-related research done at the university. The bibliography contains descriptions of all projects and follow-up publications in the categories of: agriculture, engineering, social sciences, and biological sciences.

160. California. University, Davis. Water Resources Center. Archives. **Water Resources Reports and Papers in the J. B. Lippincott Collection.** (By Gerald J. Giefer and Anelle M. Kloski) Davis, 1970. 301pp. Free. LC card No. 77-63742.

This compilation offers over one thousand studies on all aspects of water resources, citing the most important California studies.

OCEANOGRAPHY

161. California. Division of Mines and Geology. **Bibliography of Marine Geology and Oceanography.** (By Richard D. Terry) Sacramento, 1956? 146pp. $0.75. Special Report No. 44.

This is an important resource for study of the California coastal region, with over eight hundred citations.

PERSONALITIES

162. California. University, Los Angeles. Library. **Jack Benny Checklist: Radio, Television, Motion Pictures, Books, and Articles.** (By David R. Smith) Los Angeles, 1970. 33*l.* LC card No. 74-636526.

Approximately one hundred magazine articles on Jack Benny's career and private life are offered in this checklist.

POLITICS AND GOVERNMENT

163. California. Sacramento State College. Library. **Facing Right: An Annotated Bibliography of Conservative and Right-Wing Journals.** (Compiled by John Liberty) Sacramento, 1970. 21pp. Free. Bibliographic Series No. 8.

Over two hundred conservative and right-wing journals are annotated in this document. Function and content are described and beginning dates are provided.

164. California. University, San Diego. Institute of Public and Urban Affairs. **Handbook of Information Sources and Research Strategies in Public Administration.** (By M. G. Rock) San Diego, 1979. 236pp. Price on application.

This reference title reviews texts on local, state, and federal administration and includes a section on researching government publications. It lists public administration journals and compares for levels of speciality. There is emphasis on reference books and government yearbooks.

165. California. State Library. **Ombudsman: Selected Material in the California State Library.** Sacramento, 1980. 2pp. Free. Agricultural Research Library Special Bibliography No. 3.

This reading list of some important documents and books on the subject offers sixteen citations on various states.

166. California. University, Berkeley. Institute of Governmental Studies. **Proposition 13 in the 1978 California Primary: A Post-Election Bibliography.** (Compiled by Ronald J. Heckart and Terry J. Dean) Berkeley, 1981. 168pp. $12.00. LC card No. 80-27111. Occasional Bibliography No. 2.

This is a bibliography of over six hundred reports on changes brought about by the enactment of Proposition 13.

167. California. University, Berkeley. Institute of Governmental Studies. **Proposition 13 in the 1978 California Primary: A Pre-Election Bibliography.** (By Terry J. Dean and Ronald J. Heckart) Berkeley, 1979. 92pp. Price on application. LC card No. 79-12651. Occasional Bibliography No. 1.

"The taxpayer revolt of 1978 was a widespread outpouring of citizen discontent culminating in the Jarvis-Gann Initiative, Proposition 13." This bibliography lists almost six hundred items, including newspaper and journal articles, flyers, pamphlets, and state and local government documents. There are sections on the general background, unsuccessful reform, campaign, results, and general impact of Proposition 13.

168. California. University, Berkeley. Institute of Governmental Studies. **Selection of the Vice President.** (By Dorothy Campbell Tompkins) Berkeley, 1974. 26pp. $3.00. LC card No. 74-600. Public Policy Bibliography No. 6.

This bibliography is concerned with the selection of the Vice-President of the United States since the movement for and approval of the Twenty-fifth Amendment. There are specific sections relating to Lyndon Johnson, Hubert Humphrey, Spiro Agnew, and Thomas Eagleton followed by general divisions about the Twenty-fifth Amendment, special elections, Electoral College reform, and other related proposals. A thorough index completes the book.

169.   California. State University, Los Angeles. Center for the Study of Armament and Disarmament. **Spies and All That ... Intelligence Agencies and Operations: A Bibliography.** (By Donald M. DeVore) Los Angeles, 1977. 1 vol. Price on application.

This bibliography cites over five hundred monographs, reports, and articles pertaining to espionage, intelligence activities, and related subjects.

SOCIAL CONDITIONS

170.   California. University, Berkeley. Institute of Governmental Studies. **California Politics and Problems, 1964-1968: A Selective Bibliography.** (By D. R. Lester) Berkeley, 1969. 33pp. $0.50. Report No. 57.

Over 150 citations on California social and economic problems during the turbulent 1960s are collected in this volume.

171.   California. University, Berkeley. Institute of Governmental Studies. **Juvenile Gangs and Street Groups.** (By Dorothy C. Tompkins) Berkeley, 1966. 88pp. $1.00. LC card No. NUC 68-24172.

This classic bibliography on gangs and youth problems was produced in the mid-1960s when this subject was of greatest sociological and correctional interest. Over three hundred citations are included.

172.   California. University, Berkeley. Institute of Governmental Studies. **Poverty in the United States During the Sixties.** (By Dorothy Campbell Tompkins) Berkeley, 1970. 542pp. LC card No. 74-632910. $13.50.

This landmark bibliography cites over two thousand titles on all aspects of poverty in America.

173.   California. Office of Planning and Research. **Putting Social Indicators to Work: An Annotated Bibliography.** Sacramento, 1977. 79pp. $1.75.

"A survey bibliography on the use of social indicators in national, state, county, and city profiles."

TECHNOLOGY

174.   California. University, Santa Barbara. Sciences-Engineering Library. **Ergonomics Guide to the Literature in the UCSB Library.** (By Virginia R. Weiser) Santa Barbara, 1976. 32pp. $2.00. Life Sciences Guide No. 2.

Over one hundred titles from the holdings of the UCSB library are cited in this bibliography.

TRANSPORTATION

175. California. Department of Motor Vehicles. **List of Reports Published by the Research and Development Office**. Sacramento, 1983. 14*l*. Free.
This bibliography on driving offers sources for research on driver records, licensing, motor vehicles, and accidents. Most reports are available from NTIS.

WILDLIFE

176. California. Department of Fish and Game. **An Annotated Bibliography of Research on Economically Important Species of California Fish and Game**. Sacramento, 1959- . Irregular. Free.
Both the basic volume and each supplement include over five hundred well-annotated citations on California wildlife, designed mainly for use by scientists. Most of the citations are taken from important periodicals or government reports. They are divided into sections on marine fishes, marine animals, mollusks, crustaceans, kelp, anadromous and inland fishes; general game, pesticides, upland game, waterfowl, and predators.

177. California. Department of Fish and Game. **A Contribution toward a Bibliography on California Furbearers**. (By D. W. Newberry) Sacramento, 1973. 24pp. Free.
This bibliography would be useful in any natural history collection. Approximately two hundred citations are included on both large and small California furbearers.

WOMEN

178. California. Sacramento State College. Library. **Changing Role of Women**. (By Leah Freeman) Sacramento, 1971. 50pp. Free. LC card No. NUC 72-37210. Bibliographic Series No. 9.
Books, periodical articles, pamphlets, and other aids to further research are included in this collection on the changing role of women. There are over six hundred citations and a selected subject heading list for library use.

179. California. Office of Statewide Health Planning and Development. Division of Health Professions Development. **Women Physicians in the Seventies: A Selected Bibliography**. (By Julia Bauder-Nishita) Sacramento, 1980. 25pp. Free.
Malpractice, minorities, sex roles, and the feminist movement are among the seventeen categories in this bibliography of women physicians. The 250 citations are drawn from periodicals and some dissertations.

COLORADO

GENERAL

180. Colorado. University, Boulder. Graduate School of Business Administration. Business Research Division. **What's Published About Colorado.** (By C. R. Goeldner) Denver, 1973. 137pp. Price on application.

The regions, counties, cities, and other areas of Colorado are the subjects of the four hundred titles in this collection. The annotations are generous. The material is arranged in fourteen categories and there is an effective index.

AGRICULTURE

181. Colorado. Department of Game, Fish, and Parks. **Literature Review on Factors Affecting Shrub Response to Herbicides.** (By Donald G. Smith) Denver, 1966. 15pp. Free. Special Report No. 5.

There are over 150 reports and journal articles on herbicides in this review of literature "which covers shrub response to 2, 4-D, and 2, 4, 5-T." Environmental, physiological, and phenological factors are dicussed.

ANIMAL HUSBANDRY

182. Colorado. State University, Fort Collins. Ranch Science Department. **A Bibliography of the Arthropods Associated with Dung.** (By Rabinder Kuman and J. E. Lloyd) Fort Collins, 1976. 33pp. Free. Series No. 18.

"Some arthropod species that occur in manure are beneficial while others attack man and animals." The objective of this bibliography is to bring together pertinent publications on all aspects of the subject, except taxonomics. There are over five thousand citations arranged according to author.

183. Colorado. Cooperative Extension Service. **A Bibliography of the Domestic Rabbit.** (By David D. Careny and Howard L. Enos) Fort Collins, 1972. 21pp. Free. Bulletin 481A.

This is a compilation of over four hundred citations on the rabbit organized into the following sections: male and female reproduction, housing, management, disease, breeding, nutrition, and miscellaneous. Most citations are taken from journals.

ARCHAEOLOGY/ANTHROPOLOGY

184. Colorado. University of Northern Colorado, Greeley. Museum of Anthropology. **Bibliography of the 16th-20th Century Maya of the Southern Lowlands: Chol, Chol Lacandon, Yucatec, Lacandon, Quejache, Itza, and Mopan, 1542-1969.** (By Nicholas M. Hellmuth) Greeley, 1970. 114*l.* Price on application. LC card No. 71-635504. Archaeology Series No. 2.

This bibliography covers the Lacandon and the various Chol Maya groups of the tropical lowlands of Chiapas, Mexico, the Guatemalan Departamentos of the north, and Southern Belize. A major purpose of the bibliography is to point out that "there are hundreds of fragments of ethnographic data on these 16th to 20th Century people." A second purpose is to make some statement about the reliability of the data. There are over seven hundred citations, arranged alphabetically by author. Several are annotated. There is an index arranged by time period.

185. Colorado. University, Boulder. Department of Anthropology. **Language Origins: A Bibliography.** (Compiled by Gordon W. Hewes) Boulder, 1971. 139pp. $4.00.

"This bibliography is intended to include all works on the origins of language and related topics and on the gestural theory of language in particular. The sources for this work are first of all, books or articles on language origins." There is an introductory article by Hewes on the gestural origins of language. The approximately five thousand citations are arranged first by author, then by year. There is a broad subject index.

186. Colorado. University of Northern Colorado, Greeley. Museum of Anthropology. **Preliminary Bibliography of Hopewell Archaeology.** (By William R. Page) Greeley, 1976. 12pp. $0.50. Miscellaneous Series No. 21.

Hopewell archaeology has been cited in many sources. This document acts as a basic reading list to approximately one hundred prime works.

DRUG USE AND ABUSE

187. Colorado. Department of Public Health. **Alcohol Education: An Annotated Bibliography for Educators.** Denver, 1966. 35*l.* Free. Alcoholism Publication No. 3.

A topical presentation of alcohol education is presented in this bibliography. The subjects covered include: education, law, the individual, Alcoholics Anonymous, teaching outlines, books, and films.

EDUCATION AND TRAINING

188.　Colorado. University of Denver, Denver. Center for Social Research and Development. **Interagency Linkages in Vocational Rehabilitation: An Annotated Bibliography**. Denver, 1975. 1 vol. $10.00.

Annotated in this collection are more than five hundred references from the social sciences, research projects, and professional periodicals related to human services emphasizing vocational rehabilitation.

EMPLOYMENT

189.　Colorado. University of Denver, Denver. Center for Social Research and Development. **Migrant Farmworker: Social Programs, Policies, and Research**. Denver, 1973. 1 vol. $3.00. Monograph No. 7.

The emphasis of this study is on the demographics, employment, economics, housing, education, health, income, social and legal problems of the migrant farm-worker. Policy questions are addressed as well.

GEOLOGY

190.　Colorado. Geological Survey. **Bibliography and Index of Publications Related to Coal in Colorado, 1972-1977**. (By Hollis B. Fender, D. C. Jones, and D. K. Murray) Denver, 1978. 54pp. $2.00. Bulletin No. 41.

This bibliography includes approximately five hundred references to published information on the coal deposits of Colorado. The first section is arranged by author; the second is a key-word index.

HEALTH

191.　Colorado. Department of Social Services. Library. **Aging in the 70's and Beyond**. (By Alberta Denio) Denver, 1976. 52pp. $1.00. Library Counselor Series, Vol. 31, No. 1.

This bibliography contains citations on modern philosophy and research on the aged.

192.　Colorado. State Department of Public Welfare. Library. **Emotionally Disturbed Children**. Denver, 1968. 51*l*. Free. LC card No. NUC 69-79612.

Social workers and teachers are the intended audience for this bibliography empha-sizing mental health, child guidance, and psychiatry.

MINORITY GROUPS

193.   Colorado. University of Northern Colorado, Greeley. Museum of Anthropology. **Bibliography of Publications Relative to Afro-American Studies.** Greeley, 1969. 93pp. $1.00. Archaeology Monography Series No. 10.
Over four hundred titles on Afro-Americans from the early days of the slave trade are cited in this reference.

NATIVE PEOPLE

194.   Colorado. University, Boulder. Department of Anthropology. **Ethnohistorical Bibliography of the Ute Indians of Colorado.** (By Omer C. Stewart) Boulder, 1971. 167pp. LC card No. 76-636024. Anthropology Series No. 18.
This bibliography contains a list of data available in the Boulder-Denver archives and libraries. It is concerned primarily with the Colorado Utes rather than those of Utah. Not only a source of ethnological reference, this title contains all known historical references as well. There are twelve hundred citations including government publications, tribal letters, books, journal articles, and maps. There is an appendix analyzing records of the Southern Ute Agency from 1877 to 1952.

195.   Colorado. University of Denver, Denver. Center for Social Research and Development. **Indian Child Welfare: A Review of the Literature.** (By Ellen L. Slaughter) Denver, 1976. 111pp. Free.
This is a comprehensive bibliography undertaken as part of a Child Welfare Service program. Its over 225 citations include many reports from the Bureau of Indian Affairs and HEW.

RECREATION/TOURISM

196.   Colorado. University, Boulder. Graduate School of Business Administration. Business Research Division. **Bibliography of Skiing Studies.** (By C. R. Goeldner and Karen Dick) Boulder, 1978. 3 vols. $10.00.
The stated purpose of this bibliography is to "provide a ready source of references on travel, recreation, and tourism related to skiing for both business and academic fields." The citations include studies, surveys, statistical abstracts, and journal articles since 1960. The scope of the three volumes is: volume I–United States; volume II–individual states, and volume III–foreign. There is an author index.

197.   Colorado. University, Boulder. Graduate School of Business Administration. Business Research Division. **Bibliography of Tourism and Travel Research Studies, Reports, and Articles.** (By C. R. Goeldner and Karen Dicke). Boulder, 1971. 3 vols.
Volume I of this three-volume set is on national regions, volume II is on the state of Colorado, and volume III is for foreign titles. These titles were issued in cooperation with the Travel Research Association.

198.   Colorado. University, Boulder. Graduate School of Business Administration. Business Research Division. **Journal of Travel Research**. Boulder, 1965- . Quarterly. Price on application.

A regular feature of this quarterly journal is an annotated bibliography of current governmental and nongovernmental travel and tourism research materials.

199.   Colorado. Division of Wildlife. Wildlife Research Section. **Literature Review on Characteristics of Hunters**. (By Bernhard J. Schole) Denver, 1973. 16pp. Free.

This is a bibliographic attempt to determine why people hunt. It "should be of special interest to both social researchers and resource administrators in this outdoor recreation area." Factors important in participation, demographic characteristics, comparison of types, and general outdoor recreation are among the subjects covered in the 150 titles.

SOCIAL CONDITIONS

200.   Colorado. University of Denver, Denver. Center for Social Research and Development. **Review of Literature on Social Indicators**. (By Parker T. Osborn) Denver, 1972. 1 vol. Free.

This literature review serves as a guide to the broad field of indicators. Following an essay, there are thirty-three pages of citations arranged alphabetically by author. Many of the items cited are journal articles.

WILDLIFE

201.   Colorado. Department of Game, Fish, and Parks. **A Contribution toward a Bibliography on the Beaver**. (By Lee E. Yeager and Keith G. Hay) Denver, 1955. 103pp. Free. Technical Bulletin No. 1.

This older bibliography was an important contribution to the study of the beaver, with over three thousand citations. Subjects include: history, taxonomy, populations, biology, ecology, economics, and management. There is an author index.

202.   Colorado. Division of Wildlife. Wildlife Research Section. **Critical Review of Literature on Puma** *(Felis concolor)*. (By Allen E. Anderson) Denver, 1983. 91pp. Free. Special Report No. 54.

"The puma is one of the more secretive species of native wildlife in North America." This bibliography, with analysis of the material, includes almost five hundred citations. The categories include: movement, prey, nutrition, mortality, population, interaction, management, synthesis, and conclusions.

203.   Colorado Division of Wildlife. Wildlife Research Section. **Effects of Harassment on Wild Animals: An Annotated Bibliography of Selected References**. (By P. H. Neil and R. W. Hoffman) Denver, 1975. 21pp. Free. Special Report No. 37.

This bibliography includes sixty-seven lengthy annotations on wild animal harassment. The cateogries include: biological definition, off-road vehicles, free-roaming pets, urbanization, and hunting.

204. Colorado. Department of Game, Fish, and Parks. Division of Wildlife. Wildlife Research Section. **Index to Fishery Publications of the Colorado Division of Wildlife.** (By Oliver B. Cope) Denver, 1977. 100pp. $1.00. Division Report No. 8.

This is a thoroughly indexed bibliography of 1,105 reports on fish culture and fisheries. The first section is arranged alphabetically by author; the second section is by subject.

205. Colorado. Department of Game, Fish, and Parks. **Literature Review on Behavior of Mule Deer.** (By Michael J. Dorrance) Denver, 1966. 26pp. Free. Special Report No. 7.

The 145 citations in this report, arranged alphabetically by author, present a review of the literature on the behavior, daily activities, and intraspecific behavior of the mule deer.

206. Colorado. Department of Game, Fish, and Parks. **Literature Review on Bighorn Sheep Food Habits.** (By Jeffrey W. Todd) Denver, 1972. 21pp. Free. Special Report No. 27.

Published and unpublished reports pertaining to big horn sheep, especially their food habits, comprise the 115 citations in this collection.

207. Colorado. Department of Game, Fish, and Parks. **Literature Review on Cottontail Feeding Habits.** (By David S. DeCalesta) Denver, 1971. 15pp. Free. Special Report No. 25.

The greatest contribution of this review is that it "illustrates the dearth of information on the food preferences of the genus *Sylvilagus* during the spring and summer." There are 140 citations included.

208. Colorado. Department of Game, Fish, and Parks. Game Research Division. **Literature Review on Mountain Goat Ecology.** (By L. Dale Hibbs) Denver, 1966. 23pp. Free. Special Report No. 8.

This state-of-the-art bibliography includes over 250 citations on the distribution, life history, ecology, and management of the mountain goat.

209. Colorado. Department of Game, Fish, and Parks. **Literature Review on Mourning Dove Song as Related to the Coo-Count Census.** (By Charles P. Stone) Denver, 1966. 28pp. Free. Special Report No. 11.

Over 170 studies are listed and reviewed in this publication "concerned with the influents and meaning of the mourning dove." There is emphasis on the dove's song, territory, sex ratios, and populations.

210.   Colorado. Department of Game, Fish, and Parks. **Literature Review on Orchard Damage by Deer.** (By John D. Harder) Denver, 1968. 22pp. Free. Special Bibliography No. 12.

This review of 150 titles includes an introductory section followed by sections on orchard damage, investigations of damage, control methods, and summary writings.

211.   Colorado. Division of Wildlife. Wildlife Research Section. **Literature Review on the Natality Concept in Wild North American Ruminant Populations.** (By Lee K. Swenson) Denver, 1973. 10pp. Free. Special Report No. 30.

This discussion of natality stages "will be of major importance to wildlife managers and should serve as a point of departure for future research." There are sections on ovulation, fertilization, implantation, and mortality of neonatal young. There are 111 citations included.

212.   Colorado. Department of Game, Fish, and Parks. **Literature Review on the Role of Mineral Fertilizers in Big Game Range Improvement.** (By Len H. Carpenter and Gary L. Williams) Denver, 1972. 25pp. $1.00. Special Report No. 28.

One hundred thirty citations on the role of mineral fertilization on the big game range are organized into sections on forage yield, botanical composition, growth, palatability, herbicide effects, and soil ecology.

213.   Colorado. Department of Game, Fish, and Parks. **Literature Review on Vegetation Mapping in Waterfowl Biology.** (By G. G. Robinson) Denver, 1971. 15pp. Free. Special Report No. 26.

"The loss of waterfowl habitat due to increasing human population and human needs has reached a critical point." This publication reviews ninety-six sources on criteria, organization, management, and mapping.

CONNECTICUT

AGRICULTURE

214. Connecticut. Agricultural Experiment Station. **Subject and Author Index for Bulletins of the Storrs Agricultural Experiment Station.** (By Mohini Mundkur) Storrs, 1979. 68pp. Free. Bulletin No. 453.
This bibliography compiles 444 studies in 350 subject areas done at the station between 1888 and 1976. The arrangement is alphabetic within subjects. There is an author index.

EDUCATION/TRAINING

215. Connecticut. State Department of Education. Bureau of Pupil Personnel and Special Education Services. **Conn-Cept VI: A Connecticut Primer on Program Development for the Gifted and Talented, Supplement on Evaluation, and Resource Directory.** Hartford, 1978. 102pp. Free.
This publication serves as a combination manual/bibliographic guide for gifted students. Instruments for assessment are described in part I; part II is a resource directory of over 150 studies and articles.

216. Connecticut. University, Storrs. Library. **Education: Guide to Selected Sources.** (By Valorie H. Ralston) Storrs, 1977. 44pp. $2.00. University Bibliography Series No. 8.
Over two hundred citations to important educational studies and information services are provided in this selective bibliographic guide.

HEALTH

217. Connecticut. University, Storrs. Library. **Aging: A Guide to Reference Sources, Journals, and Government Publications.** (By B. McIlvaine and Mohini Mundkur) Storrs, 1978. 162pp. Price on application.
This bibliography of over five hundred titles related to aging and gerontology was sponsored by the University Center for Gerontology.

LAWS AND LEGISLATION

218.   Connecticut. Department of Corrections. **Corrections: A Resource Guide to Materials, Arranged by Topic on Corrections with Objectives and Learning Activities Included.** Hartford, 1980. 181p. Free.

This resource guide to over 110 books, documents, and films is divided into units on history, the correctional process, prison life, probation and parole, arrest, reform, and so on.

MINORITY GROUPS

219.   Connecticut. University, Storrs. Center for Real Estate and Urban Economic Studies. **Minority Groups and Housing: Bibliography 1950-1970.** Storrs, 1972. 202pp. Price on application. LC card No. 72-76557.

All aspects of real estate are covered in this comprehensive bibliography of over six hundred books, pamphlets, reports, periodical articles, government documents, and unpublished works. This bibliography is published in response to the "increasing need for knowledge about the scope and nature of housing minority groups." Categories include housing segregation, socioeconomic characteristics, attitudes, and finance. Each chapter is preceded by a bibliographic summary; there are author and subject indexes.

NATURAL RESOURCES

220.   Connecticut. University, Storrs. Institute of Water Resources. **A Bibliography of Publications Relating to Water Resources in Connecticut, 1900-1970.** Storrs, 1970. 125pp. Free. Report No. 16.

This is an important, comprehensive bibliography of over one thousand citations concerning Connecticut waters. An author index and appendix of state, federal, and private organizations concerned with the study of Connecticut water are included.

SAFETY

221.   Connecticut. Public Fire Education Committee. **A Catalog of Fire Education Resources: Materials, Programs, People and Products of the Connecticut Fire Education Committee.** Meriden, 1980. 76pp. Free.

This bibliography of books, general materials, and film catalogs concerned with fire safety could be useful for teachers or any specialists in fire safety.

SOCIAL CONDITIONS

222.   Connecticut. Department of Children and Youth Services. **Child Abuse: An Annotated Bibliography.** (By Jerry Seagrave) Hartford, 1980. 4pp. Free.

This is a bibliography of seventy key books and documents (most dated since 1975) on child abuse, with emphasis on treatment. All are annotated with many reviews taken from the preface or introduction of the book described.

WETLANDS

223.   Connecticut. Department of Environmental Protection. Natural Resource Center. **Annotated Bibliography of Source Materials for Wetland Habitats in Connecticut.** Hartford, 1979. 37p. Free.

"This bibliography was prepared in support of the State wetland and habitat element." Entries are organized under six classifications: techniques, regulations, classification, general references, illustrated guides, and tools. The over four hundred citations (some annotated) make this bibliography useful for anyone interested in wetland research.

WOMEN

224.   Connecticut. University, Storrs. Library. **Women's Studies: A Guide to Reference Sources.** (By Kathleen Burke McKee) Storrs, 1977. 112pp. Free. LC card No. 77-1747. Bibliographic Series No. 6.

The 364 citations on women's studies included in this collection are organized into handbooks, directories, statistics, indexes and abstracts, and twenty subject categories. A supplement on feminist serials in the University of Connecticut Library's Alternative Press Collection is appended.

DELAWARE

AREA STUDIES

225.   Delaware. University, Newark. Department of Anthropology. **Bibliography on Liberia.** (By Svend E. Holsoe) Newark, 1971. 123pp. LC card No. 79-636057. Liberian Studies Research Paper No. 1.

This bibliography on Liberia was published in cooperation with the Liberian Studies Association in America, Inc.

EMPLOYMENT

226.   Delaware. Department of Labor. **Bibliography of Wage Information.** (By Sally Straughn) Newark, 1981. 5pp. Free.

This list of publications, microfiche, and computer printouts containing information about wages for selected industries and jobs would be helpful to individuals and firms. Most are U.S. Bureau of Labor Statistics or Delaware State titles.

OCEANOGRAPHY

227.   Delaware. University, Newark. College of Marine Studies. **Bibliography for the Coastal Circulations of the Eastern North Pacific.** (By Kenneth Vierra) Newark, 1980. 77pp. Free. LC card No. 83-620742.

Included among the three hundred citations in this compilation are reports and articles on coastal currents, tides, waves, sediment, chemical and biological transports, and climate.

228.   Delaware. University, Newark. College of Marine Studies. **Marine Publications.** Newark, 1977. 61pp. Free.

This is a useful reference to over 275 marine research titles available from the college, covering coastal zone management, fishery economics, mariculture, marine education, biology, geology, remote sensing, and Delaware Bay. Short content descriptions are provided for each citation and there is a title index.

229.   Delaware. University, Newark. College of Marine Studies. **Tidal Marsh Bibliography.** (By Franklin C. Daiber) Newark, 1976. 281pp. DEL-SG-21-76. (Available from NTIS, accession No. PB 263386/AS).
This is an important bibliography of over eight hundred works on tidal marshes.

PLANNING

230.   Delaware. State Planning Office. **Bibliography of Delaware State Agency Publications.** Dover, 1971. 1 vol. Out-of-Print.
This is a listing of several hundred official publications with emphasis on Delaware planning and economic growth.

231.   Delaware. State Planning Office. **Bibliography of Reports Issued by the Office of Management, Budget, and Planning (State Planning Office), December 1962 through April 1977.** Dover, 1977. 25pp. Free.
Over four hundred reports on Delaware recreation, demographics, and specific comprehensive plans are provided in this collection. The reports are listed by category in part I and chronologically in part II.

GENERAL

232.   Florida. Department of Education. **Florida in Fact and Fiction**. Talla-
        hassee, 1972. 18pp. Free.
Designed as a bibliographic aid for school media specialists and teachers, this brief
document contains over 175 recommended books on Florida. There is a section on
guidance by interest levels.

DISABLED

233.   Florida. Department of Education. Bureau of Education for Exceptional
        Children. **Annotated Bibliography of Books about Exceptional Children**.
        Tallahassee, 1981. 38pp. Free.
Nondisabled children are seeing more of their exceptional peers in the classroom.
"To assist teachers, librarians, and parents in selecting literature about handicapped
children, this bibliography has been compiled." There are 160 citations divided
according to age group. A publisher's list and title index are other features.

234.   Florida. Department of Health and Rehabilitative Services. **Catalog of
        Materials for the Severely Handicapped**. Tallahassee, n.d. 1 vol. Free.
The materials in the first two sections of this bibliography have been selected as
being appropriate for the severely handicapped. Assessment, language, motor
skills, and self-help are addressed. There are sections on infants, preschoolers,
parents, behavior modification, and the multiply handicapped. The appendix
provides citations to useful articles.

235.   Florida. Department of Education. Bureau of Education for Exceptional
        Children. **Clearinghouse Catalog: Resources for Exceptional Student
        Education**. Tallahassee, 1982. 363pp. Free.
This catalog provides annotated entries of approximately four hundred currently
available materials. There is emphasis on parent training, counseling, advocacy,
and home activities. There is a useful subject index with many citations on
mainstreaming of the handicapped.

236. Florida. Department of Education. Bureau of Education for Exceptional Children. **Speech and Language Impaired, Volume II-C.** Tallahassee, 1979. 78pp. Free.

This document is useful both as a resource manual for the development and evaluation of special programs for the speech- and language-impaired and as a bibliography of fifty-seven citations of use to teachers and administrators.

EDUCATION AND TRAINING

237. Florida. Department of Education. **Material for Literacy Education: An Annotated Bibliography.** (By Edwin H. Smith) Tallahassee, 1971. 53pp. Free. Bulletin No. 71-F3.

This is a selected annotated bibliography of instructional literacy materials for adult basic education. Over one hundred fifty titles are included.

238. Florida. Division of Vocational, Technical, and Adult Education. **A Selected Bibliography of Instructional Literacy Materials for Adult Basic Education.** (By Edwin Smith and Welden Bradmueller) Tallahassee, 1968. 52pp. Out-of-Print.

This source of "easy-reading" materials appropriate for adults is divided into three levels: introductory (levels 1-3), elementary (levels 4-6) and intermediate (levels 7-9). There are sections on English as a Second Language, general language arts, reading, practical math, money management, citizenship, social studies, and pre-vocational orientation.

HEALTH

239. Florida. Division of Vocational, Technical, and Adult Education. **Resource Guide for Food and Nutrition.** Tallahassee, n.d. 66pp. Free.

This guide to three hundred basic sources on food and nutrition is useful for teachers and social workers as well as nutritionists.

LAWS AND LEGISLATION

240. Florida. State Library. **Crime Prevention: A Bibliography.** Tallahassee, 1982. 1 vol. Free.

This selective bibliography of books and films on crime prevention is designed for public library use. It was issued in cooperation with the Florida Federation of Women's Clubs.

OCEANOGRAPHY

241.   Florida. Department of Natural Resources. Marine Research Laboratory. **Bibliography and Checklist of Polychaetous Annelids of Florida, the Gulf of Mexico, and the Caribbean Region.** (By Thomas H. Perkins and Thomas Savage) St. Petersburg, 1975. 62pp. Free. Florida Marine Research Publication No. 14.

There are 280 citations for this marine biota in this document. Primary arrangement is alphabetical according to author. There is also a checklist of annelids (marine worms).

242.   Florida. Board of Conservation. Division of Salt Water Fisheries. **Discussion and Selected Annotated References of Subjective or Controversial Marine Matters.** (By Kenneth D. Woodburn) St. Petersburg, 1965. 50pp. Free. Technical Series No. 46.

This specialized bibliography of thirty-eight citations on such diverse marine matters as dredging, fish mortality, trawling, oil pollution, and oyster culture is designed for all oceanographic collections. Arrangement is alphabetic according to author. The annotations average half a page each.

243.   Florida. Atlantic University, Boca Raton. Sea Grant College. **Florida Marine Education Resource Bibliography.** Boca Raton, 1983. 115pp. $3.00. Report No. 51.

This multidisciplinary, annotated bibliography is offered for K-12 teachers, other educators, and librarians. Included are commercial materials, government documents, and unpublished materials prepared by teachers. The documents are divided into five sections; each entry includes entry number, an annotation, and source.

244.   Florida. University, Gainesville. Sea Grant Marine Advisory Program. **Marine Education Resources Bibliography.** (By Marjorie R. Gordon and Leni L. Bane) Gainesville, 1982. 116pp. $3.00.

This reference work is the result of a statewide survey of seven hundred elementary and secondary school teachers to identify printed teaching resources which have proven to be most successful and effective in Florida marine education. Subject areas are not only marine biology and oceanography, but also literature, the arts, and engineering. Nearly five hundred citations are included; each item is annotated with information on subject, grade level, and application.

245.   Florida. Department of Natural Resources. Marine Research Laboratory. **Publications of the Bureau of Marine Research, Marine Research Laboratories.** (By Mark G. Krost) St. Petersburg, 1983. 95pp. Free.

Despite being issued as a publication list, this is a valuable bibliography of 546 studies on marine research completed by division scientists. Topics covered include algae, aquaculture, clams, crabs, coloration, *Gastropoda,* lobsters, and the Gulf of Mexico. Arrangement is alphabetic by author with separate author and subject indexes.

246. Florida. Board of Conservation. **Selected References Concerning Florida's Marine Resources.** (By Robert M. Ingle) St. Petersburg, 1969. 117pp. Free. Special Scientific Report No. 24.

This work is intended to provide an introduction to extensive research resources on thirty-two important marine subjects. There are over two thousand citations offering basic bibliographic information on titles in the areas of physiology, ecology, and arthropods.

TRANSPORTATION

247. Florida. University, Gainesville. Sea Grant Marine Advisory Program. **Sail Assisted Commercial Marine Vehicles: Bibliography and Abstracts.** (By John W. Shortall) Gainesville, 1982. 110pp. $2.00. TP No. 28.

This publication contains abstracted citations to 331 articles published on commercial sailing vessels and sail-assisted work boats of all types. It contains a brief discussion of both modern and historical commercial sailing, reasons for serious interest in this subject, and commercial sailing and fishing vessels.

WILDLIFE

248. Florida. Department of Natural Resources. Marine Research Laboratory. **Annotated Bibliography of Dolphin and Porpoise Families** *Delphinedae* **and** *Plantanistidae.* (By William K. Whitfield, Jr.) St. Petersburg, 1971. 104pp. Free. Special Scientific Report No. 26.

This unique bibliography of 1,185 entries highlights "all important sources to 1969." Material is divided into sections on acoustics, anatomy, behavior, reproduction, pathology, physiology, and related subjects, with fifty-five subheadings and a short subject index.

249. Florida. Department of Natural Resources. Marine Research Laboratory. **An Annotated Bibliography of** *Sirenia.* (By William K. Whitfield, Jr. and Sandra L. Farrington) St. Petersburg, 1975. 43pp. Free. Special Publication No. 7.

The emphasis of this collection is on the manatee. There are 488 citations, arranged primarily by author.

250. Florida. Department of Natural Resources. Marine Research Laboratory. **Annotated List of Post-1950 Literature Pertaining to Distribution of Gulf of Mexico Fishes.** (By Robert W. Topp and Robert Ingle) St. Petersburg, 1972. 17pp. Free. Special Scientific Report No. 33.

This collection presents 201 citations on a wide range of fishes, arranged alphabetically by author with a geographic index.

251. Florida. Game and Fresh Water Fish Commission. **Endangered Species: Concepts, Principles, and Programs—a Bibliography.** Tallahassee, 1981. 228pp. Free.

"This bibliography is designed for use by biologists, planners, administrators, and others who may be involved in making management or research decisions relative to endangered species." This is an invaluable work with 3,135 citations, arranged alphabetically by author. The emphasis is on journal articles, but books and documents are also reviewed. The index is cross-referenced to enable easy location of needed references.

252.   Florida. University, Gainesville. Sea Grant Marine Advisory Program. **Indexed Bibliography of Snapper (*Lutjanidae*) and Grouper-Sea Bass (*Serranidae*) Biology.** (By Stephen A. Bortone, Karen A. Armsby, and Mildred B. Bortone) Gainesville, 1980. 297pp. $5.00. SGR No. 30.

A comprehensive, computer-produced list of 1,192 snapper/grouper sources for both commercial and scientific interests. Key-word-in-context, subject, and species indexes are included.

253.   Florida. University, Gainesville. Sea Grant Marine Advisory Program. **Indexed Bibliography of the Spiny Lobsters, Family *Palinuridae*.** (By Paul Kanciruk and William F. Herrnkind) Gainesville, 1976. 101pp. Free. Report No. 8.

This master reference list consists of 1,111 references by first author. There are author, key-word-in-context, and subject indexes.

254.   Florida. Department of Natural Resources. Marine Research Laboratory. **Partial Bibliography of Oysters, with Annotations.** (By Edward A. Joyce, Jr.) St. Petersburg, 1972. 846pp. Free. Special Scientific Report No. 34.

This bibliography provided a significant contribution to the literature on oysters. Forty-five percent of the 4,117 references are annotated. The bibliography was prepared to update J. L. Baughman's work of 1948; thus most citations were written between 1948 and 1970.

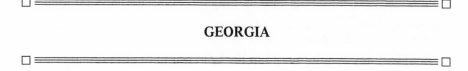

GEORGIA

GENERAL

255. Georgia. University, Athens. Libraries. **Checklist of Basic Reference Sources.** Athens, 1982. 8pp. Free. University of Georgia Libraries Bibliographies Series No. 22.

This is a highly selective list of some basic reference tools. Over one hundred citations are reviewed; most consist of general reference sources.

256. Georgia. University, Athens. Libraries. **Selected U.S. Documents Reference Sources.** Athens, 1981. 26pp. Free. University of Georgia Libraries Bibliographies Series No. 16.

This is a bibliography of 167 important government reference works and aids. Each citation has a short annotation and there is a subject index.

AGRICULTURE

257. Georgia. University, Athens. College of Agriculture. Experiment Stations. **Horticultural Use of Bark Softwood: A Bibliography.** (By Franklin A. Pokorny) Athens, 1982. 91pp. Free. Research Report No. 402.

A major bibliography of over fifteen hundred citations on the use of tree bark—both softwood and hardwood—over a two-decade period. References are listed by fifteen major categories, followed by over one hundred specific crops. Minimal bibliographic information is provided.

258. Georgia. University, Athens. College of Agriculture. Experiment Stations. **List of Theses and Dissertations on Peanuts and Peanut Related Research.** (By Emory Cheek) Athens, 1969. 38pp. Free. Research Report No. 54.

Over two hundred theses representing valuable research on the peanut are reviewed in this publication designed for research scientists in the field. The arrangement is primarily by author, followed by a subject list.

259. Georgia. University, Athens. College of Agriculture. Experiment Stations. **List of Theses and Dissertations on Peanuts and Peanut Related Research— III.** (By Emory Cheek) Athens, 1973. 20pp. Free.

This bibliography updates a 1969 title (Bulletin No. 54). It adds eighty-three new titles, mostly graduate theses, to the approximately 331 titles previously reviewed. International coverage is offered with a short subject index.

AREA STUDIES

260. Georgia. State University. Department of Geography. **Bibliographic Aid to the Study of the Geography of Africa.** (By Sanford H. Bederman) Atlanta, 1972. 287pp. Price on application. LC card No. 72-612816.

This is an important bibliography of 2,690 citations arranged to "ameliorate the difficult and time-consuming research problem of searching this subject." Primary arrangement is according to forty-six separate countries, with arrangement alphabetical by author within each category. There is an author index.

ECONOMY/ECONOMICS

261. Georgia. Office of Planning and Budget. **Index of Georgia Statistical Data.** Atlanta, 1980. 1 vol. Free.

This edition includes a detailed bibliography of research titles on the people and economy of Georgia. There are approximately three hundred printed sources, as well as data files. Instructions for acquisition are provided.

EDUCATION AND TRAINING

262. Georgia. University, Athens. Geography Curriculum Project. **Bibliography for Geographic Education.** (By John M. Ball) Athens, 1969. 113pp. Price on application. Revised Publication No. 2.

This is an effort to include all articles, books, and pamphlets published since 1950 on the subject of geography education. Almost one thousand citations are provided. Major categories are teaching methods and research in geography education. There is an author index.

263. Georgia. University, Athens. Geography Curriculum Project. **Inventory of Recent U.S. Research in Geographic Education.** (By Robert N. Saveland and Clifton W. Pannell) Athens, 1975. 1 vol. Price on application. Occasional Paper No. 4.

This is a bibliography of approximately one thousand citations on geographic education arranged according to the following subjects: history and philosophy, curriculum, materials, methods, evaluation, and teacher training. Most citations were obtained from the ERIC database. An author index is included.

EMPLOYMENT

264. Georgia. University, Athens. College of Education. Rehabilitation Counselor Training Program. **Job Placement Bibliography.** (By Timothy F. Field and W. Sears) Athens, 1979. 89pp. $1.00.

This bibliography covers pertinent sources from the past twenty years, providing a comprehensive review of job placement literature for rehabilitation. Over 850 citations are grouped according to nine categories: attitude, counseling, development, placement, surveys, affirmative action, job searching, and miscellaneous.

ENERGY

265. Georgia. University, Athens. Libraries. **Sun Power: A Bibliography of U.S. Government Documents on Solar Energy Located in the University of Georgia Libraries.** (By Sandra McAninch) Athens, 1978. 55pp. Free. Libraries Bibliography No. 18.

This bibliography offers a comprehensive listing of over eleven hundred citations divided into eighteen subject categories. There are lengthy listings on solar conversion, technology, radiation, heating, and cooling.

ENVIRONMENT

266. Georgia. University, Athens. Libraries. **Bibliography of the Published Contributions on the Alapaha Experimental Range.** (By Emory Cheek) Athens, 1977. 7*l*. Free. University of Georgia Bibliographies Series No. 11.

The Alapaha Experimental Range is located near Alapaha, Georgia, on a 2,750-acre tract. This is a complete bibliography of fifty-eight citations dating from the early 1940s to 1977, arranged chronologically.

GEOLOGY

267. Georgia. Department of Natural Resources. Georgia Geological Survey. **Annotated Bibliography of Georgia Geology through 1959.** (By H. R. Cramer, A. T. Allen, Jr., and J. G. Lester) Atlanta, 1967. 368pp. $3.00. Bulletin No. 79.

This is a major bibliography of over one thousand citations on Georgia geology divided into thirteen categories, with published reports and maps.

268. Georgia. Department of Natural Resources. Georgia Geological Survey. **Annotated Bibliography of Georgia Geology through 1970.** (By Ross Cramer) Atlanta, 1976. 84pp. Free.

Approximately two hundred recent studies on all areas of Georgia geology are listed. This list updates Bulletin No. 79 (above) to include material from 1960 through 1970.

269.   Georgia. Department of Natural Resources. Georgia Geologic Survey. **Publications of the Georgia Geologic Survey.** (Compiled by Eleanore Morrow) Atlanta, 1983. 25pp. Free. Circular No. 1 (18th edition).

This is a complete bibliography of over three hundred studies completed by the Georgia Geological Survey since 1907. Major publication series, out-of-print reports, and open-file reports, and maps are listed. Instructions for acquisitions are provided.

LAWS AND LEGISLATION

270.   Georgia. University, Atlanta. Institute of Government. **Literature on Parole.** (By Frank K. Gibson) Atlanta, 1967. 95pp. Price on application.

This collection documents over twelve hundred citations on the literature of parole. Many of the works cited are government publications. Part I offers the origin and history of parole; part II reviews important literature (1923 to 1967); and part III documents current literature.

271.   Georgia. University, Athens. Institute of Government. **Police Literature: An Annotated Bibliography.** (By A. Lee McGehee) Athens, 1970. 65pp. Out-of-Print. LC card No. 72-633912.

This bibliography includes over five hundred citations on police training and on-the-job expectations.

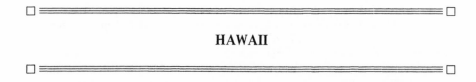

HAWAII

GENERAL

272.   Hawaii. Department of Education. Multimedia Services Branch. **Bibliography for Hawaiian Studies**. Honolulu, 1981. 87pp. Free.
Over four hundred current reference books and curriculum sources are listed by author with annotations in this bibliography. It would be of use to both public and school libraries in selecting materials on Hawaiian studies.

273.   Hawaii. Department of Planning and Economic Development. **Directories of Hawaii**. Honolulu, 1972. 10pp. Free.
Sixty-three directories are listed in this bibliography, arranged by business, commerce, government, and general. All are adequately annotated.

274.   Hawaii. Department of Planning and Economic Development. **Hawaii State Research Inventory, 1961-1966**. Honolulu, 1967. 199*l*. Free.
This bibliography "lists all research reports completed and/or published by or for the State of Hawaii, between July 1, 1961, and December 31, 1966, or in progress."

275.   Hawaii. State Library. **What to Read About Hawaii: A Bibliography**. Honolulu, 1982. 20pp. Free.
A core collection of readings about Hawaii is found in this 250-item bibliography. There are short annotations for books in the following subject areas: bibliography, description and travel, history, biography, natural history, industry, land, people, language and legend, music, and the arts.

AGRICULTURE

276.   Hawaii. Agricultural Experiment Station. **Bibliography of Macadamia**. (By B. H. Krauss and R. A. Hamilton) Honolulu, 1970. 2 pts. Free.
This bibliography was issued in two station bulletins, part I (No. 541) includes the author index and part II (No. 572) contains the subject index.

277.   Hawaii. University, Manoa. College of Tropical Agriculture and Human
        Resources. **Bibliography of the Sweet Potato (*Ipomea batatas*).** (By Peter
        R. Rotar and Barbara Bird) Manoa, 1981. 1 vol. Price on application.
Literature on the sweet potato published before 1956 is followed by that of the
1956-1966 period, and finally 1967-1077 in this bibliography. The compilers
reviewed bulletins, journals, books, and diaries from many sources. The main part
of the bibliography is available on microfiche.

278.   Hawaii. University, Manoa. College of Tropical Agriculture and Human
        Resources. **Bibliography of Taro and Other Edible Aroids.** (By Barbara
        K. Bird) Honolulu, 1982. 123pp. Single free copy to Hawaiian residents.
        LC card No. 82-21173. Research Series No. 18.
Four hundred citations from 1977 to 1982 comprise this bibliography. There are
author, key-word-in-context, and source indexes.

279.   Hawaii. Agricultural Experiment Station. **Bibliography of the Hawaii
        Agricultural Experiment Station: Publications 1901-1976.** (By Catherine
        A. Hughes) Honolulu, 1980. 238pp. Free.
"This volume is testimony to the longstanding productivity of the research efforts
of the College of Tropical Agriculture and Human Resources." The 749 titles
cover ten series offered over seventy-five years. The bibliography is in four parts:
master file, title file according to series, author index with citation numbers, and
the key word index also indexed to the master file. An addendum updates the
material to 1980.

ECONOMY/ECONOMICS

280.   Hawaii. Department of Planning and Economic Development. **A Bibliog-
        raphy of Foreign Investment in Hawaii.** (By Helen Uchihara) Honolulu,
        1978. 21pp. Free. International Business Series No. 9.
Over three hundred newspapers, periodicals, reports and publications, testimonies,
opinion polls, and miscellaneous reports are cited in this bibliography on foreign
investment in Hawaii. The *Honolulu Star-Bulletin* is heavily cited; most testimony
was before state legislative committees.

281.   Hawaii. State Library. **PPB Bibliography.** Honolulu, 1970. 53pp. Free.
Planning-programming-budgeting (PPB) became the official budgeting system for
Hawaii in 1970. The State Library has a large collection of materials on PPB of
which over eight hundred are listed in this bibliography. There are sections on
accounting, agriculture, computers, education, finance, health, housing, justice,
planning, and transportation. A supplemental section lists statistical methods;
there is an author index.

282.   Hawaii. Agricultural Experiment Station. **Research Methodology for
        Market Potentials and Market Development: A Bibliography with Primary
        References to Food Products.** (By M. A. Chaudhary and F. S. Scott)
        Honolulu, 1974. 128pp. Free. Bulletin No. 348.

This is a general bibliography on the marketing potential of a wide range of Hawaiian crops.

EDUCATION AND TRAINING

283. Hawaii. Department of Education. Office of Library Services. **Publications of the Department of Education, State of Hawaii—1964 through June 1972.** Honolulu, 1972. 83pp. Free.

Although a publication list, this title also serves as a useful bibliography to Hawaii education over a nine-year period. There are 576 studies and guides accompanied by a thorough subject index. Many relate to instruction and building services.

EMPLOYMENT

284. Hawaii. State Library. **Collective Bargaining in the Public Sector: A Bibliography.** (By Masae Gotanda and Kent Nakamura) Honolulu, 1972. 6pp. Free. Contemporary Affairs Bibliography Volume II, No. 2.

This is a guide to exploratory works on public sector bargaining.

ENERGY

285. Hawaii. University, Honolulu. Hawaii Institute of Geophysics. Geothermal Project. **Geothermal Power Economics: An Annotated Bibliography.** (By N. El-Ramly, R. Peterson, and K. K. Seo) Honolulu, 1974. 2 vols. Free. Institute Technical Report No. 21.

Each volume of this two-volume work abstracts over one hundred important research titles, listing major findings and subject coverage. Volume I provides 192 geothermal references and volume II, 198.

ENVIRONMENT

286. Hawaii. Department of Planning and Economic Development. **Selected Bibliography on the Environment of Hawaii.** Honolulu, 1973. 17pp. Free. Research Report No. 73-3.

Intended primarily for planners and research workers, this volume provides a basic background on thirteen environmental subjects. Minimal bibliographic information is provided for the 186 citations on climate, geology, land, slope, soils, vegetation, surface and ground water, shoreline, water biota, and insects and general wildlife.

GEOLOGY

287.   Hawaii. University, Honolulu, Hawaii Institute of Geophysics. **Geology and Geophysics in Hawaii: A Bibliography of Theses and Dissertations, 1909-1977.** (By Unni Havem Rowell) Honolulu, 1978. 78pp. Free.
A total of 278 theses are included in the bibliography—89 percent from the University of Hawaii and 11 percent from academic institutions outside of Hawaii. The bibliography has two main sections—one chronological and one arranged by subject—and eighteen subject categories. Full bibliographic information is supplied. There are geographical, author, and institutional indexes.

HISTORY

288.   Hawaii. State Library. **Genealogical Sources in the Hawaii and Pacific Collection of the Hawaii State Library: A Bibliography.** Honolulu, 1981. 15pp. Free.
Almost two hundred citations arranged by general sources, ethnic groups, special interest groups, and guides for genealogical research are included in this very useful bibliography. There are sections on Chinese and Japanese names; a category of special interest groups includes various professions.

289.   Hawaii. Department of Land and Natural Resources. Division of State Parks. **Hawaii Register of Historic Places, Bibliography of Hawaiiana.** Honolulu, 1970. 94pp. $2.50. *Hawaiian State Archaeological Journal* 70:3.
This working bibliography of historic sites was designed for the researcher in anthropology, archaeology, sociology, geography, and history. Many unpublished manuscripts are included. Arrangement is by author with minimal bibliographic information supplied.

MINORITY GROUPS

290.   Hawaii. State Library. **Blacks in Hawaii: A Bibliography.** Honolulu, 1975. 4pp. Free.
There are thirty-six citations in this seventh bibliography on Hawaiian ethnic groups; most are government publications or from the University Press.

291.   Hawaii. State Library. **Chinese in Hawaii: A Bibliography.** Honolulu, 1979. 12pp. Free.
The third in a series on ethnic groups that constitute the people of Hawaii, this study of the Chinese has 160 citations arranged by author. These include a wide range of books and articles on social and economic life. There are also selections from *Mid-Pacific Magazine.*

292.   Hawaii. State Library. **Filipinos in Hawaii: A Bibliography.** (By P. A. Strona) Honolulu, 1974. 12pp. Free.

This bibliography of 127 citations offers books and documents relating to Filipinos in Hawaii. Arrangement is alphabetic by author. There are articles from *Mid-Pacific Magazine.*

293.   Hawaii. University, Honolulu. Social Sciences and Linguistics Institute. **The Filipinos in Hawaii: An Annotated Bibliography.** (By Ruben R. Alcantara) Honolulu, 1977. 152pp. $5.00. Hawaii Series No. 6.

This is a comprehensive bibliography of over six hundred citations on all aspects of Filipino life in Hawaii.

294.   Hawaii. State Library. **Japanese in Hawaii: A Bibliography.** Honolulu, 1982. 12pp. Free.

Part of series on the ethnic groups of Hawaii, this volume contains 136 citations arranged alphabetically by author. Information on other sources of Japanese information and popular festivals is provided.

295.   Hawaii. State Library. **Koreans in Hawaii: A Bibliography.** Honolulu, 1975. 8pp. Free.

This bibliography of materials relating to Koreans in Hawaii is the sixth in a series of bibliographies on major ethnic groups. The sixty citations have short annotations. A section on statistics and sources for further information are included.

296.   Hawaii. State Library. **Portuguese in Hawaii: A Bibliography.** Honolulu, 1979. 10pp. Free.

There are sixty-six citations in this fourth in a series of bibliographies on major ethnic groups of Hawaii. Arrangement is alphabetical by author with some short annotations. There are some common Portuguese expressions.

297.   Hawaii. State Library. **Samoans in Hawaii: A Bibliography.** Honolulu, 1980. 6pp. Free.

There are forty-one citations in this bibliography from a series on Hawaiian ethnic groups. Most are government publications. Sources of further information on Samoans are included.

NATURAL RESOURCES

298.   Hawaii. University, Honolulu. Institute of Geophysics. **Annotated Bibliography of Uses of Hawaiian Lavas Including a Report and Recommendations.** (By A. T. Abbott) Honolulu, 1957. 92pp. Out-of-Print. Contribution No. 4.

Many of the 163 citations in this bibliography are related to the fertilizing value of lava, its use in concrete, and other economic functions. Most of the citations are from journals; many of the abstracts are of several paragraphs. Arrangement is alphabetical by author. There are author and subject indexes.

299.   Hawaii. University, Honolulu. Water Resources Research Center. **Bibliography of Water Resources of the Hawaiian Islands.** (By Rose T. Pfund and Dorothy L. Steller) Honolulu, 1971. 142pp. Free. Technical Report No. 50.

This bibliography of the water resources of Hawaii includes approximately 750 citations arranged alphabetically by author, with short annotations. An index for all authors, descriptor listing, and a lengthy subject index are appended.

OCEANOGRAPHY

300.   Hawaii. University, Honolulu. Hawaii Institute of Marine Biology. **An Annotated Bibliography of Kaneohe Bay.** (By Joleen Aldous Gordon and Philip Helfrich) Honolulu, 1970. 260pp. Free. Technical Report No. 20.

This collection of seven hundred items cites all pertinent materials on Kaneohe Bay. Topics covered include archaeology, biology, geology, history, waste disposal, land-use studies, public health, transportation, meteorology, plus bibliographies and maps.

301.   Hawaii. University, Honolulu. Hawaii Institute of Marine Biology. **Annotated Checklist of Hawaiian Barnacles (Class *Crustacea*: Subclass *cirripedia*) with Notes on Their Nomenclature, Habitats, and Hawaiian Localities.** (By Joleen Aldous Gordon) Honolulu, 1970. 130*l*. Free. Technical report No. 19.

The subject of Hawaiian barnacles is addressed in abstracts of over one hundred reports and a 125-citation bibliography.

302.   Hawaii. University, Honolulu. Hawaii Institute of Marine Biology. **Bibliographic Species List for the Biota of Kaneohe Bay.** (By Joleen Aldous Gordon and Philip Helfrich) Honolulu, 1970. 70*l*. Free. Technical Report No. 21.

This publication contains a bibliographic list of the species found in Kaneohe Bay as recorded in papers and reports. The twelve hundred citations for the twenty phylum are arranged phylogenically according to the Edmondson system.

303.   Hawaii. University, Honolulu. Hawaii Institute of Geophysics. **Bibliography to the Preliminary Catalog of Tsunamis Occurring in the Pacific Ocean.** (By Iida Kimizi, Doak C. Cox, and George Pararas-Carayannis) Honolulu, 1967. 27pp. Free. HIG Report No. 67/25.

This is an important bibliography concerning the tsunamis—the violent Pacific storm—with over 150 citations.

304.   Hawaii. University, Honolulu. Hawaii Institute of Geophysics. **An Introduction to Oceanographic Literature.** (By Malvern Gilmartin) Honolulu, 1966. 33pp. Free. Institute Report 66-15.

This document's stated purpose is to "provide an introduction for graduate students on books related to oceanography." About 450 titles are arranged alphabetically by author with descriptors relating to applied oceanography, biology, chemistry, geology, and physical studies.

305.   Hawaii. State Library. **Marine Environment: A Bibliography**. Honolulu, 1976. 16pp. Free.
"Hawaii's blue waters always have been a source of pleasure to Island people." This bibliography reflects a wide range of interests in helping to maintain those waters. The 230 citations cover aquaculture, fishing, periodical literature, marine life, and oceanography.

306.   Hawaii. University, Honolulu. Hawaii Institute of Geophysics. **Oceanography of the Tropical Pacific: A Bibliography of Theses and Dissertations 1935-1978**. (By Unni Havem Rowell) Honolulu, 1979. 78pp. Free. Data Report No. 37.
All doctoral dissertations and master's theses accepted by the institute's Department of Oceanography to 1978 are cited here. Key-word-in-context subject index includes over 250 reports, authors, and geographic place names.

307.   Hawaii. University, Honolulu. Sea Grant College. **Program Bibliography 1968-1981**. Honolulu, 1981. 27pp. Free.
This is a listing of over one hundred reports that were sponsored by the Sea Grant College dealing with the Pacific Ocean and oceanographic research generally.

308.   Hawaii. University, Honolulu. Hawaii Institute of Geophysics. **Publications 1983**. Honolulu, 1983. 172pp. Free.
This publication list also serves as a comprehensive bibliography of oceanographic physics and waves in the Pacific. Over one thousand studies are listed according to type of report: technical, data, sea grant, and biennial. There is an author index.

RECREATION/TOURISM

309.   Hawaii. Department of Planning and Economic Development. Research and Economic Analysis Division. **Bibliography of Tourism Projections Issued Since 1969**. Honolulu, 1976. 8pp. Free.
This bibliography lists seventeen tourism studies prepared by consultants at the DPED focusing on implications for state planning.

310.   Hawaii. State Library. **Ethnic Culinary Art in Hawaii: A Bibliography**. Honolulu, 1980. 12pp. Free.
Arranged alphabetically by author, this is a unique bibliography to eighty-five recommended cookbooks on the Hawaiian style available from the Hawaii State Library. Ample annotations are provided.

311.   Hawaii. University, Manoa. Social Science Research Institute. **Tourism in the Pacific: A Bibliography.** (By B. H. Farrell et al.) Honolulu, 1983. 293pp. Free.

The forerunner of this work was a volume published by the Center for South Pacific Studies called *Source Materials for Pacific Tourism*. This bibliography presents a mass of articles, books, and special studies on seventeen specific Pacific localities and nine related geographic areas. There are almost three thousand citations, mostly annotated. There are specific sections on general publications, reports, serials, journals, and magazines.

SOCIAL CONDITIONS

312.   Hawaii. Department of Planning and Economic Development. **Bibliography of Population Forecasts and Projections for Hawaii, 1981.** Honolulu, 1982. 16pp. Free.

This is a useful bibliography for planners and educators with approximately one hundred citations to population-related materials.

313.   Hawaii. University, Manoa. Social Science Research Institute. **Culture and Behavior in Hawaii: An Annotated Bibliography.** (By Judith Rubano) Honolulu, 1971. 147pp. Out-of-Print. LC card No. 79-634604. Hawaii Series No. 3.

This bibliography is still useful for studying the culture of Hawaii as it emerged into statehood.

WILDLIFE

314.   Hawaii. University, Honolulu. Hawaii Institute of Marine Biology. **Bibliography of the Hawaiian Monk Seal.** (By George H. Balaz and G. Causey Whittow) Honolulu, 1978. 27*l.* Free. Marine Biology Technical Report No. 35.

"There is considerable interest in the monk seal due to its restricted range and designation as an endangered species." These 340 citations listed alphabetically by author include articles from the Honolulu newspapers.

WOMEN

315.   Hawaii. University, Honolulu. Library. **Status of Women in Higher Education: A Working Bibliography.** (By Linda Engelberg, Ellen Chapman, and Janice Powell) Honolulu, 1971. 7pp. Free.

This basic bibliography on salaries and advancement offers approximately one hundred citations.

IDAHO

ENVIRONMENT

316. Idaho. University, Moscow. Forest, Wildlife, and Range Experiment Station. **Full Forest Utilization: A Bibliography.** (By John P. Howe) Moscow, 1978. 19pp. Free. Bulletin No. 16.

These current references of biomass interest emphasize some little-known writings. The four hundred entries are arranged alphabetically by author.

GEOLOGY

317. Idaho. Bureau of Mines and Geology. **Graduate Theses on the Geology of Idaho, 1900-1973.** (By Mary P. Gaston) Moscow, 1979. 25pp. Free. Information Circular No. 32.

Several hundred theses on all aspects of Idaho geologic research are included in this bibliography.

HISTORY

318. Idaho. University, Moscow. Library. **Check List of Western Americans in the Day-NW Collection, University of Idaho Library.** (By Charles A. Webbert) Moscow, 1970. 664pp. Price on application. LC card No. 72-634814.

The Day-NW collection includes materials relating to the exploration, settlement, and development of the country west of the Mississippi River. The emphasis of the collection is on Idaho, with secondary emphasis on the Oregon Territory. Over six thousand citations arranged alphabetically by author are included here, and there is a useful subject index.

MINORITY GROUPS

319. Idaho. University, Moscow. Library. **Basque Collection: A Preliminary Checklist.** (By Charles A. Webbert) Moscow, 1971. 100pp. Out-of-Print. Library Publication No. 9.

The University of Idaho Library holds a large collection on Basque-Americans and the Basques of Spain, many of whom settled in Idaho to work in the sheep industry.

POLITICS AND GOVERNMENT

320. Idaho. University, Moscow. Bureau of Public Affairs Research. **Selected Bibliography on Politics and Government in Idaho.** (By James Weatherby) Moscow, 1972. 24pp. Free.

This bibliography includes studies on Idaho governmental structure and function as well as state personalities. Most of the titles are official state documents. Listed are over 260 books, periodicals, manuscripts, and government publications divided into chapters on Idaho politics, election statistics, natural resources, economic and demographic data, and general government information.

WILDLIFE

321. Idaho. Fish and Game Department. **A Partial Bibliography of Idaho Wildlife.** (By Paul D. Dalke) Boise, 1973. 132pp. Free. Wildlife Bulletin No. 6.

This document provides a valuable resource for Idaho wildlife research. Part I is an author index; part II is arranged by over one hundred subjects. Most research from the Fish and Game Department is included along with titles from the University of Idaho and Washington State University collections.

ILLINOIS

GENERAL

322. Illinois. Office of the Superintendent of Public Instruction. **An Annotated Listing of Free and Inexpensive Materials for Teaching about Illinois.** Springfield, 1980. 13pp. Free.
Useful for teachers and public libraries, this is a descriptive bibliography of almost one hundred booklets, guidebooks, and audiovisual materials useful for studying Illinois. Many of the booklets, particularly those from the Conservation Department, are free of charge.

323. Illinois. University, Urbana-Champaign. Graduate School of Library Science. **Federal and State Government Publications of Professional Interest to the School Librarian: A Bibliographic Essay.** (By Marilyn Lester) Urbana, 1971. 31pp. LC card No. 72-610415.
Over two hundred titles are included in this bibliography.

AGRICULTURE

324. Illinois. University, Urbana-Champaign. Department of Agricultural Economics. **Agricultural Economics 1981, Publications.** (By E. H. Gussing) Urbana, 1982. 16pp. Free.
This document is both a publication list and a bibliography to over two hundred studies on agriculture in Illinois and general agricultural/rural problems.

325. Illinois. University, Urbana-Champaign. Water Resources Center. **Bibliography of Optimization of Irrigation Systems.** (By Dale O. Meredith) Urbana, 1973. 123pp. Free. WRC No. 71.
This is a bibliography of 1,918 references (some annotated) pertaining to irrigation systems. The arrangement is by author and the topics covered include plant response to the physical environment and methodologies.

326.   Illinois. Natural History Survey. **Literature of Arthropods Associated with Soybeans.** (By M. P. Nichols and M. Kogan) Urbana, 1972. 20pp. Out-of-Print. Biological Notes No. 7.

Over fifty citations on the Mexican Bean Beetle, *Epilachna varivestis,* are included in this bibliography.

AREA STUDIES

327.   Illinois. Office of the Superintendent of Public Instruction. **Non-Western Cultures: A Bibliography.** (By James A. Spears) Springfield, n.d. 18pp. Free.

The history of nonwestern civilizations, their geographical environments, governments, and cultural and behavioral structures are among the subjects covered in this 166-item bibliography of nonwestern cultures. The arrangement is by country.

ARTS

328.   Illinois. State Library. **Illinois Authors: A Publication of Read Illinois.** Springfield, 1983. 228pp. Free.

The Read Illinois program was initiated in 1981 by the Illinois Secretary of State and the State Library to promote the reading of Illinois authors. The 825 citations provide background information about the authors—including their Illinois connections—and a list of books published by the writers with publishing dates. Arrangement is alphabetic by author. This biobibliography is a "must" for school, public, and college libraries in Illinois.

DISABLED

329.   Illinois. Sangamon State University. Library. **Special Needs Bibliography.** Springfield, 1978. 41pp. Free.

This is a useful bibliography of over 320 guides, books, and kits useful for planning vocational education for the handicapped and deprived. Most have a paragraph of description. Availability information is provided. This is an excellent source for teachers, guidance personnel, and rehabilitation workers.

DRUG USE AND ABUSE

330.   Illinois. Department of Mental Health. **Bibliography on Drugs—Stash Book List.** Chicago, 1970? 5pp. Free.

This popular listing of books on drugs and drug education contains a keyed evaluation as to whether the works are geared for high schools, colleges, or as general reference works and indicates whether the contents are average, good, or excellent.

ECONOMY/ECONOMICS

331.   Illinois. Department of Commerce and· Community Affairs. **Recycling Bibliography**. Springfield, 1983. 6pp. Free.
The recycling of glass, paper, metals, oil, rubber products, and other products are addressed in the seventy-one citations contained in this recycling bibliography. Many of the items listed are available free of charge.

EDUCATION AND TRAINING

332.   Illinois. Sangamon State University. Vocational Curriculum Center. **Accounting Bibliography**. Springfield, 1978. 9pp. Free.
Both print and audiovisual resources are represented in this bibliography on the bookkeeping and accounting professions. Completely annotated citations, including cost and availability information, are provided for seventy-three items.

333.   Illinois. Sangamon State University. Vocational Curriculum Center. **Adult Education Bibliography**. Springfield, 1978? 25pp. Free.
Over 175 recommended titles in the holdings of Vocational Curriculum Center Library are highlighted in this compilation. Arrangement is by subject. The annotations are brief—usually one sentence.

334.   Illinois. Department of Public Instruction. **An Annotated Bibliography for Health Occupations**. (By Lindy Solon) Springfield, 1975. 1 vol. Free.
Print and audiovisual materials related to fifteen health occupations are cited in this bibliographic guide designed to assist teachers and students at the secondary level. Over 150 sources are listed with brief introductions, annotations, and evaluations.

335.   Illinois. State Board of Education. Department of Adult, Vocational, and Technical Education. **Annotated Bibliography of Instructional Materials in Cooperative Vocational Education**. Available from Western Illinois University, Macomb, 1977. 1 vol. $3.00.
This annotated bibliography "designed to assist teachers working in cooperative vocational education" is useful for selecting, utilizing, and recommending instructional materials. Materials received from over seven hundred publishers were evaluated by experienced teachers. The looseleaf format allows for easy updating. The project was carried out cooperatively with the Curriculum Publications Clearinghouse of Western Illinois University.

336.   Illinois. Department of Mental Health. Learning Media Center. **Annotated Bibliography on Television and Videotaping in Psychiatry**. (By Floy Jack Moore) Springfield, 1970. 58pp. Free. Publication No. 70-4.
Seventy-two citations on the ways in which television and videotape can be used in psychiatric training programs are included in this thoroughly annotated listing. There is a separate section on psychiatric videotape indexing.

337.   Illinois. Office of the Superintendent of Public Instruction. **Bibliographies:
        Elementary School Mathematics.** (By Frances Hewitt) Springfield, 1969.
        66*l.* Free.

This publication would be interesting as a guide to historic mathematics resources,
many from the years 1950 to 1960. There are sections on aids for the classroom,
curriculum revision guides, method guides, in-service materials, textbooks, and
films. Over eight hundred items have been included.

338.   Illinois. Western Illinois University, Macomb. Curriculum Publications
        Clearinghouse. **Bibliography of Bilingual Materials for Career/Vocational
        Education.** Macomb, 1980. 1 vol. $1.35.

Counselors, vocational instructors, and ESL teachers will find these materials
dealing with career education, vocational training, vocational ESL, crosscultural
counseling, and assessment valuable. A list of publishers is included.

339.   Illinois. Office of the Superintendent of Public Instruction. **A Bibliography
        of Materials on the Year-Round School.** (By James L. Ranney) Springfield,
        1970. 27pp. Free. LC card No. 74-634209.

This annotated bibliography of over four hundred entries was compiled in response
to an increased interest by many educators in Illinois for further information on the
year-round school. A number of different programs that were in existence in the
period 1960 to 1969 are described.

340.   Illinois. Sangamon State University. Vocational Curriculum Center.
        Bilingual Materials. Springfield, n.d. 16pp. Free.

The 115 citations in this useful bibliography of bilingual materials are mostly
related to career education and designed for Spanish-Americans. Arrangement is
alphabetic by title; short annotations are provided.

341.   Illinois. Sangamon State University. Vocational Curriculum Center.
        Cosmetology Bibliography. Springfield, 1978. 4pp. Free.

A bibliography that both describes the requirements of the profession and lists
specific course outlines, this title would be useful for most vocational education
collections. The titles are annotated and availability information is provided.

342.   Illinois. State Board of Education. Department of Adult, Vocational,
        and Technical Education. **ECCMC Special Bibliography in Vocational
        and Career Education: Sex Equality.** Springfield, 1978. 28pp. Free.

This annotated bibliography of the Education and Curriculum Career Materials
Center (ECCMC) lists 316 citations useful to teachers, counselors, administrators,
and students. Books, documents, journal articles, and audiovisual materials are
listed. Each entry has at least a one-sentence annotation; arrangement is alphabetic by title. Many of the citations are related to guidance, non-sexist textbooks,
and the woman at work.

343.   Illinois. Sangamon State University. Vocational Curriculum Center.
        Food and Nutrition. Springfield, 1980? 28pp. Free.

These 260 citations center around vocational preparation for food services. They
are arranged alphabetically by title with short annotations. There is stress on
specific occupational titles, curriculum guides, and bilingual foods.

344.   Illinois. Sangamon State University. Vocational Curriculum Center. **Personal Preparation, Attitudes, and Life Skills.** Springfield, 1980. 22pp. Free.

The publications in this collection are useful as resources for the study of human and family relations and as aids to securing employment and discovering goals. There are over two hundred titles arranged by title; most are annotated and include acquisition information.

345.   Illinois. Sangamon State University. Vocational Curriculum Center. **Police and Fire Sciences.** Springfield, 1977. 11pp. Free.

Here is a bibliography of one hundred annotated citations related to police and fire occupations. Many of the items included are educational materials and curriculum guides. All of these materials are available on loan from the center.

EMPLOYMENT

346.   Illinois. Sangamon State University. Library. **Guide to Sources: Work and Employment.** Springfield, 1975. 12pp. Free.

Federal, state, and international documents are cited in this general pathfinder and bibliographic guide to indexes, abstracts, journal articles, and government publications on work.

347.   Illinois. Sangamon State University. Library. **Work Bibliography.** Springfield, 1978. 23pp. Free.

Over 160 print and audiovisual resources have been reviewed for this well-annotated bibliography on the meaning of work in America, the changing work ethic, and various manpower plans and systems.

ENERGY

348.   Illinois. Department of Commerce and Community Affairs. **Commercial and Industrial Energy Conservation Bibliography.** Springfield, 1983. 4pp. Free.

This is a guide to over fifty basic books on the subject of energy conservation. Commercial, industrial, and general sources have been researched. Addresses, cost, and in some cases short annotations have been provided.

ENVIRONMENT

349.   Illinois. State Geological Survey Division. **Coal Fly Ash: A Review of the Literature and Proposed Classification System With Emphasis on Environmental Impacts.** (By William R. Roy, Richard G. Thiery, Rudolph M Schuller, and John J. Suloway) Urbana, 1981. 69pp. Free. Environmental Geology Note No. 96.

This bibliography offers a comprehensive review of scientific literature on fly ash generated by coal-burning power plants reported in 284 titles since September 1980. General conclusions are formulated, on the basis of these reviews, on the physicochemical characteristics of the solid waste and possible environmental effects. Most of the citations are government publications or periodical articles.

HEALTH

350.　Illinois. Department of Mental Health. Learning Media Institute. **Acquisition List of Care and Rehabilitation Materials.** Springfield, 1971. 212pp. Free. Publication No. 71-2.

A wide range of literature on the rehabilitation of the mentally retarded and mentally ill are included in this list. It is useful for historic comparisons.

351.　Illinois. State Council on Nutrition. **The Art of Food Selection: A Bibliography for Consumers and a Guide for Librarians to Help Consumers.** (By Sherwood Kirk) Springfield, 1982. 7pp. Free.

This functional bibliography was designed for public libraries and includes many government publications.

HISTORY

352.　Illinois. Southern Illinois University, Carbondale. **Sources of Mormon History in Illinois, 1839-48.** (By Stanley B. Kimball) Carbondale, 1964. 76pp. Price on application.

This bibliography is an annotated account of the microfilm collection at Southern Illinois University. "The chief purpose is to acquaint scholars and students of Mormon history with the many sources, mostly primary." The material is divided by letters and documents, newspapers, theses and dissertations, and indexes. There is a name index.

LAWS AND LEGISLATION

353.　Illinois. Southern Illinois University, Carbondale. Center for the Study of Crime, Delinquency, and Corrections. **Bibliography on Classification of Offenders.** (By Thomas G. Eynon) Carbondale, 1970. 31*l.* Price on application.

This collection of over one hundred citations on different types of offenders was designed for professional criminologists and judges as background readings before sentencing.

354.　Illinois. Legislative Council. **Legal Research Materials: Availability of Legal Research Materials in the Illinois State Library, Supreme Court Library, and Legislative Reference Bureau.** (By Camilla Carr) Springfield, 1979. 44pp. Free.

This document, besides describing the library's holdings, serves as a current bibliographic guide to important Illinois legal sources. It could serve as well as an evaluative guide for law libraries.

MINORITY GROUPS

355. Illinois. Commission on Human Relations. **Bibliography on Hispano-America: History and Culture**. Chicago, 1972. 32pp. Free.
These 145 annotated entries recognize Hispano-Americans as a legitimate culture. There are sections on general history and culture, the Puerto Rican experience, and Chicano-Americans. Most of the titles are by Spanish-American authors.

356. Illinois. Illinois-Chicago Project for Inter-Ethnic Dimensions in Education. **Ethnic Resources Guide: An Annotated Bibliography for Teachers**. Chicago, 1977. 42pp. Out-of-Print.
This is a bibliographic guide to selective titles on major minority groups for teachers.

357. Illinois. Commission on Human Relations. Education Services Department. **Selected Books for Children With Emphasis on Black History and Culture**. Chicago, 1973. 12pp. Free.
This annotated bibliography was designed for use by elementary through junior high school students, teachers, librarians, and parents. "Materials that portray an accurate picture of Blacks are included." There are approximately 220 citations on literature, poetry, African roots, biographies, and student history references.

NATIVE PEOPLE

358. Illinois. Commission on Human Relations. **Bibliography on the Native American Experience**. Chicago, 1973. 28pp. Free.
This is a bibliography of recommended books on the Indians of North America for high schools, colleges, public libraries, and personal reading. Many of the authors whose works are included in the 117 entries are themselves Indian. Sections include general history, specific nations, contemporary literature and culture. The arrangement is alphabetical by author and the entries have short annotations. There are separate sections listing periodicals published by Indian associations and films.

NATURAL RESOURCES

359. Illinois. State Geological Survey Division. **Selected and Annotated List of Industrial Minerals, Publications**. (By J. E. Lamar) Urbana, 1972. 24pp. Free. Industrial Mineral Note No. 47.
Over one hundred industrial mineral studies on Illinois are listed in this publication of the State Geological Survey.

POLITICS AND GOVERNMENT

360.   Illinois. Northern Illinois University, De Kalb. Center for Governmental
       Studies. **Chicago's Politics and Society: A Selected Bibliography.** (By
       Vernon Simpson and David Scott) De Kalb, 1972. 81pp. $1.50.
The almost eight hundred citations in this bibliography on Chicago focus on works
of social scientists, historians, journalists, and geographers. Most of the citations
are from the post-1940 period. The first section is an alphabetical listing of books
and articles; part II lists official documents. There is a broad subject index.

361.   Illinois. State Library. Legislative Research Unit. **The Constitution of
       Illinois: A Selective Bibliography.** (By Charlotte B. Stilwell) Springfield,
       1974. 171pp. Free.
Books, federal and state documents, monographs, pamphlets, and periodical articles
comprise the fifteen hundred descriptive citations in this bibliography of the Illinois
constitution. The scope is both historical and current. The arrangement is by year,
for the various constitutions. There is an author index.

362.   Illinois. Northern Illinois University, De Kalb. Center for Governmental
       Studies. **Political Campaigns: A Bibliography.** (By Robert Agranoff) De
       Kalb, 1972. 241pp. $1.50.
This bibliography is designed to assist both academic researchers and political
practitioners. It contains over two hundred selective sources on the subjects of campaign strategies, techniques, media, advertising, and finance.

363.   Illinois. Constitutional Convention. Public Information Committee. **A
       Selected Bibliography on Constitutional Conventions.** Springfield, 1970.
       12pp. Out-of-Print.
The sixth Illinois State Constitutional Convention was held in 1970. This is a bibliographic record of the Proceedings and related documents.

RECREATION/TOURISM

364.   Illinois. Southern Illinois University, Carbondale. Library. **American
       Travellers Abroad: A Bibliography of Accounts Published before 1900.**
       (By Harold F. Smith) Carbondale, 1969. 166pp. $4.00. LC card No.
       70-630365.
The Old World played host to many notable Americans in the nineteenth century.
This bibliography collects in one place over five hundred accounts—diaries, articles,
and books—by these travelers.

SOCIAL CONDITIONS

365.   Illinois. Office of the Superintendent of Public Instruction. **Resource
       Materials: Parenting, Child Abuse, and Birth Defects.** Springfield, 1978.
       16pp. Free.

Child neglect, parenthood, and proper prenatal care are the subjects addressed in this useful bibliography. Over sixty books, articles, pamphlets, and films are reviewed, with cost noted.

WOMEN

366.   Illinois. Sangamon State University. Library. **Guide to Sources: Women's Studies**. Springfield, 1974. 11pp. Free.

In addition to books and government publications, this guide to women's studies sources provides a pathfinder to the card catalog and indexes.

367.   Illinois. Secretary of State. **On Women ... New Books Received**. Springfield, 1984. 4pp. Free.

The latest in an ongoing series, this 1984 title includes current books, pamphlets, government documents, and journal articles on women. Some are annotated. Arrangement is by subject. Major categories include day care, feminism, motherhood, poverty, and religion. Usually fifteen to twenty subjects are covered in each edition.

INDIANA

AREA STUDIES

368.   Indiana. Indiana University, Bloomington. Department of Spanish and Portuguese. **U.S. Political Ideas in Spanish America before 1830: A Bibliographic Study**. (By Merle Simmons) Bloomington, 1977. 86pp. Price on application. LC card No. 76-27513.

This collection of over three hundred citations was designed for historians and political scientists researching the development of democratic thinking in Latin America.

ARTS

369.   Indiana. Indiana University, Bloomington. Chicano-Riqueño Studies. **Bibliography of Hispanic Women Writers**. (By Norma Alcarcon and Sylvia Kossnar) Bloomington, 1980. 86pp. Price on application. LC card No. 80-138062. Bibliographiy No. 1.

Writings of some fifty important Latin-American woman writers are cited in this bibliography.

ECONOMY/ECONOMICS

370.   Indiana. Purdue University, West Lafayette. Krannert Graduate School of Management. **Corporate Failure Prediction: The State of the Art**. (By Christine V. Zavgren) West Lafayette, 1983. 72pp. Free. Paper No. 828.

"This paper surveys empirical research concerning the predictions of bankruptcy." The extent to which the assumptions of these techniques are met in the various studies are discussed. There are thirty-five references included.

371.   Indiana. Purdue University, West Lafayette. Krannert Graduate School of Management. **Two Decades of Research at Krannert: A Bibliography**. (Edited by John M. Houkes) West Lafayette, 1980. 165pp. Free.

"This bibliography documents the outstanding research productivity of the Krannert School." It is a compilation of all research papers and publications of the faculty, amounting to 1,482 studies. Included are institute papers, reprints, working papers, monographs, and information privacy working papers. Arrangement is by author and there is a broad subject index.

EDUCATION AND TRAINING

372.   Indiana. State Board of Health. **Report of Health, Physical Education, and Recreation Research Projects Completed or In Progress in the State of Indiana.** Indianapolis, 1966- . Annual. Free.

Each annual issue of this publication acts as a bibliography to over 150 reports and research papers completed by Indiana physical education personnel. Each report includes the researcher's title, description of the project, status, and publication plans. Many of the reports are on sports medicine.

HISTORY

373.   Indiana. Indiana University, Bloomington. Folklore Institute. **Ozark Folklore: A Bibliography.** (By Vance Randolph) New York, Humanities Press, 1972. 572pp. $25.00. LC card No. 68-64531.

This major bibliography of over three thousand citations on the Ozark region is important for all folklore collections. The subject sections include: songs and ballads, folk speech, place names, tall tales, games and riddles, buried treasure, folk art, fiction, plays, verse, bibliographies, and miscellaneous. There is a combination author-title index.

LAWS AND LEGISLATION

374.   Indiana. Purdue University, West Lafayette. Krannert Graduate School of Management. **Age Discrimination: A Review and Synthesis of the Legal and Psychological Literatures.** (By Robert H. Faley, Lawrence S. Kleiman, and Mark L. Lengnick) West Lafayette, 1983. 39pp. Free. Paper No. 823.

This first installment of a proposed larger future work reviews and synthesizes over fifty legal cases on age discrimination, with some related literature.

MINORITY GROUPS

375.   Indiana. State University, Terre Haute. Cunningham Memorial Library. **Insight—The Negro in the United States; a Selected Bibliography.** Terre Huate, 1970. 45pp. Free. LC card No. 78-633592.

Designed to provide a starting point for the student who is researching black studies, this bibliography lists older standard works as well as current titles "that offer varied viewpoints." Included are books, documents, and newspaper articles. There are sixteen subject categories for the 425 citations.

IOWA

AGRICULTURE

376.   Iowa. State University, Ames. Center for Agricultural and Rural Develop-
        ment. **Selected Bibliography on the Relationships Between Agriculture
        and Water Quality.** (By Craig V. Fulton) Ames, 1973. 130pp. Free.
This selected bibliography offers one thousand unannotated entries on the nature
of water, cycles, supply, management, planning, resource data, engineering, manpower, scientific information, parameters, and background.

EDUCATION AND TRAINING

377.   Iowa. Department of Public Instruction. **Behavioral Objectives: An Anno-
        tated Bibliography.** Des Moines, 1971. 65pp. Free.
The goal of this bibliography is to help teachers to understand their school curriculum assignments relative to developing positive behavior..."to bring about desirable
changes in pupils and teachers." Part I includes "how-to-do-it" publications; part
II focuses on issues relating to objectives; part III on classification of objectives and
part IV presents appropriate audiovisuals.

378.   Iowa. Department of Public Instruction. Alternative Programs Section.
        **Selected Bibliography: A Bibliography of Selection Sources for School
        Library Media Centers.** (By Betty Jo Buckingham) Des Moines, 1979.
        35pp. Available on loan from the State Library of Iowa.
This bibliography is in its fourth edition. Over one hundred books, audiovisuals,
and teaching aids specific to grade level are recommended.

GEOLOGY

379.   Iowa. Geological Survey. **Annotated Bibliography of Source Materials
        in Locating Abandoned Mine Problems in Iowa.** (By J. Lemish and T.
        A. Cloud) Iowa City, 1979. 1 vol. Price on application.

Abandoned mines have become both a challenge and a danger in many states. The over two hundred citations in this collection would be useful for geologists and public officials in those states affected.

381. Iowa. Geological Survey. **Bibliography of Pennsylvania Geology and Coal of Iowa.** (By Paul E. VanDorpe) Iowa City, 1980. 125pp. Price on application. LC card No. 72-621353.

This is an important bibliography of over fifteen hundred citations on the economics and geology of Iowa coal. It updates a 1909 bibliography by J. H. Lees published in the 1908 Annual Report. It is an open-file report. There are divisions according to Iowa counties followed by sections on flora and fauna, geochemistry, regions, stratigraphy, structure, and utilization. There is a short author index.

381. Iowa. Geological Survey. **Bibliography of the Geology of Iowa, 1960-1964.** (By Paul J. Horick, J. C. Prior, and E. E. Hinman) Iowa City, 1967. 49pp. $1.35. Miscellaneous Publication No. 5.

Over four hundred publications on all aspects of Iowa geology, many offered by the state Survey, are described in this Geological Survey publication.

382. Iowa. Geological Survey. **Bibliography of the Pleistocene Geology of Iowa.** Iowa City, n.d. 55pp. 1 vol. Miscellaneous Publication No. 3.

Over three hundred citations are included in this bibliography of Pleistocene geology, with essays on the Pre-Illinoian and Post-Illinoian geology of Iowa.

HISTORY

383. Iowa. Department of Public Instruction. **Iowa History: A Guide to Resource Material.** Des Moines, 1972. 102pp. Free.

Books, pamphlets, folders, periodicals, and audiovisual materials for all age levels on wide variety of historical subjects described in this guide to resource material. Part I contains over four hundred titles; part II describes periodicals.

NATURAL RESOURCES

384. Iowa. Geological Survey. **Bibliography of Gypsum.** Iowa City, n.d. 1 vol. Out-of-Print. Annual Report No. 28.

This important bibliography is appended to the USGS annual report focusing on gypsum in Iowa.

SOCIAL CONDITIONS

385.   Iowa. State University, Ames. Gerontology Center Project. **A Guide to Gerontology Information: Selected Sources in Iowa and Other States.** (Edited by Patricia Apt) Ames, 1979. 80pp. Free.

This document was "designed to be a learning tool for those providing services for elderly people, students, teachers, researchers, and administrators." The major focus is on gerontology resources in Iowa but numerous general sources, government publications, and films available nationally have been included. There are over fifteen hundred citations and many of them are annotated. Arrangement is alphabetic by author within seven format categories.

386.   Iowa. University, Iowa City. Department of Home Economics and Division of Continuing Education. **Social Science Aspects of Clothing for Older Women: An Annotated Bibliography.** (By Adeline Mildred Hoffman) Iowa City, 1977. 1 vol. Free.

The uniqueness of this bibliography on the sociology of clothes makes it a useful addition for academic or textile/fashion libraries. It includes over two hundred citations.

KANSAS

GENERAL

387. Kansas. Emporia State University. School of Library Science. **Selected Government Publications for the Elementary School.** (By Kathleen S. Guthrie et al.) Emporia, 1980. 19pp. Free.
"This booklet has been designed as a possible aid in the choice and use of federal documents for elementary schools. Documents included are a composite of items to be utilized by children, parents, teachers, and librarians." The bibliography contains over ninety useful titles.

388. Kansas. Emporia State University. School of Library Science. **Selected U.S. and Kansas Publications for School and Public Libraries.** (By Donald P. Saselbuhn and Bruce Flanders) Emporia, 1980. 19pp. Free.
This is a useful selection guide of over two hundred pamphlets and government books considered useful for school and public libraries.

389. Kansas. Emporia State University. School of Library Science. **Statistical Data in Kansas State Documents: A Select Annotated Bibliography.** (By Bruce L. Flanders) Emporia, 1981. 39pp. Free. Monograph Series No. 3.
The purpose of this select annotated bibliography of 153 titles is to provide easy access, by specific subject areas, to pertinent Kansas state documents. Related directories, annual reports, and lists of publications have also been included. Categories include: demographics, business and industry, education, energy, environment, government data, recreation, and transportation/communication.

AGRICULTURE

390. Kansas. State University, Manhattan. Institute for Systems Design and Optimization. **Feedlot Manure and Other Agricultural Wastes as Future Material and Energy Resources: Introduction and Literature Review.** (By W. P. Walawender, L. T. Fan, and L. E. Erickson) Manhattan, 1972. 13*l*. LC card No. 72-612202. Report No. 36.
This fifty-item bibliography was an early work on the use of feedlot wastes.

391.   Kansas. State University, Manhattan. Food and Feed Grain Institute. **Losses Which Occur during Harvesting and Storage of Grains: A Bibliography.** (By A. N. Mphuru) Manhattan, 1976. 73pp. Free.

This bibliography on grain was prepared for the Agency for International Development and was designed primarily for use by developing nations. Over 250 citations are included.

AREA STUDIES

392.   Kansas. Agricultural Experiment Station. **Farmer in the Semi-Arid Tropics of South Africa: A Partially Annotated Bibliography.** (By David W. Norman) Manhattan, 1982. 122pp. Free. Research Bulletin No. 4, Contribution No. 1.

This bibliography, authored in cooperation with the International Crop Research Institute, contains over five hundred citations.

393.   Kansas. University, Lawrence. Libraries. **International Bibliography of Vegetation Maps: Vegetation Maps of the Union of Soviet Socialist Republics, Asia, and Australia.** (By A. W. Kuchler) Lawrence, 1968. 389pp. $7.50. LC card No. 65-63240. Library Series No. 29.

This is a major bibliography for biologists and geographers with over one thousand vegetation maps and descriptions.

394.   Kansas. University, Lawrence. Libraries. **Maps of Costa Rica: An Annotated Cartobibliography.** (By Albert E. Palmerlee) Lawrence, 1965. 358pp. Price on application.

This is a guide to over eight hundred maps on Costa Rica with bibliographic aids. Most of the maps are in the University Libraries.

HISTORY

395.   Kansas. Emporia State University. School of Graduate and Professional Studies. **Collapse of the Small Towns on the Great Plains: A Bibliography.** (By Nancy Burns) Emporia, 1982. 36pp. Price on application. LC card No. 82-623111.

After World War II, the small towns comprising the heartland of the Midwest began to decrease in population and industry. This bibliography of over three hundred citations helps to interpret the causes.

LAWS AND LEGISLATION

396.   Kansas. Emporia State University. School of Library Science. **United States and Kansas Legislative Publications**. Emporia, 1981. 30pp. Free. Monograph Series No. 4.

Over fity citations on both federal and Kansas sources related to legislation, including bills, hearings, journals, session laws, and codes, are included in this bibliographic guide.

GENERAL

397. Kentucky. University, Lexington. Libraries. **Kentucky in Fiction: An Annotated Bibliography 1951-1980.** (By Mary Donna Foley) Lexington, 1981. 1 vol. $10.00.

Eighty-six adult books and forty-three children's books related to Kentucky are thoroughly abstracted and indexed in this collection.

GEOLOGY

398. Kentucky. Geological Survey. **Bibliography and Index of Kentucky Geology for 1980.** (By American Geological Institute) Lexington, 1983. 48pp. $2.50. Report of Investigation Series No. 11.

This compilation offers a current listing of publications on all aspects of Kentucky geology with a useful index.

HISTORY

399. Kentucky. Department of Justice. State Law Library. **Index to Kentucky Legal History: References to Selected Sources of Information concerning the Eighteenth and Nineteenth Centuries.** Frankfort, 1983. 167pp. Free.

This is a comprehensive bibliography of noteworthy books and case materials covering two centuries of Kentucky legal history. Helpful appendixes include an explanation of abbreviations and sample entries. There is a thorough subject index.

LAND USE

400. Kentucky. University, Lexington. Libraries. **Landscape Architecture Book Catalog: A Bibliography.** (By Antoinette Powell) Lexington, 1982. 355pp. $10.00. LC card No. 83-620717.

Over one thousand citations on all aspects of landscape architecture are included in this comprehensive work.

NATURAL RESOURCES

401. Kentucky. Geological Survey. **Bibliography of Coal in Kentucky.** Lexington, 1970. 73pp. $2.00. LC card No. 70-634886. Special Publication No. 19.

Coal is very important to the economy of Kentucky. This publication of the Geological Survey presents over five hundred citations on the regions, economy, and geology of coal in Kentucky.

402. Kentucky. Geological Survey. **Bibliography of Industrial and Metallic Minerals in Kentucky through August 1973.** (By Preston McGrain) Lexington, 1975. 1 vol. $2.00. Special Publication No. 23.

This is a useful bibliography on economic geology with over four hundred citations.

403. Kentucky. University, Lexington. Institute for Mining and Mineral Research. **KCERL Bibliography of Oil Shale Literature.** Lexington, 1982. 1 vol. $2.00. Research Report No. 82-69.

The volume of oil shale literature is rapidly increasing. This basic bibliography with quarterly updates is valuable for current awareness. The materials cited are located in the Kentucky Cabinet on Energy Research Library (KCERL).

404. Kentucky. University, Lexington. Institute for Mining and Mineral Research. **Literature Review of Coal Refuse Dikes.** Lexington, 1980. 73pp. $6.50. Research Report No. 80-51.

This report reviews over three hundred citations on building and maintaining coal refuse dikes.

POLITICS AND GOVERNMENT

405. Kentucky. Department of Libraries and Archives. **Reading List for Kentucky Federation of Women's Clubs: A Bibliography.** (By Jo Rawlings) Frankfort, 1983. 16pp. Free.

This is a topical bibliography of eighty items on issues of public interest for those interested in in-depth reading.

GENERAL

406. Louisiana. Secretary of State. **List of Public Documents of Louisiana, 1967-1972.** (By Margaret T. Lane) Baton Rouge, 1973. 316pp. Free. Official Publications No. V.

This is a compilation of over two thousand Louisiana state documents published over a five-year span. These cumulations are required by law. There is an author-subject-title index.

407. Louisiana. Secretary of State. **List of Public Documents of Louisiana, 1973-1979.** (By Grace Moore) Baton Rouge, 1982. 376pp. Price on application. Official Publications No. VI.

This is another in a series of official Louisiana bibliographies of state documents. This list offers a comprehensive record of fifteen hundred official Louisiana documents from the years 1973 through 1979.

ARTS

408. Louisiana. State University and A and M College, Eunice. LeDoux Library. **Puppets and Puppetry.** (Compiled by Shirley C. Harrison) Eunice, 1981. 13pp. Free. Bibliography No. 13.

There are 236 citations arranged alphabetically by author in this functional bibliography on the construction and operation of puppets.

409. Louisiana. State University and A and M College, Eunice. LeDoux Library. **Sculpture and Sculptors: A Bibliography.** (Compiled by Thomas C. Hobbs) Eunice, 1974. 11*l.* Free. Bibliography No. 7.

This bibliography on sculpture and sculptors offers over two hundred citations arranged alphabetically within categories on sculpture in general, the history of sculpture, individual scuptors, and so on.

ECONOMY/ECONOMICS

410.   Louisiana. State University and A and M College, Baton Rouge. College of Business Administration. Division of Research. **Selected Bibliography on the Louisiana Economy.** (By Louis J. Rodriquez and Michael E. Abadie) Baton Rouge, 1972. 30*l.* Price on application. LC card No. 72-610573. Occasional Paper No. 5.

Six hundred citations on agriculture, employment, income, finance, government, labor, natural resources, population, the economy, and transportation are included in this bibliography on the Louisiana economy.

EDUCATION AND TRAINING

411.   Louisiana. University of Southwestern Louisiana. Office of Institutional Research. **Institutional Research: A Comprehensive Bibliography.** (By Jack Testerman, Robert Blackmon, and Terry White) Lafayette, 1972. 131pp. LC card No. 72-611550. Research Series No. 12.

Over four hundred citations related to institutional research in higher education are highlighted in this comprehensive collection.

412.   Louisiana. State University and A and M College, Eunice. LeDoux Library. **Public Speaking: A Bibliography.** (Compiled by Shih Yang) Eunice, 1971. 12*l.* Free. Bibliography No. 3.

Debates and debating, speechmaking, quotations, parliamentary practice, communication, language, and oratory, orations, and orators are among the topics covered in this 145-item collection on public speaking.

413.   Louisiana. Department of Education. **Selected Resources in Career Education.** (By James S. Cookston) Baton Rouge, 1973. 17*l.* Free. Bulletin No. 1230.

This bibliography is designed for school librarians. Many of the 450 sources are textbooks and curriculum guides. The material is divided into grades 5-8 and grades 9-12.

414.   Louisiana. Department of Education. **Teaching Outline and Resource Guide for Health Education, Grades 9-12.** Baton Rouge, 1967. 85pp. Free. Bulletin No. 1107.

"This publication reflects a coordinated effort in the health field to help teachers overcome difficult problems in instruction." There are almost two hundred specific citations along with supplemental sources.

ENVIRONMENT

415.   Louisiana. State University and A and M College, Baton Rouge. School of Forestry and Wildlife Management. **Fire Ecology and Fire Use in the Pine Forest of the South: A Chronological Bibliography.** (By A. Bigler Crow) Baton Rouge, 1982. 131pp. Free.

"The pattern of a year-by-year listing portrays the history of fire ecology and fire use in southern (roughly Delaware to Texas) pine forests." A year-reference numbering system enhances the author and subject indexes.

HISTORY

416.   Louisiana. Louisiana State University and A and M College, Baton Rouge. School of Home Economics. **Dress and Adornment of the Head: An Annotated Bibliography.** (By Miriam Morris and Eleanor Kelley) Baton Rouge, 1970. 33pp. LC card No. 78-633793.

Issued in cooperation with the Agricultural Experiment Station, this specialized bibliography presents over three hundred citations on hats, helmets, and head adornments.

417.   Louisiana. University of Southwestern Louisiana. **Selected Bibliography of Scholarly Literature on Colonial Louisiana and New France.** (By Glenn R. Conrad and Carl A. Brasseaux) Lafayette, 1982. 138pp. Price on application. LC card No. 82-73751.

This is an important bibliography for all collections dealing with the history of the South and Louisiana. The over five hundred citations include much material on the early French settlers.

NATIVE PEOPLE

418.   Louisiana. Department of Conservation. Geological Survey. **Bibliography Relative to Indians of the State of Louisiana.** (By Robert W. Neuman and Lanier A. Simmons) Baton Rouge, 1969. 72pp. Free. Anthropological Study No. 4.

This anthropological study from the Geological Survey contains 456 entries, most of which are annotated. Entries are arranged according to author. Journal articles and documents comprise the bulk of the citations. Translations from the French are provided. There is no index.

NATURAL RESOURCES

419.   Louisiana. Department of Natural Resources. Office of Forestry. **School Bibliography and Order Blank.** Baton Rouge, 1981. 1 vol. Free.

Many of the items cited in this collection would be useful in general vertical files. Over one hundred current studies on Louisiana forestry and natural resources are offered.

OCEANOGRAPHY

420. Louisiana. State University and A and M College, Baton Rouge. Coastal Studies Institute. **Selected Bibliography on Beach Features and Related Nearshore Processes**. (By Robert Dolan and James McClory) Baton Rouge, 1965. 59pp. Free.

"This bibliography is believed to contain seventy-five percent of the most pertinent filtration on beach citations through 1965." More than thirteen hundred citations on coastal and beach morphology, measurement techniques, sediment properties, transport, coastal engineering, and beach processes are reviewed.

PLANNING

421. Louisiana. University of New Orleans. School of Urban and Regional Studies. Earl K. Long Library. **Guide to Studies in Urban and Public Affairs**. New Orleans, 1983. 13pp. Free.

This bibliography of fifty-five planning studies and books (mostly on Louisiana) addresses the topics of flood control, recreation, transportation, and housing among others. There is a general index.

SPACE EXPLORATION

422. Louisiana. State University and A and M College, Eunice. LeDoux Library. **Man Probes the Universe**. (Compiled by Shih Yang) Eunice, 1970. 8*l*. Free. LC card No. 79-633481.

This bibliography represents a preliminary selection on space exploration with 120 citations divided among astronomy, instruments, astrophysics, and teaching.

WOMEN

423. Louisiana. State University and A and M College, Eunice. LeDoux Library. **And John, Don't Forget the Ladies: An Annotated Bibliography on Women**. (By Martha Rosen) Eunice, 1980. 46*l*. Free. LC card No. 80-623568. Bibliography No. 12.

This bibliography on women annotates over two hundred government documents on women generally, child care, battered children, alcohol use, education, employment, equal rights, media, midlife, minorities, older women, rape, statistics, sexual preference, teenage pregnancy, and public welfare.

MAINE

GENERAL

424. Maine. Department of Educational and Cultural Services. **All about Maine.** (By Clyde W. Swett and Mary L. Haskell) Augusta, 1969. 90pp. Free.
This guide to print and film resources for Maine studies was designed primarily for elementary and junior high grades. There are over three hundred citations organized into the categories of biography, fiction, folklore, literature, maps, natural history, and general background. There is a title index.

425. Maine. University, Orono. Folger Library. **Bibliography of Maine, 1960-1975.** (By Eric S. Flower) Orono, 1976. 1 vol. Price on application.
"A union list of books about Maine or by Maine authors found in four of the largest libraries in the State: Bangor Public, Maine State Library, Portland Public, and the Folger Library."

426. Maine. State Planning Office. **Critical Areas Program List of Publications 1975-1982.** Augusta, 1982. 14pp. Free.
The Critical Areas Program has produced over two hundred reports, brochures, and fact sheets related to Maine's significant botanical, geological, zoological, and scenic resources.

427. Maine. State Library Bureau. **Maine In Print Index 1976-1979.** Augusta, 1982. 49pp. Free.
This is a comprehensive bibliography to a wide variety of books and documents on Maine arranged according to author and title with a separate section of town histories. There is one index to all titles.

428. Maine. Department of Educational and Cultural Services. **Maine Resources: Print and Non-Print.** Augusta, 1977. 261pp. Price on application.
"Prepared because of the huge interest in studying Maine," this bibliography includes over two thousand books, bibliographies, periodical articles, and audiovisuals on the people, economics, fiction, folklore, literature, and history of Maine. There is a combined author-title index.

AREA STUDIES

429.   Maine. University, Orono. New England-Atlantic Provinces-Quebec Center. **Atlantic Provinces of Canada, Union List of Materials in the Large Libraries of Maine.** Orono, 1971. 70pp. Out-of-Print.

"This bibliography includes the holdings on the Atlantic Provinces of Canada in periodicals, serials, newspapers, and non-fiction books." Approximately fourteen hundred citations are included on the Acadia region, all Atlantic provinces, New Brunswick, Nova Scotia, and Prince Edward Island. There is a special section of theses as well.

OCEANOGRAPHY

430.   Maine. University, Orono. Marine Advisory Program. **Education and the World: A Partial Bibliography for Marine Educators.** (By Richard M. Schlenker) Orono, 1979. 1 vol. Price on application. MSG-M-No. 7/77.

Over fifty of the most useful current books on oceans are highlighted in this selective listing.

431.   Maine. University, Orono. Marine Advisory Program. **Maine Sea Grant Publications Index, 1972-1980.** Orono, 1980. 9pp. Free.

The 112 citations in this bibliographic/publications list are arranged by principal series. Prices are provided and there is a subject index.

RECREATION/TOURISM

432.   Maine. Department of Conservation. Bureau of Parks and Recreation. Community Recreation Division. **References for Recreation Services.** Augusta, 1976. 18pp. Free.

Some three hundred citations on recreation, administration, camping, leisure, management, outdoor education, playgrounds, and special populations are referenced in this document. Date of publication and pagination are provided.

WILDLIFE

433.   Maine. University, Orono. Department of Oceanography. Migratory Fish Research Institute. **Bibliography of the Eggs, Larval, and Juvenile Stages of Fishes: Including Other Pertinent References.** (By Richard F. Shaw) Orono, 1980. 266pp. Price on application. Technical Report No. 61.

This important bibliography, which contains over forty-one hundred citations, is an effort to bring together the vast amount of existing literature on ichthyoplankton. Coverage is international. Basic bibliographic information is provided; there are author, subject, and scientific name indexes.

434.   Maine. University, Orono. Marine Advisory Program. **Partial Bibliography of the Bay Scallop,** *Argopecten irradians* **Lamarck, 1960-1980.** Orono, 1982. 14pp. Free. RF-MSG-82-5.

This partial bibliography on the bay scallop presents approximately seventy-five citations.

435.   Maine. University, Orono. Marine Advisory Program. **Preliminary Bibliography of the Soft Shell Clam For the Years 1960-1978.** (By Les Watling et al.) Orono, 1979. 1 vol. Free. MSG-TR-44/79.

Over one hundred works on the soft-shell clam, from the years 1960 through 1978, are cited in this bibliography.

ARTS

436. Maryland. University, College Park. College of Library and Information Services. **Children's Literature: Selected Essays and Bibliographies.** (By Anne S. MacLeod) College Park, 1977. 153pp. $9.75. LC card No. 620023.
Over one hundred bibliographies on children's literature are reviewed in this "guide to selection of materials by media specialists."

DISABLED

437. Maryland. State Law Library. **Guide to Sources of Information on Education and the Handicapped Child.** (By Mary L. Yoder) Annapolis, 1982. 8pp. Free.
The eighty-two citations in this collection are mostly treatises and government documents. There is also a section of looseleaf services for current legal information in specialized fields.

438. Maryland. State Department of Education. Division of Special Education. **Pick-a-Title: A Collection of Media about the Handicapped.** Baltimore, 1980. 28pp. Free.
This collection was prepared in response to an educators. Over two hundred films, filmstrips, cassettes, and books on the handicapped have been arranged according to preschool, intermediate, and young adult activities. There are also sections for parents and professionals, with many annotated citations.

EDUCATION AND TRAINING

439. Maryland. State Department of Education. **Maryland Instructional Materials List.** Baltimore, 1971. 32pp. Free.
This list was designed to be a "time-saving compendium of pamphlets, books, periodicals, maps, films, and teaching kits for use in Maryland classrooms." It is useful for general Maryland studies. The six hundred sources are available from fifty-seven official and semi-official agencies. Several citations are annotated; prices are included for all.

ENERGY

440.   Maryland. Department of Natural Resources. Power Plant Siting Program. **A Bibliography of the Maryland Plant Siting Program**. (Edited by Thomas Magette) Annapolis, 1982. 54pp. Free.

The fourth edition of this bibliography includes 427 reports on eleven specific site-monitoring programs. There are chapters on air monitoring, power plant studies in the Upper Chesapeake and Lower Susquehanna regions, the Potomac fisheries, radiological monitoring, and regional siting. The NTIS ordering number is provided for many of the entries.

LAWS AND LEGISLATION

441.   Maryland. State Law Library. **Divorce: Maryland Divorce Law: A Selected Bibliography of Materials**. Annapolis, 1982. 6pp. Free.

This bibliography on divorce in Maryland presents a total of fifty-five citations from the state law library. Legal texts and forms, recent court cases, encyclopedic sources, and legal periodical articles are documented.

POLITICS AND GOVERNMENT

442.   Maryland. Commission on the Status of Women. **Educational Materials on Citizenship**. Baltimore, 1971. 27pp. Free.

This basic reading list of citizenship and women's rights includes approximately seventy-five citations.

EDUCATION AND TRAINING

443. Massachusetts. Department of Education. Dissemination Project. **Resources for Schools: Everyone's Guide to Peer Counseling.** (By Sylvester DiDiego) Boston, 1982. 73pp. Free. Dissemination Report No. 23.
Over one hundred sources provide "information on how to set up a peer counseling program in a school or community setting and resources needed."

444. Massachusetts. Department of Education. Dissemination Project. **Resources for Schools: Framework for Health Education in Massachusetts Schools.** Boston, 1982. 108pp. Free. Dissemination Report No. 26.
A bibliography of over 125 curriculum guides, books, and media sources augments this overview of Massachusetts health teaching.

445. Massachusetts. Department of Education. Dissemination Project. **Resources for Schools: Resources for Training Educators of Children with Special Needs.** (By Cecilia M. DiBella and Elizabeth J. Maillett) Boston, 1978? 88pp. Free. Dissemination Report No. 9.
This bibliographic directory to twenty-five categories of special education highlights early childhood education, parents, needs of the severely handicapped, testing, mainstreaming, and vocational education.

446. Massachusetts. Amherst College, Amherst. Center for Urban Education. **Selected Bibliography of Urban Education.** (By Byrd L. Jones) Amherst, 1971. 17l. Free.
The staff of the Center for Urban Education at Amherst has selected fifty books and documents they deem most important to the study of urban education. Many are classics of the 1960s and early 1970s.

447. Massachusetts. Department of Education. Dissemination Project. **Teaching Speaking and Listening Skills in the Elementary and Secondary School.** (By Kenneth L. Brown) Boston, 1981. 85pp. Free.
The first section of this study is an overview of teaching and listening skill research. The second section is a bibliography of over one hundred sources for teaching speaking and listening at the elementary and secondary levels. Most of the entries are briefly annotated.

ENERGY

448. Massachusetts. Department of Education. Dissemination Project. **Focus on: Classroom Energy Materials.** Boston, 1980. 46pp. Free.

The 130 citations in this collection focus on timely energy resources for public schools. Bibliographies, classroom materials, and funding sources are covered. All citations are annotated and acquisition addresses are provided.

449. Massachusetts. Solar Action Office. **Solar Bibliography.** Boston, 1978. 13pp. Free.

This is a basic reading list on solar energy of use for media and public libraries.

ENVIRONMENT

450. Massachusetts. Amherst College, Amherst. Institute for Man and Environment. **Wetlands—Uses and Misuses: A Selected Bibliography.** (By Richard B. Newton) Amherst, 1977. 1 vol. Free.

This bibliography addresses key topics in wetlands use and misuse including assessment, protection, and management. It is not exhaustive and some topics are emphasized more than others. Useful for planners, scientists, and others with responsibility for wetland use.

HEALTH

451. Massachusetts. General Court. Science Resource Office. **Health Effects of Asbestos Inhalation: A Review of the Literature.** (By Douglas Gilbert) Boston, 1976. 26*l.* Free.

Occupational hazards of asbestos, especially lung cancer, are reviewed in this seventy-five-item bibliography. It was authored cooperatively with the State Asbestos Commission.

LAWS AND LEGISLATION

452. Massachusetts. Department of Education. Bureau of Equal Educational Opportunity. **Bibliography of Multi-Ethnic and Sex-Fair Resource Materials Available.** Boston, 1976. 35pp. Free.

This useful guide for all school systems recommends curricular materials to be used in the implementation of Chapter 622 of Massachusetts law.

453. Massachusetts. Bureau of Library Extension. **Prison Reform: A Selective Bibliography.** (By Dina G. Malgeri and Mary A. Litterst) Boston, 1972. 12*l.* Free.

This is a ready-reference guide to over fifty citations on prison reform, from a state that was in the forefront of the movement.

NATIVE PEOPLE

454.   Massachusetts. Department of Education. Bureau of Curriculum Innovation. **Selected Media about the American Indian for Young Children, K-3.** (By Suzanne S. Cane) Boston, 1970. 21pp. Free.

The "best" books for young children presenting a nonbiased view of the American Indian are suggested in this brief bibliography. Approximately seventy-five titles are described.

SOCIAL CONDITIONS

455.   Massachusetts. Holyoke Community College Library. **Bibliography on Gerontology: Pamphlets and Articles on the Incapacitated Elderly.** Holyoke, 1978. 10pp. Free.

Fifty citations, with emphasis on the homebound elderly, are included in this brief gerontology bibliography.

456.   Massachusetts. Rehabilitation Commission. Library. **Productivity in Human Service Agencies: A Bibliography.** (By David Cain) Boston, 1983. 7pp. Free.

The eighty entries included in this collection are relevant to productivity in human service agencies with emphasis on local government agencies. The titles cited also have implications for productivity in all vocational rehabilitation agencies.

WILDLIFE

457.   Massachusetts. Agricultural Experiment Station. **Bibliography of the Recent Literature on Beaver.** Amherst, 1980. 128pp. Free. Research Bulletin No. 665.

This is an important current bibliography on beavers, with over three hundred citations.

MICHIGAN

GENERAL

458.   Michigan. Department of Education. State Library Services. **Michigan Literature in the Sixties.** Lansing, 1971. 32pp. Free. Bibliography Vol. 9, No. 5-10.
This bibliography contains over three hundred briefly annotated citations arranged into the following categories: Literature of the Sixties, Michigan in Novels, Poetry, Writing for the News, Underground, What's New With Books and Writers, Friends of the Arts, and A Subjective Mirror.

459.   Michigan. Department of Education. State Library Services. **Selected Bibliography of Non-Sexist Fiction: Preschool through Sixth Grade.** Lansing, 1980. 32pp. Free.
Over two hundred authors and 250 works are represented in this selective bibliography of nonsexist fiction. Arrangement is alphabetic by author; adequate annotations are provided. Material is divided evenly between early and upper elementary. A list of selection sources is appended.

460.   Michigan. Department of Education. State Library Services. **Selected Bibliography of Non-Sexist Fiction: Seventh through Twelfth Grade.** Lansing, 1980. 26pp. Free.
This bibliography includes the work of two hundred authors whose works appear in one or more selection source and who meet the criteria of the Kalamazoo Public Schools. Over 260 books are annotated. Grade level is indicated for each title. The Kalamazoo guidelines are also included.

461.   Michigan. Department of Education. State Library Services. **Selected List of Basic Inexpensive Materials on Michigan.** Lansing, 1971. 8pp. Free. Library Tool Bibliography No. 5.
Seventy annotated citations in twenty-three categories provide a good basic list on Michigan.

462.   Michigan. Department of Education. Office for Sex Equity in Education. **Sex Equity in Education: An Annotated Bibliography**. Lansing, 1980. 50pp. Free.

This is an alphabetical listing by title and subject of over two hundred sources aiding a bias-free curriculum. Each entry includes a call number in the Michigan collection, titles, format, source, and cost. There is a broad subject index and a listing of addresses for acquisition.

AREA STUDIES

463.   Michigan. State University, East Lansing. Department of Agricultural Economics. **Bibliography on Rural Development in Tanzania**. (By James E. Kocher and Beverly Fleischer) East Lansing, 1979. 77pp. Free. MSU Rural Development Paper No. 3.

Demographics, villages and settlements, farm management, and policy are among the twenty-eight subjects covered in this bibliography. The over one thousand citations include books, periodical articles, and documents. An author list is provided.

464.   Michigan. State University, East Lansing. Department of Agricultural Economics. **Rise and Fall of Community Development in Developing Countries, 1950-65: A Critical Analysis and an Annotated Bibliography**. (By Lane E. Holdcroft) East Lansing, 1978. 72pp. Free. MSU Rural Development Paper No. 2.

"The community development approach was directed at the promotion of better living for the whole community with active participation." There are 180 citations with discussions of origins, implications, and the decade of prominence.

DISABLED

465.   Michigan. State University, East Lansing. Institute for International Studies in Education. Non-Formal Education Information Center. **Non-Formal Education and the Handicapped in Developing Countries: A Selected Annotated Bibliography**. East Lansing, 1982. 38pp. $1.75.

Seeking to assist in establishing a transnational network of practitioners, the center has prepared an annotated bibliography citing references regarding disability issues in developing countries. Many of the reports were produced in developing countries. Topics discussed include community-based training, special needs, and attitude studies.

EDUCATION AND TRAINING

466.   Michigan. Department of Education. **Bibliography of Elementary Guidance Materials**. Lansing, 1976. 15pp. Free.

"Often elementary guidance materials have been difficult to obtain." These fifty citations are mainly for "office use only."

467. Michigan. Department of Education. State Library Services. Education Resources Information Center. **Bilingual Education: A Bibliography of Non-English Books in the State Library.** Lansing, 1983? 3 vol. Price on application.

These useful bibliographies include non-English books other than Spanish or Native American, Spanish language books, and Native-American language books.

468. Michigan. Department of Education. State Library Services. **Bilingual Education: A Bibliography of Non-English Books in the State Library, Non-English Books Other than Spanish or Native American.** Lansing, 1982. 41pp. Free.

This bibliography is divided according to fifty-six important languages and includes primarily introductory texts and dictionaries. There are also appendixes for Arabic series and dictionaries.

469. Michigan. Department of Education. State Library Services. **Bilingual Education: Books for Educators, an Annotated Bibliography.** Lansing, 1981? 39pp. Free.

This bibliography of resources for bilingual educators include books and booklets available at the State Library that were added to the collection since 1976. There are 290 citations, arranged alphabetically by title. A good mix between theory and practical materials is achieved. There is a broad subject index.

470. Michigan. Department of Education. Office for Sex Equity in Education: **Content Specific Bibliographies: Mathematics.** Lansing, 1983. 10pp. Free.

This compilation of supplementary materials for both elementary and secondary mathematics curricula is designed to provide sex-fair and sex-affirmative print and nonprint resources for educators. Persons seeking nonbiased mathematics material should find it useful. The 135 citations are divided into curriculum materials, games, biographies, career information, national resource projects, workshop materials, math anxiety, and research studies. Acquisition information is provided.

471. Michigan. State University, East Lansing. Institute for International Studies in Education. Non-Formal Education Information Agency. **Evaluation of Non-Formal Education: A Selected Annotated Bibliography.** East Lansing, 1983. 79pp. Price on application. Annotated Bibliography No. 13.

"A four section annotated bibliography is comprised of sources of information on evaluation, intended for non-formal education specialists." The difficulty of isolating impacts, the question of qualitative versus quantitative data, and cost effectiveness are among the themes addressed in this compilation. Nearly 250 citations are included.

472. Michigan. State University, East Lansing. Institute for International Studies in Education. Non-Formal Education Information Agency. **Non-Formal Education and Radio: A Selected, Annotated Bibliography.** East Lansing, 1983. 47pp. Price on application. Annotated Bibliography No. 14.

The first section of this bibliography includes 118 citations from twenty-five nations. Materials concern the use of radio and mass communication for adult education and are intended for those actively involved in nonformal education and development. The second section describes ten newsletters, section III lists twelve organizations in eight countries to contatct for further information.

EMPLOYMENT

473. Michigan. State University, East Lansing. College of Agriculture and Natural Resources. Department of Sociology.. Rural Manpower Center. **Rural Manpower: An Annotated Bibliography**. East Lansing, 1968. 42pp. Free.

The scope of this publication is migrant and rural labor in the Midwest and other high rural manpower areas. The three hundred items cited include bibliographies, books, journals, bulletins, and government reports. Short annotations are supplied for the majority of the entries. Action-oriented publications are emphasized over comprehensive coverage.

GEOLOGY

474. Michigan. Michigan State University, East Lansing. Soil Science Department. **Research Library Reference Materials for Data Pertaining to the Movement of Nutrients through Earth Materials**. East Lansing, 1972? 43pp. Out-of-Print.

This list of library reference materials was issued in cooperation with the state Water Resources Commission. Over 150 citations are included.

HEALTH

475. Michigan. University, Ann Arbor. Medical School. Office of Educational Resources and Research. Learning Resource Center. **Audiovisual Resources for Diabetes Education**. Ann Arbor, 1980. 344pp. Price on application.

This bibliography, in its second edition, lists several hundred titles on diabetes. It was issued cooperatively with the Michigan Diabetes Research and Training Center.

HISTORY

476. Michigan. Department of Education. State Library Services. **Michigan's Deprived: A Selected Bibliography**. Lansing, 1971. 3pp. Free.

Here is a historical bibliography indicating some fifty of the most important works on the culturally deprived. It was prepared during the heyday of the federal programs.

LAWS AND LEGISLATION

477. Michigan. Eastern Michigan University, Ypsilanti. Library. **How to Find Information on Juvenile Delinquency.** Ypsilanti, 1974. 7*l.* Free.

This is a bibliographic guide to materials in the EMU Library, including indexes, periodicals, selected government publications, and pamphlets.

478. Michigan. Eastern Michigan University, Ypsilanti. Library. **Right of Privacy in an Open Society.** (By Arlys Evans) Ypsilanti, 1971. 10*l.* Free. Bibliographic Series No. 16.

This title is a basic bibliography on privacy laws.

MINORITY GROUPS

479. Michigan. State University, East Lansing. College of Agriculture and Natural Resources. Department of Sociology. Rural Manpower Center. **Mexican-Americans in the Midwest: An Annotated Bibliography.** (By Nancy Salana) East Lansing, 1969. 60pp. Free. Special Paper No. 10.

This is a "selective bibliography of sources dealing with Mexican-Americans living in Michigan and other parts of the Midwestern U.S. emphasizing those factors most significant in migration and settlement." There are 120 citations abstracted, dating from 1920. There are thirteen chapters including demography, employment, culture, education, and language subjects.

480. Michigan. Department of Education. State Library Services. **Negroes in Michigan: A Selected Bibliography.** Lansing, 1969. 6pp. Out-of-Print.

This is a partial bibliography of books, pamphlets, and periodical articles in the library's holdings, including some good historical studies; the arrangement is by author.

NATIVE PEOPLE

481. Michigan. Department of Education. State Library Services. **Native Americans in Michigan.** Lansing, 1972. 4*l.* Free.

The Michigan Collection materials are divided into basic sources, recent materials, Indian periodicals, and newspapers. Some classic sources are included. Arrangement is by author within each category.

PLANNING

482. Michigan. Eastern Michigan University, Ypsilanti. Library. **City and Regional Planning.** (By Hannelore B. Rader) Ypsilanti, 1970. 39*l.* LC card No. 75-634374.

This is an annotated listing of books and documents on city planning, with emphasis on urban renewal.

SOCIAL CONDITIONS

483. Michigan. Agricultural Experiment Station. **Farmers Organizations and Movements: Research Needs and a Bibliography of the United States and Canada.** (By Denton E. Morrison) East Lansing, 1970. 116pp. Free. North Central Regional Research Publication; Research Bulletin No. 24.

This bibliography has weathered the passage of time. It is still valuable for its citations related to the farm movement, the Grange, and populists.

484. Michigan. Eastern Michigan University, Ypsilanti. Library. **Militarism in Contemporary America.** Ypsilanti, 1971. 9*l.* Free. Bibliography Series No. 17.

The emphasis of this one hundred-item collection is the Vietnam War period.

TECHNOLOGY

485. Michigan. Department of Education. State Library Services. **Automation Data Processing.** Lansing, 1970. 9pp. Free.

This is a bibliography of 119 citations on data processing and system management, arranged by author.

TRANSPORTATION

486. Michigan. University, Ann Arbor. College of Engineering. Department of Naval Architecture. **Naval Architecture and Marine Engineering.** Ann Arbor, 1981. 22pp. Free. Department Report Series.

This is both a publication list and a bibliography to 237 studies on marine architecture, specific transportation problems, and the physics of water. Full bibliographic information and prices are included.

WETLANDS

487. Michigan. Department of Natural Resources. **Coastal Wetland Value Study Annotated Bibliography.** (By Eugene Jaworski, et al.) Lansing, 1977. 667pp. Free.

These 667 abstracted titles reflect a comprehensive collection of materials on wetland values in coastal Michigan. This volume had been designed to supplement the author's *Coastal Wetland Value Study*. There is a subject index.

WOMEN

488. Michigan. Department of Education. Office for Sex Equity in Education. **American History Bibliography.** Lansing, 1983. 1 vol. Free.

Both elementary and secondary materials are part of this bibliography on women in American history. Included are biographical references, statistical studies, lesson plans, and pilot programs.

489.   Michigan. Department of Education. Office for Sex Equity in Education. **Media Fair Bibliography**. Lansing, 1982. 1 vol. Free.

The Media Fair is an excellent exhibit of sex-fair materials suitable for large gatherings of teachers and librarians. The bibliography cites books, games, and other nonbiased educational materials that are part of this exhibit.

490.   Michigan. Department of Education. Office for Sex Equity in Education. **Minority Women Bibliography**. East Lansing, 1983. 1 vol. Free.

This bibliography specifically addresses the academic interests and needs of minority women. Included are both elementary and secondary materials. The over two hundred citations include contributions of minority women to society through biographical and statistical studies, research, and lesson plans addressing sex equity questions.

491.   Michigan. State University, East Lansing. Department of Agricultural Economics. **Rural Women Workers in the 20th Century: An Annotated Bibliography**. East Lansing, 1973. 64pp. Free. Special Publication No. 15.

Only citations that consider both rural manpower and womanpower are included in this collection. The first section is on preparation for work while the second is on the subject of qualitative and quantitative work. There are over six hundred citations, all with short annotations.

492.   Michigan. State University. Institute for International Studies in Education. Non-Formal Education Information Center. **Women in Development: A Selected Annotated Bibliography and Resource Guide**. (By Linda Gire Vavrus and Ron Cadieux) East Lansing, 1980. 69pp. Free.

Issued on cooperation with the U.S. Office of Education and the Office of Women in Development of the Agency for International Development, this title reviews over four hundred materials on women in developing countries.

MINNESOTA

GENERAL

493.　Minnesota. Department of Education. Division of Instruction. Educational Media Unit. **Reference Books for the Elementary School Library or Media Center.** St. Paul, 1976. 13pp. Free.

This is a useful guide to recommended reference books appropriate for young children. Ordering information is included.

AGRICULTURE

494.　Minnesota. University, Minneapolis. Department of Agricultural and Applied Economics. **Bibliography of Economic Regulations or Agricultural and Nonagricultural Industries, 1960-1979.** (By W. W. Grant and D. C. Dahl) Minneapolis, 1980. 50pp. $1.00.

This is a worthwhile bibliography on government regulations on industry.

495.　Minnesota. University, Minneapolis. Institute of Agriculture, Forestry, and Home Economics. **List of Departmental Publications in Agricultural and Applied Economics, July 1979-June 1980.** (Prepared by Nancy Van Hemert) Minneapolis, 1980. 52pp. Free.

A publication list and a subject-indexed bibliography to over 450 experiment station bulletins, extension service publications, economic reports, staff papers, journal articles, books, and theses. There is also an author index.

496.　Minnesota. Agricultural Experiment Station. **Method and Materials for the Maintenance of Turf on Highway Right-of-Way: An Annotated Bibliography.** (By Margaret H. Smithberg and Donald B. White) St. Paul, 1971. 102pp. Free. LC card No. 71-637087. Miscellaneous Report No. 105.

Maintenance of sufficient turf along highways presents a challenge to maintenance planners. This report offers over two hundred citations on the subject.

AREA STUDIES

497. Minnesota. University, Minneapolis. Center for Population Studies. **Taiwan Demography, 1946-1971: A Selected Annotated Bibliography of Government Documents.** (By Henry C. Cheng) Minneapolis, 1973. 60pp. Free. Occasional Studies Paper No. 1.

"Included are 150 items selected for their high academic reference value, the most recent of which was published in 1971." Subjects include general demographics, fertility, mortality, family planning, and population policies. All are amply annotated.

DRUG USE AND ABUSE

498. Minnesota. Department of Education. Division of Instruction. **Bibliography of Resource Materials for Educators.** St. Paul, 1976. 27pp. Free.

Included in this bibliography are over one hundred citations for teachers on the wise use of drugs. The titles were recommended by the Affective Drug Abuse Prevention Team.

EDUCATION AND TRAINING

499. Minnesota. Instructional Materials Center. **Annotated Bibliography of Consumer Homemaking Materials in Home Economics.** (By Norma Baker) White Bear Lake, 1976. 151pp. Free.

This is an annotated bibliography of child development, clothing textiles, consumer education, family life education, food and nutrition, housing, and home furnishings materials for K-Adult.

500. Minnesota. Minnesota Curriculum Services Center. **Annotated Bibliography of Prevocational-Vocational Materials for Students with Special Needs.** White Bear Lake, 1977. 1 vol. Price on application.

Materials in reading/language arts, math survival skills, and vocational and instructional resources for students with special needs comprise this annotated bibliography.

501. Minnesota. Department of Education. Pupil Personnel Services Section. **Resource Guide for Career Development in the Junior High School.** (By Arland Benson) St. Paul, 1972. 161pp. Out-of-Print.

While designed for junior high school students, these five hundred citations on career development guidance could also be useful for advising older students and adults.

EMPLOYMENT

502. Minnesota. University, Minneapolis. Industrial Relations Center. **The Whole Center Catalog: 25 Years of Industrial Relations Center Staff Publications, a Bibliography, 1945-1970.** (By Georgianna Herman, Mary Joan Flynn Peterson, and Barbara Krueger Jeppesen) Minneapolis, 1972. 131*l*. Free.

The subject emphasis of these five hundred reports and reprints is on collective bargaining and public negotiating.

HISTORY

503. Minnesota. University, Minneapolis. Immigration History Research Center. **Hungarians in the United States and Canada: A Bibliography.** (By Joseph Szeplaki) Minneapolis, 1977. 113pp. $6.00. LC card No. 77-89096. Ethnic Series No. 2.

There are entries from 701 books, 198 serials, and eighteen manuscripts in this bibliography, based on the holdings of the Immigration History Research Center Library. There is emphasis on history, language, textbooks, literature, religion, associations, music, and manuscripts. An index of names is provided.

504. Minnesota. University, Minneapolis. Immigration History Research Center. **Romanii Din America: Bibliogrfie Comentata.** (By Radu Toma) Minneapolis, 1976. 234pp. Free. ($2.00 mailing)

This is a thorough bibliography of Romanian life in America—in the Romanian language. History, religion, organizations, and reference works are among the topics covered.

505. Minnesota. University, Minneapolis. Immigration History Research Center. **Serbs in the United States and Canada: A Comprehensive Bibliography.** (By Robert Gakovich and Milan Radovich) Minneapolis, 1977? 129pp. $6.00.

Categories in this five hundred-entry bibliography include biographies, archives, the press, directories, general works on Serbs, organizations and societies, regional works, Serbian-American literature, textbooks, readers, and works on Yugoslavia by American and Canadian Serbs.

506. Minnesota. University, Minneapolis. Immigration History Research Center. **Slovenes in the United States and Canada: A Bibliography.** (By Joseph D. Dwyer) Minneapolis, 1978. 196pp. $7.00. Bibliography Series No. 3.

The six hundred citations in this collection are organized into the following categories: biographies, manuscripts, newspapers, reference works, religion, arts and music, Slovenian-American history, language, organizations, society, and works by Slovenian-Americans on Slovenia and Yugoslavia.

507.   Minnesota. University, Minneapolis. Immigration History Research Center. **Ukrainians in North America: A Select Bibliography.** (Compiled by Halyna Myroniuk and Christine Worobec) Minneapolis, 1980. 236pp. $10.00.

This bibliography on Ukrainians in North America offers over one thousand citations on the arts, language, general reference works, emigrés, and Ukrainians in Canada and the United States.

LAWS AND LEGISLATION

508.   Minnesota. Agricultural Experiment Station. **Bibliography of Agricultural and Food Law, 1968-1978.** (By Winston S. Grant and Dale C. Dahl) St. Paul, 1978. 1 vol. Price on application. Minnesota Economic Regulation Series.

Over five hundred citations on a wide variety of state and federal food laws are included in this collection.

NATIVE PEOPLE

509.   Minnesota. University, Minneapolis. Training Center for Community Programs. **Review of Recent Research on Minneapolis Indians: 1968-1969.** (By Richard G. Woods and Arthur M. Harkins) Minneapolis, 1969. 34*l*. LC card No. 72-612365.

Approximately 150 citations on problems of urban Indians in Minneapolis are reviewed in this document.

NATURAL RESOURCES

510.   Minnesota. University, Minneapolis. Water Resources Research Center. **Publications Related to Water Resources Research Center Projects, 1965-71: Abstract-Index.** Minneapolis, 1971. 59pp. LC card No. 79-636712. Bulletin No. 32.

Many valuable studies related to the Great Lakes are described in this bulletin.

SOCIAL CONDITIONS

511.   Minnesota. University, Minneapolis. Department of Political Science. Center for Comparative Political Analysis. **Bibliography on Planned Social Change: With Special Reference to Rural Development and Educational Development.** Minneapolis, 1967. 3 vol. Out-of-Print.

The Center has worked closely with AID—the Agency for International Development. This bibliography was compiled to provide background information for the AID Rural Project. It contains periodicals, books, and government and United Nations publications. It is annotated in considerable detail and indexed.

DRUG USE AND ABUSE

512.   Mississippi. University. School of Pharmacy. Research Institute of Pharmacy. Research Institute of Pharmaceutical Sciences. **Annotated Bibliography of Marihuana, 1964-1970.** (By Coy W. Waller) University, 1971. 301pp. Price on application.

The emphasis of this project is on chemistry, the synthesis of the tetrahydrocannabinols and the use of new analytical tools to identify them. Most of the 1,112 citations are from scientific journals or documents; many have short annotations. Arrangement is alphabetical by author and there is a subject index.

513.   Mississippi. University. School of Pharmacy. Research Institute of Pharmaceutical Sciences. **Annotated Bibliography of Marihuana, 1971 Supplement.** (By Coy W. Waller, Jacqueline J. Denny, and Marjorie Ann Walz) University, 1971. 155pp. Price on application.

This 1971 supplement to the *Annotated Bibliography of Marihuana, 1964-1970* was "designed to continue serving those interested in the latest technical knowledge." It contains 467 annotated references with emphasis on metabolism and pharmacology. There are subject and author indexes.

ECONOMY/ECONOMICS

514.   Mississippi. University, Bureau of Business and Economic Research. **Publications on the Economy of the State of Mississippi in the 1960's: A Selected Bibliography.** (By Kenneth W. Hollman and Edward E. Milam) University, 1973. 1 vol. Price on application.

This is a comprehensive bibliography of both government documents and nongovernmental sources on Mississippi economic change.

ARCHAEOLOGY/ANTHROPOLOGY

515. Missouri. University, Columbia. Museum of Anthropology. **A Guide to the Reading and Study of Historic Site Archaeology.** (By Richard Hulan and Stephen S. Lawrence) Columbia, 1970. 90pp. $3.50.
This study guide provides over two hundred bibliographic references to historic archaeology in the southeastern United States, with an emphasis on Missouri.

ECONOMY/ECONOMICS

516. Missouri. Division of Commerce and Industrial Development. **Bibliography of Economic Reports in the State of Missouri.** Jefferson City, 1965. 101pp. Out-of-Print.
The scope of this report is 1955 to 1965. The more than five hundred titles are organized by subject.

517. Missouri. State Library. **Investments, Real Estates, Stocks and Bonds, Small Business: A Compilation of Bibliographies.** (By C. Edward Carroll et al.) Jefferson City, 1979. 62*l.* Free.
This collection illustrates the diversity of information sources in the field of business. There are some 750 citations divided into three categories: selected sources for a larger library; marketing; basic reference sources; how to keep current; building and updating the collection; and real estate. Most of the citations are annotated and most date from the late 1970s.

518. Missouri. University, Columbia. **Marketing: A Selected Annotated Bibliography.** (By June DeWeese) Columbia, 1979. 6pp. Free.
These fifty citations include the most important handbooks and abstracts in the field of marketing. They would be useful for even small business libraries. All entries are adequately annotated.

519. Missouri. University, Columbia. Public Information. **One Hundred Books on Advertising.** (Compiled by Robert Haverfield) Columbia, 1976. 30pp. Free. University of Missouri Bulletin No. 183.

"This annotated bibliography offers a selected list of books in the principal fields of advertising." The twenty categories are designed for the student or the professional advertising practitioner. More lengthy sections include: advertising management, layout and graphics, and public relations.

520. Missouri. University, Columbia. School of Library and Information Science. **Selected Business Reference Sources for the Larger Library.** (By C. Edward Carroll and Lynne Holzschuh) Columbia, 1979. 6pp. Free.

This bibliography is intended to "provide a picture of diversity of information sources in the field of business." The eighty-three citations are all important titles or services; acquisition information is included.

EDUCATION AND TRAINING

521. Missouri. Department of Education. Division of Career and Adult Education. **Missouri Career Education Career Resource Center Bibliography.** Jefferson City, 1981. 187pp. Free.

This is a current bibliography of excellent career education materials for elementary, junior high, and senior high students. There are also sections on stereotyping and on materials for special needs students. The over twelve hundred citations have ample annotations. There are sections of publishers and sources of free materials.

LIBRARIES

522. Missouri. University, Columbia. Museum of Anthropology. **Libraries for Small Museums.** (By Linda Anderson and Marcia R. Collins) Columbia, 1975. 48pp. $2.50.

This publication serves as a basic handbook of information and procedures for the establishment and maintenance of a small museum library, along with a list of suggested books.

WILDLIFE

523. Missouri. Department of Conservation. **Indexed Bibliography of the Paddlefish (*Polodon spathula*).** (By Kim Graham and Patrick Bonislawsky) Jefferson City, 1978. 12pp. Free.

"This listing of technical and popular literature on the paddlefish was compiled to serve as a ready reference to fishery managers, researchers, and individuals." Many references listed were obtained by contacting the fishery biologists. There are 335 citations and a subject index to sixteen main categories.

GENERAL

524.   Montana. State Library. **Montana in Print**. Helena, 1972. 35pp. Free.
These titles act as a selection guide for librarians and teachers to books about Montana. A select list, it revises the 1966 publication *Montana as It Is and Was.* Sections cover adult, juvenile, nonfiction, and periodical works. There are over four hundred citations, with reading levels indicated.

NATIVE PEOPLE

525.   Montana. Superintendent of Public Instruction. **The Indian in the Class-room: Readings for the Teacher with Indian Students**. Helena, 1972. 312pp. Price on application.
This is a useful reference for all teachers with Indian students. The first section consists of seven articles on Indian culture; the second section is a bibliography of over five hundred citations divided into seventeen subjects. Most of the entries are annotated and publishers are included.

POLITICS AND GOVERNMENT

526.   Montana. University of Montana, Missoula. Bureau of Government Research. **Working Bibliography for Montana Local Government Commissions**. (By Art Weydemeyer) Missoula, 1975. 24pp. Free. Occasional Paper No. 6.
This 340-item bibliography is designed as a reference to be drawn on by Montana local officials and other public servants. It contains a brief listing of books and documents on local government with application for all local areas.

NEBRASKA

AGRICULTURE

527.   Nebraska. Library Commission. Nebraska Publications Clearinghouse. **How Does Your Garden Grow?** Lincoln, 1980. 4pp. Free. NLC Documents Bibliography No. 2.
This list features selected U.S. and Nebraska government publications dealing with gardening. The subject categories are fruits and vegetables, flowers, gardening basics, and additional sources. There are short annotations and prices are provided.

528.   Nebraska. Department of Agriculture. **Teacher's Resource Guide for Nebraska Agriculture, Grades K-3**. Lincoln, 1983. 15pp. Free.
Prepared in a joint effort with the Department of Education, this resource guide was compiled to promote the use of agricultural materials in Nebraska schools. It is designed for K-3 teachers; grade level is noted along with ordering information. There are fifty-six citations, divided by ten types of food. (A companion volume, for grades 4-6, is cited below.)

529.   Nebraska. Department of Agriculture. **Teacher's Resource Guide for Nebraska Agriculture, Grades 4-6**. Lincoln, 1983. 11pp. Free.
Subtitled "Let's Take a Look at Nebraska Agricultural Products," this bibliography includes 102 current citations divided by sixteen food groups. Each listing includes a contact person, the complete address, and a description of the kind of information available. The material has not been screened.

530.   Nebraska. Agricultural Experiment Station. **World Bibliography of the Genus** *Phyllophaga*. (By K. S. Pike et al.) Lincoln, 1976. 21pp. Miscellaneous Publication No. 31.
This is a useful bibliography of over one hundred citations on this large genus of beetles which includes the common June Beetles of the northern United States.

ARTS

531.   Nebraska. University, Lincoln. **John O'Keefe: A Bibliography.** (By
        Frederick M. Link) Lincoln, 1983. 144pp. Free. University of Nebraska
        Studies, New Series No. 65.
"This bibliography of John O'Keefe's works is considered more than a check-list
and something more than a full analytic bibliography." There are over six hundred
works arranged in four sections: collected plays, individual plays, poetry, and auto-
biographies. Entries for each play are preceded by a brief headnote.

532.   Nebraska. Library Commission. **Nebraska Authors.** Lincoln, 1972. 16*l.*
        Out-of-Print.
Approximately 350 Nebraska authors are arranged alphabetically in this directory.
Cities and some street addresses are provided. Selected titles are included along
with designations for those residing out of state.

ECONOMY/ECONOMICS

533.   Nebraska. University, Lincoln. Bureau of Business Research. Business
        Development Center. **Bibliography of Economic Publications for Small
        Businesses.** (By Keith K. Turner) Lincoln, 1981. 8pp. Free.
Fifty basic citations on starting and managing a small business are included in this
brief bibliography.

534.   Nebraska. Library Commission. **Cornucopia.** Lincoln, 1980. 4pp. Free.
        LLC Document Bibliography No. 6.
This brief reading list on the canning, freezing, drying, and storing of fruits and
vegetables offers twenty-five citations.

535.   Nebraska. Library Commission. **Getting Your Money's Worth.** Lincoln,
        1980. 4pp. Free. NLC Documents Bibliography No. 4.
This short bibliography of twenty citations on personal finance/bugeting, credit,
housing, and estate planning is designed for the average citizen. Most are Nebraska
and U.S. government documents.

EDUCATION AND TRAINING

536.   Nebraska. Library Commission. **Careers—Education and Opportunities.**
        Lincoln, 1980. 4pp. Free. NLC Bibliography No. 10.
The emphasis of this bibliography is on exploring careers using state and federal
document titles. Approximately fifty titles with sources are included.

537.   Nebraska. Department of Education. Curriculum Development Section.
        Equipment, Texts, and Reference Materials. (By Duane H. Schmidt)
        Lincoln, 1978. 10pp. $0.90.
Teachers are the target audience for this useful bibliography of equipment, supplies,
and booklets for use in drive education curricula.

ENERGY

538. Nebraska. Library Commission. **Be Energy-Wise**. Lincoln, 1980. 4pp. Free. NLC Documents Bibliography No. 7.

Gasohol, solar energy, and recycling are among the topics covered in this collection of practical documents on energy for the beginner.

539. Nebraska. University, Lincoln. Department of Agricultural Economics. **Cost of Production of Fuel Ethanol in Farm-Size Plants**. (By Joseph A. Atwood) Lincoln, 1980. 58pp. Free.

Current data and references on the costs of producing ethanol in small-scale, on-farm plants are supplied in this publication.

ENVIRONMENT

540. Nebraska. Agricultural Experiment Station. **Drought in the Great Plains**: **A Bibliography**. (By Donald A. Wilhite and Richard O. Hoffman) Lincoln, 1979. 75pp. Price on application. Miscellaneous Publication No. 39.

"Drought is a recurring phenomenon in the Great Plains of North America." Approximately twenty-seven hundred titles on drought in the Great Plains are included in this bibliography. Only basic information is provided; there are author and subject indexes. (A supplement, issued in 1980, is listed below.)

541. Nebraska. Agricultural Experiment Station. **Drought in the Great Plains**: **A Bibliography, Supplement**. (By Donald A. Wilhite and Deborah A. Wood) Lincoln, 1980. 48pp. Free.

This supplement to an exhaustive 1979 bibliography includes materials produced to 1982. There are 632 bibliographic entries, arranged alphabetically by author.

HEALTH

542. Nebraska. Library Commission. **To Your Good Health**. Lincoln, 1980. 4pp. Free. NLC Documents Bibliography No. 5.

This is a reading list of twenty-four citations on nutrition, physical education, fitness, exercise, and miscellaneous health issues. Federal documents are accompanied by prices.

HISTORY

543. Nebraska. State Historical Society. **Selected Bibliography of General Genealogical Reference Materials, 1978**. Lincoln, 1978. 1 vol. Free. Reference Leaflet No. 7.

This is a ready-reference guide to seventy-eight general genealogical reference sources.

NATURAL RESOURCES

544. Nebraska. University, Lincoln. Water Resources Center. **Water Resources Research in Nebraska**. Lincoln, 1979. 101pp. Free.

This is a summary of current water resources-related research in Nebraska. The annotations include the name of project, principal investigator, source of funding, source address, and abstract of study. Indexes are provided for agency, author, subject, and key words.

POLITICS AND GOVERNMENT

545. Nebraska. University, Lincoln. Political Science Department. Government Research Institute. **Nebraska Government: Sources and Literature**. (By Robert Miewald and Robert Sittig) Lincoln, 1983. 1 vol. $5.00.

Here is an extensive bibliography of over six hundred citations on Nebraska government and politics.

546. Nebraska. Library Commission. Nebraska Publications Clearinghouse. **Your State Legislature**. Lincoln, 1980. 2pp. Free. NLC Bibliography No. 1.

Ample annotations and availability information are features of this basic bibliography of Nebraska official legislative publications.

RECREATION/TOURISM

547. Nebraska. Library Commission. **Travelin', the Good Life**. Lincoln, 1980. 4pp. Free. NLC Bibliography No. 3.

This is a bibliography of selected U.S. and Nebraska government publications dealing with traveling and the outdoors. Although the emphasis is on Nebraska there are useful general titles under the headings of recreation, parks, backpacking, the handicapped traveler, and general information.

SOCIAL CONDITIONS

548. Nebraska. Library Commission. **Child Abuse and Neglect**. Lincoln, 1980. 4pp. Free. NLC Bibliography No. 8.

Annotated federal documents comprise the bulk of the eighty citations in this bibliography on child abuse and neglect.

GENERAL

549.　Nevada. University, Reno. Library. **Preliminary Union Catalog of Nevada Manuscripts.** (By Robert D. Armstrong) Reno, 1967. 218pp. Price on application.

This is a preliminary listing of all important Nevada documents and manuscripts from the time of statehood.

ARCHAEOLOGY/ANTHROPOLOGY

550.　Nevada. University, Reno. Western Research Center. **Great Basin Anthropology: A Bibliography.** (By Catherine S. Fowler) Reno, 1970. 418pp. Price on application. LC card No. 78-634802.

Issued in cooperation with the Agricultural Experiment Station of Massachusetts and the U.S. Department of Agriculture, this is a major bibliography with over one thousand titles on anthropology and archaeology.

ARID LANDS

551.　Nevada. University, Reno. Desert Research Institute. **Desert Research Institute Publications of the Water Resources Center.** Reno, 1983. 32pp. Free.

The 350 studies on Nevada dry lands and southwestern deserts in this collection represent a wealth of dryland research. Most titles are currently available.

ENVIRONMENT

552.　Nevada. Agricultural Experiment Station. **Vegetation of Nevada: A Bibliography.** (By Paul T. Tueller, Joseph H. Robertson, and Benjamin Zamora) Reno, 1978. 28pp. Free. Report No. 78.

This update of a 1971 bibliography offers 672 citations in the categories of general information, taxanomy, ecology, range and pasture improvement, and paleobotany.

HISTORY

553.   Nevada. University, Reno. Library. **Oral History Project of the University of Nevada, Reno, Library: A Bibliography.** (By Mary Ellen Glass) Reno, 1972. 16*l.* Free.

This document supplies over fifty citations on gathering local history.

NEW JERSEY

GENERAL

554. New Jersey. State Library. **Federal Government Reference Tools**. Trenton, 1979. 4*l*. Free. Special Bibliography No. 12.
These nineteen annotated citations of the most useful titles in the State Library attempt to supply "everything you want to know about the federal government but were afraid to ask."

555. New Jersey. State Library. Reference Section. **Popular Names Index to New Jersey State Documents**. Trenton, 1977. 7pp. Free.
This bibliography has been compiled and published at the suggestion of the Government Document Association of New Jersey. The eighty-five citations are based on the card file of the State Library. Full bibliographic information on each document is provided.

DISABLED

556. New Jersey. State Library. **The Handicapped**. (By Stephen Breedlove) Trenton, 1977. 2pp. Free. Special Bibliography No. 3.
This is a current-awareness reading list with eleven annotated citations. The subjects covered include education, recreation, and college guides.

ECONOMY/ECONOMICS

557. New Jersey. State Library. **Fund-Raising: Bibliography**. (By Stephen Breedlove) Trenton, 1980. 3pp. Free. Special Bibliography.
Designed as a functional bibliography, this collection on fund raising would be useful for professionals as well as community groups. There are over twenty citations on successful events.

558. New Jersey. State Library. **Zero Base Budgeting: A Selective Bibliography**. (By Harold Dunn) Trenton, 1978. 2pp. Free. Special Bibliography No. 5.
This is a basic reading list on a logical approach for budget making. The twelve sources include both books and documents.

EDUCATION AND TRAINING

559.　New Jersey. Department of Education. Urban Education Observatory. **Home Environment, Self-Concept, and Urban Student Achievement: A Bibliography and Review of Research.** (By Carol Shapiro and Joel S. Bloom) Trenton, 1977. 66pp. Urban Education Research Report No. 5.

Urban student achievement is addressed in the three hundred citations of this report.

560.　New Jersey. Montclair State College. National Multimedia Center/National Adult Education Clearinghouse. **Metric Bibliography.** (By Beverly Schwartz) Upper Montclair, 1979. 13pp. $1.00. LC card No. 79-624952.

This is a short, ready-reference for teachers, public libraries, and media centers on metric measurement and the background of the metric system.

561.　New Jersey. Office of Equal Educational Opportunity. **Resources for Nonsexist/Interethnic Multicultural Education.** (Compiled by Pamela Leggio, Theodora F. Martin, and Susan Davis) Trenton, 1979. 47pp. Free.

This current guide to over two hundred citations on nonsexist education could be used along with the Michigan Department of Education nonsexist bibliographies listed elsewhere in this volume.

EMPLOYMENT

562.　New Jersey. State Library. **Job Hunt.** (By Betty Steckman) Trenton, 1983. 4pp. Free. Special Bibliography.

This is a reading list of thirty-six books and directories concerned with obtaining a job. Arrangement is according to author; all titles are found in the State Library.

563.　New Jersey. State Library. **Job Seeking and Resume Writing.** Trenton, 1978. 2pp. Free. Special Bibliography No. 8.

This brief compilation highlights twenty-five citations useful for job seeking and resume writing. The books on resumes investigate the subject in depth.

ENERGY

564.　New Jersey. State Library. **Wind Power.** (By Stephen Breedlove) Trenton, 1977. 2pp. Free. Special Bibliography No. 1.

The generation of electricity by wind power is addressed in the fourteen citations of this brief bibliography.

HEALTH

565.   New Jersey. Library for the Blind and Handicapped. **Deafness: An Anno-
        tated Bibliography.** Trenton, 1982. 11pp.
All aspects of deafness are covered in this current bibliography of over fifty
citations.

566.   New Jersey. State Library. **Health Services—Delivery and Cost.** (By Robert
        Fortenbaugh) Trenton, 1977. 2pp. Free. Special Bibliography No. 4.
Fourteen annotated citations on the nature of health costs, right to care, and
Medicaid are included in this bibliography.

567.   New Jersey. Department of Environmental Protection. **Literature Survey
        of the Hazards and Risks Associated with Exposure to Asbestos.** (By
        Peter W. Preuss and Michael Graber) Trenton, 1977. 35pp. Free.
This current bibliography of seventy-seven citations on asbestos dangers—cancer,
intensity of exposure, latent period, interactions, indirect exposure, and community exposure—includes a section on regulations and standards.

HISTORY

568.   New Jersey. State Museum. **Folklife in New Jersey: An Annotated Bibliog-
        raphy.** (By David Steven Cohen) Trenton, 1982. 108pp. $3.00.
"The first publication of the Commission's New Jersey Folklife Program, this is a
guide for folklorists, historians, teachers, students, and the general public." It lists
477 published works in the categories of: traditional occupations and activities,
folk narratives, folk speech, placenames, music, dance, Indian folklore, ethnic folklore, medicine, foodways, architecture, art and artifacts, proverbs, riddles, and
jokes.

569.   New Jersey. Historical Commission. **From Point to Cape, New Jersey:
        A Selected Bibliography of the Resources on New Jersey in the Sarah
        Byrd Askew Library, William Paterson College.** Trenton, 1982. 31pp.
        Price on application. LC card No. 82-621932.
This is an important bibliography of over two hundred New Jersey historical materials found in the Askew Library.

LAWS AND LEGISLATION

570.   New Jersey. State Library. **Exclusionary Zoning.** (By William Forman)
        Trenton, 1983. 6pp. Free. Special Bibliography.
"The Mount Laurel decisions declared unconstitutional those laws which restrict
the building of low and moderate income housing." Forty-seven citations on the
Mount Laurel decisions and exclusionary zoning generally—goverment documents,
periodical articles, and newspaper clippings—are included.

571.   New Jersey. State Library. **Legalized Gambling**. (By Beverly Railsback) Trenton, 1977. 4pp. Free. Special Bibliography No. 2.

Eighteen journal articles and government documents with emphasis on New Jersey discuss the pros and cons of legalized gambling.

POLITICS AND GOVERNMENT

572.   New Jersey. Department of Community Affairs. Office of Public Information. **Publications Directory: A Bibliography of Periodicals, Publications, Legislation, and Maps Available from the New Jersey Department of Community Affairs**. Trenton, 1970. 39pp. Out-of-print.

This document is both a bibliography and a publication list to several hundred sources on New Jersey urban affairs.

TECHNOLOGY

573.   New Jersey. State Library. **Computers**. Trenton, 1983. 4pp. Free. Special Bibliography.

The thirty-five computer titles in this list all have imprints from the 1980s. They are divided into sections on business and personal use, professional use, computer-assisted instruction, programs and programming, and word processing.

ECONOMY/ECONOMICS

574. New Mexico. Agricultural Experiment Station. **Impact of Relative Price Changes of Feeds and Cattle on the Marketing of U.S. Beef, 1975-1981: An Annotated Bibliography.** Las Cruces, 1982. 58pp. Free. LC card No. 83-622166. Western Regional Beef Research Project No. W145.

There are approximately three hundred titles on the economics of modern beef production in this Regional Research Publication.

ENERGY

575. New Mexico. Energy Research and Development Institute. **Bibliography for Low-Temperature Geothermal Resource Assessment in New Mexico.** (By Larry Icerman) Las Cruces, 1982. 48pp. Free.

This 150-item bibliography is a compilation of the references cited in three other Energy Institute reports. Divided into three sections, part I is a listing of original contributions to the three summary reports, part II contains an alphabetical compilation of references, and part III contains a reference list for Quartenary and late-Pliocene geology.

ENVIRONMENT

576. New Mexico. Cooperative Extension Service. Range Improvement Task Force. **Bibliography of Forest and Rangeland as Nonpoint Sources of Pollution.** (By James M. Fowler and M. Karl Wood) Las Cruces, 1980. 37pp. Free. Report No. 4.

This bibliography is a comprehensive compilation of relevant published literature that reports on some facet of the erosion and resultant sedimentation that can be generated from forest or rangeland. The sources cover approximately fifty years of published literature. There are 472 citations arranged alphabetically by author. Most were published by the Forest Service, the Environmental Protection Agency, and journals.

GEOLOGY

577.　New Mexico. State Bureau of Mines and Mineral Resources. **Bibliography of Geophysics for New Mexico through 1970.** (By D. J. Cash) Socorro, 1971. 27pp. $1.25. LC card No. 72-611171.

Over one hundred geophysical studies collected by the State Bureau of Mines comprise this bibliography.

LAWS AND LEGISLATION

578.　New Mexico. University, Albuquerque. Institute for Social Research and Development. **Basic Selected Bibliography of Crime and Delinquency.** (By P. R. David) Albuquerque, 1971. 1 vol. Out-of-Print.

References dealing with crime and delinquency prevention, correction and rehabilitation, law enforcement, and the judicial process are included in this bibliography.

579.　New Mexico. State Library. **Right to Die: A Bibliography.** (By Margaret C. Kutcher) Santa Fe, 1977. 4pp. Free.

"One aspect of death which has attracted a considerable amount of attention is the so called 'right to die.'" This bibliography has been prepared for those wishing to make a decision about mercy killing and euthanasia. The twenty-four citations are evenly divided between books and journal articles.

NATURAL RESOURCES

580.　New Mexico. State University, Las Cruces. Water Resources Research Institute. **Bibliography of Dissertations and Theses on Water and Water Related Topics from New Mexico State University through December 1980.** (By Robert G. Myers and Karen M. Pinckley) Las Cruces, 1981. 28*l.* Free. WRRI Report No. 138.

This bibliography was compiled using the titles available in the New Mexico State University Library. There are almost three hundred unannotated citations with a departmental author index.

POLITICS AND GOVERNMENT

581.　New Mexico. University, Albuquerque. Division of Government Research. **A Bibliography of New Mexico State Politics.** (By T. Philip Wolf) Albuquerque, 1974. 95pp. $2.50. Publication No. 82.

Intended to compliment Frederick C. Irions' *Bibliography of New Mexico Politics,* this title includes 350 entries arranged by author, with full bibliographic information and abstracts of various lengths. Categorical listings of subject matter include: general articles, state executive, legislative, legal, local politics, planning, public opinion, pressure groups, ethnic groups, political leaders, and policy areas.

WOMEN

582. New Mexico. State Library. **Writings on Women: A Selected Bibliography.** (By Margaret C. Kutcher) Santa Fe, 1976. 29pp. Free.

Directed primarily to political, cultural, and economic aspects of females, the items in this collection were selected to represent various viewpoints. All were published in the 1970s. There are approximately 450 citations including reference sources, sexual politics, women in the arts, women as a minority group, women and the church, and women in education. Many government publications are included.

GENERAL

583. New York. State Library. **Bibliographies and Lists of New York State Newspapers: An Annotated Guide.** (By Paul Merce) Albany, 1981. 7pp. $3.00. LC card No. 82-620637.

This is a unique annotated guide to over four hundred state newspapers. There is a title index.

584. New York. State University of New York, Geneseo. School of Library and Information Sciences. **Federal Publications for School Media Centers.** (By Rebekah Butler) Geneseo, 1977. 37*l.* Price on application.

The departments, offices, and agencies of the federal government produce thousands of pamphlets, books, and reports of an educational nature. This bibliography annotates over 135 of these titles. The arrangement is according to ten broad subject headings; acquisition processes are described.

585. New York. State Library. **Official Publications of New York State: A Bibliographic Guide to Their Use.** (By Dorothy Butch) Albany, 1981. 31pp. Free.

This guide includes selected publications, both official and unofficial, which promote awareness of government history and which facilitate identification of government publications reflecting that history. Topics excluded from consideration relate to New York State statutes, administrative law, judicial decisions, and legislative history.

586. New York. State Library. Division of Library Development. **Reference Books for a Regional Reference Collection.** (By Edward C. Nelson) Albany, 1967. 282pp. LC card No. 70-632925.

This core collection of basic reference works is still valuable because many entries have been updated. It is useful for public and small college libraries.

ARCHAEOLOGY/ANTHROPOLOGY

587. New York. State University of New York, Geneseo. Library. **Anthropology.** (By David W. Parish) Geneseo, 1972. 9*l.* Free. Collection Description Series No. 4.

The scope of this bibliography encompasses anthropology, archeology, and anthropogeographical titles. All of the 140 citations are of government publications—state, federal, and Canadian.

AREA STUDIES

588.   New York. State Education Department. Bureau of Educational Integration. **Annotations on Selected Aspects of the Culture of Puerto Rico and Its People.** Albany, 1972. 1 vol. Free.
This bibliography provides citations regarding various aspects of Puerto Rican life.

589.   New York. School of Industrial and Labor Relations. **Bibliography of Industrial Relations in Latin America.** (By James O. Morris and Efren Cordova) Ithaca, 1967. 308pp. $10.00. ILR Bibliography No. 8.
Material on labor economics, manpower problems, labor-management relations, labor law, social security, and management are listed for twenty-one Latin American countries.

590.   New York. State Education Department. Foreign Area Materials Center. **The Geography of China: A Selected and Annotated Bibliography.** (Edited by Theodore Herman) Albany, 1967. 44pp. Out-of-Print. Occasional Publication No. 7.
This bibliography is designed as a guide to important materials and writings on the geography of China for those with little geographical training. There are four hundred annotated citations in sections on bibliographies, atlases, textbooks, human geography, physical geography, and useful periodicals. An author index is included.

591.   New York. State Education Department. Foreign Area Materials Center. **Language and Area Studies: A Bibliography.** (By Lyman H. Legters) Albany, 1967. 43pp. Out-of-Print. Occasional Publication No. 5.
This is a lengthy bibliography of mostly periodical articles explaining area and language studies, along with readings on eight areas of the world. Arrangement is by author within each section. There are approximately eight hundred citations.

592.   New York. State Education Department. Foreign Area Materials Center. **Science in South Asia, Past and Present: A Preliminary Bibliography.** (By Patrick Wilson) Albany, 1966. 100pp. Out-of-Print. Occasional Publication No. 3.
This work includes writings on the history of science and technology in South Asia, translations of ancient scientific works, and present-day writings. Some fourteen hundred citations are divided by the branch of science and by country, with full bibliographic information. There is an author index.

ARTS

593.   New York. State University of New York, Geneseo. **Bibliography of
        Novels about New York State**. (By Walter Harding) Geneseo, 1970?
        17pp. Out-of-Print.

Approximately 450 novels about the Empire State are arranged by author with
minimal bibliographic information in this publication.

594.   New York. State Education Department. Foreign Area Materials Center.
        Indian Novels in English. (By Donald Johnson and Jean Johnson) Albany,
        1970. 16pp. Free.

This is a bibliography of novels from India recommended for American schools
and colleges. Suggested educational levels are presented. Arrangement is by author
with in-depth annotations.

DISABLED

595.   New York. Institute for Basic Research in Mental Retardation. **Bibliog-
        raphy of Bibliographies on Mental Retardation, 1963-June 1975**. Staten
        Island, 1975. 21*l*. Free.

Approximately one hundred bibliographies on all aspects of retardation are
included in this useful guide to collection building in the field of retardation.

DRUG USE AND ABUSE

596.   New York. State University, Albany. Institute for Traffic Safety Manage-
        ment and Research. **Alcohol and the Young Driver: A Select Annotated
        Bibliography**. Albany, n.d. 26pp. Free.

This useful bibliography for all types of libraries (including school libraries) offers
thirty-six amply annotated citations discussing risks by teenage drivers, education,
night driving, and lowering the legal drinking age. Most of the citations are taken
from journals.

597.   New York. State University, Albany. Institute for Traffic Safety Manage-
        ment and Research. **Alcohol and Traffic Safety: A Select Annotated
        Bibliography**. (Robert Herman, director) Albany, 1980. 8pp. Free. TSSB
        3-1180.

This is a functional bibliography of readable articles from journals and government
publications. Effects of blood alcohol and driver attitudes are stressed in this
collection of lengthy abstracts published in conjunction with activities of the
Governor's Alcohol and Highway Safety Task Force.

598.   New York. State Education Department. Bureau of Drug Education.
        Drug Education Curriculum: Materials Cost List, Elementary Level.
        Albany, 1981. 13pp. Free.

This is a list of over 150 up-to-date teaching materials arranged according to
distributor followed by titles, grade level, format, and price. There is also a
summary of suggested ordering procedures. (The companion item for the secondary
level is below.)

599.   New York. State Education Department. Bureau of Drug Education.
       Drug Education Curriculum: Materials Cost List, Secondary Level. Albany,
       1981. 13pp. Free.
This bibliography of curriculum materials for junior and senior high school cites
grade level, format, and price for approximately two hundred teaching aids and
books on drugs and alcohol.

600.   New York. State Library. Legislative Reference Library. **Establishment**
       and Administration of Narcotic Rehabilitation Programs. Albany, 1974.
       5pp. Price not available.
This is a list of books, periodicals, and documents on narcotic rehabilitation to aid
New York State in program development.

601.   New York. State Education Department. **Multimedia Reference History**
       of Materials on Drug Education. Albany, 1971. 149pp. Free.
Over eighteen hundred basic sources on drug education–audiovisuals, books, kits,
essays, films, general articles, papers, professional articles, and handbooks for
teachers–comprise this collection.

602.   New York. Narcotic Addiction Control Commission. **Suggested Starting**
       Bibliography in Narcotic Education. (By Henry Brill) Albany, 1969.
       5pp. Free.
Still useful for a core education collection, this bibliography listed approximately
one hundred guides and background materials on narcotic education.

ECONOMY/ECONOMICS

603.   New York. Agricultural Experiment Station. **Annotated Bibliography of**
       Writings on Peasant Economy. (By Donald K. Freebairn, Mariann Love-
       land, and Elyse Tepper) Ithaca, 1980. 51pp. Free. Cornell Agricultural
       Economics Staff Paper No. 80-29.
This is a bibliography for scholars of over 250 amply annotated studies on the politics of peasantry, case studies, theories, the historical process, production, organization, agrarian structure, and peasant movements. Many are foreign citations.

604.   New York. Department of Commerce. **Bibliography of Demographic and**
       Economic Projections for New York State and Areas. Albany, 1969.
       39pp. Free. LC card No. 71-628422.
Reflecting the widespread interest in growth projections into the 1980s, this bibliography provides over two hundred citations on planning statistics, population
documents, and statistical methods for the State of New York and regional areas.

605.   New York. School of Industrial and Labor Relations. **Project Management:**
       An Annotated Bibliography. (By Lee Dyer and Gary D. Paulson) Ithaca,
       1976. 48pp. $2.75. ILR Bibliography No. 13.
This annotated list of publications on managing temporary projects in organizations
provides a broad view of relatively new forms of organizational design.

606.   New York. Department of State. **Compendium of New York State's Consumer Oriented Publications.** Albany, 1981. 29*l.* Free.
This bibliography lists over three hundred consumer-related titles issued by thirteen New York State agencies. Brief descriptions are provided for most with lengthy annotations for the most important. Availability is indicated. This bibliography would be of use to most public libraries.

607.   New York. State University, Albany. Research Foundation. **Sponsored Fund Administration: A Bibliography.** Albany, 1976. 18pp. Free.
This bibliography of seventy-five citations on the operation of the Research Foundation and its administration under the State University of New York would be most helpful to university personnel and other researchers interested in obtaining grants.

EDUCATION AND TRAINING

608.   New York. State University, Albany. Division of Education for the Disadvantaged. **Annotated Bibliography: Educating the Disadvantaged Child.** (By Linda Regan and Barbara White) Albany, 1969. 88pp. Out-of-Print.
This collection of over three thousand studies on the culturally disadvantaged was designed for teacher use as an aid to developing federal programs.

609.   New York. State University, Albany. Division of Education for the Disadvantaged. **Annotated Bibliography: Educating the Disadvantaged Child, Supplement No. 1.** Albany, 1969. 88pp. Out-of-Print.
"Prepared for teachers and educators as a source of current reports," the objective of this bibliography is to aid urban educators generally. There are two hundred citations in nineteen subject categories.

610.   New York. State Education Department. Bureau of Bilingual Education. **An Annotated Bibliography of Audiovisual Materials for Bilingual Programs.** Albany, 1982. 70pp. Free.
ESL, Puerto Rican materials, reference books, curriculum materials, and audiovisual materials comprise the two hundred instructional materials, articles, and kits in this bilingual bibliography. Short annotations and a list of publishers are provided.

611.   New York. State Education Department. Division of School Supervision. **Bibliography of Current Literature on the Education of Young Children.** Albany, 1968. 7pp. Free.
There are fifty annotated sources in this bibliography, divided into sections on child development, early childhood education, disadvantaged children, and journals of interest to early childhood education.

612.   New York. Division of Human Rights. **Bibliography on Education.** Albany, 1972. 60pp. Free. Special Collection No. 2.
Part of a planned series, this title includes over three hundred reports and documents on equal education programs.

613. New York. State Education Department Bureau of Elementary Curriculum Development. **Books That Count.** (By Gretchen Savage and others) Albany, 1969? 20pp. Out-of-Print.

This once-popular bibliography lists attractive books recommended for teachers as resources in teaching mathematics.

614. New York. State Education Department. Cultural Education Center. **Books to Change Your Future: Selected Bibliographies for Career and Job Information, Options for Education, Study Skills and Research Techniques, Financial Aid.** Albany, 1979. 28pp. Free.

This is an excellent guidebook and bibliography of one hundred books and documents on occupational choice and implementation objectives. Emphasis is placed on materials that aid in adjusting to change. A coding key is used for quick reference to selecting a career. There are job descriptions and suggestions for the job hunt.

615. New York. State University, Albany. Institute for Traffic Safety Management and Research. **Child Automobile Restraints: A Select Annotated Bibliography.** (Richard Steinrer, director) Albany, 1979. 8pp. Free. TSSB 1-0479.

These thirty-three citations offer a mixture of readings on child behavior, child restraints (such as belts and airbags), and education. Documents, journal articles and conference proceedings are included; many of the abstracts are quite lengthy.

616. New York. State University of New York, Buffalo. Department of Education. **Comparative Higher Education.** Buffalo, 1983. 14pp. Free.

This bibliography is designed for use with a comparative education course. Over 150 citations are included providing a broad crosscultural reading list with emphasis on the United States, Europe, and the Third World, but including case studies on China and India.

617. New York. School of Industrial and Labor Relations. **Education and Training for Effective Manpower Utilization: An Annotated Bibliography.** (By Emil Mesics) Ithaca, 1969. 164pp. $2.50. ILR Bibliography No. 9.

"A basic source of literature in the training field," this bibliography is primarily intended for personnel administrators and training specialists in business, industry, and government. There are over three hundred citations.

618. New York. State Education Department. Division of Intercultural Relations in Education. **Materials, Programs, Services for Multicultural Education.** Albany, 1977. 34pp. Free.

Multicultural education strives to develop knowledge, understanding, and sensitivity regarding ethnic groups. This bibliography lists over 170 multimedia materials, publications, and programs useful for all teachers. There are lengthy annotations and sources for all materials.

619. New York. State Education Department. Bureau of Migrant Education. **Migrant Bilingual Annotated Bibliography.** Albany, 1976. 1 vol. Free.

Information on resources for migrant bilingual students from pre-K to grade 12 is provided in this annotated volume.

620. New York. State Library. Legislative and Governmental Services. **Reform of Educational Finance.** (By Colin Campbell) Albany, 1981. 11*l*. Price not available. Selected, Annotated Bibliography No. B81.

Ample annotations are provided for the eighty-one documents, books, and journal articles in this bibliography emphasizing educational equality, vouchers, federal and state reform, and the future of school finance.

621. New York. State Education Department. Bureau of School Health Education and Services. **Resource List: Family Life Education Program.** Albany, 1981. 76pp. Free.

A listing of materials on family education and adolescent pregnancy used by schools in New York State. There are over seven hundred citations. There is a separate audiovisual section. Indexes include producers, title, and a listing of regional health and nutrition coordinators.

EMPLOYMENT

622. New York. School of Industrial and Labor Relations. **Bibliography of Collective Bargaining in Hospitals and Related Facilities.** (By William A. Tothman) Ithaca, 1976. 164pp. $4.25.

This extensive collective bargaining bibliography of over five hundred publications stresses organized labor drives, bargaining, strikes, contract terms, federal and state laws, arbitration, and the training of the health services staff. There are annotations for the more important contributions.

623. New York. School of Industrial and Labor Relations. **Bibliography of Industrial Relations in the Railroad Industry.** (By James O. Morris) Ithaca, 1975. 172pp. $5.00. ILR Bibliography No. 12.

The author presents a comprehensive selection of the "best published and unpublished nonfiction materials on this subject from 1880 to 1975."

624. New York. Division of Human Rights. **Bibliography on Employment and Related Subjects.** Albany, 1973. 198pp. Free. Special Collection No. 3.

Almost two thousand titles on equal employment and affirmative action are annotated and arranged by author in this publication. Over half of the entries are government publications.

625. New York. State Library. Legislative Reference Bureau. **Chronological Bibliography of Official New York State Publications concerning the Taylor Law.** (Compiled by Gladys Ann Welles Lescak) Albany, 1974. 1 vol. Out-of-Print.

This is an important bibliography on one of the pioneer laws allowing public employees to negotiate. The time period covered is 1966 to 1974 and general studies, official New York State documents, and laws are included.

626. New York. School of Industrial and Labor Relations. **Historical Sources of Personnel Work: An Annotated Bibliography of Development Since 1923.** (By Frank B. Miller and Mary Ann Coghill) Ithaca, n.d. 116pp. $2.00. Bibliography Series No. 5.

This bibliography offers some 550 citations under thirteen topical headings, with brief introductions to each topic. Categories include: the personnel function, employment, systematic job study, training, employee representation, profit sharing, communications, personnel research, and recordkeeping. There is an index of authors.

627. New York. School of Industrial and Labor Relations. **Mediation: An Annotated Bibliography.** (By Edward Levin and Daniel V. DeSantis) Ithaca, 1978. 32pp. $3.25. ILR Bibliography No. 15.

The purpose of this document was to present "the most significant publications since 1964 as well as the major early works on mediation." Short descriptions and a subject index are provided.

628. New York. School of Industrial and Labor Relations. **Personnel Research Abstracts.** (By Richard A. Shafer and Mary Ann Coghill) Ithaca, 1973. 60pp. $3.00. ILR Bibliography No. 10.

Compiled for administrators and students, this work offers a convenient reference to over two hundred studies on personnel problems.

629. New York. School of Industrial and Labor Relations. **Public Employment: Bibliography I.** (By Richard Pegnetter) Ithaca, 1971. 60pp. $2.00.

This listing of materials was published between 1966 and 1970 and covers federal, state, and local employees, as well as professionals and nonprofessionals in education, libraries, and health care.

630. New York. School of Industrial and Labor Relations. **Public Employment: Bibliography II.** (By Robert V. Pezdek) Ithaca, 1973. 185pp. $7.00. LC card No. 73-620038. Bibliography Series No. 11.

The scope of this bibliography is primarily the period between late 1970 and late 1972. There are over seventeen hundred citations arranged in nine categories according to professions and occupations.

ENVIRONMENT

631. New York. Department of Health. **Annotated Bibliography of Periodical Literature Dealing with Algae of New York State and Contiguous Waters.** (By John Kingsbury) Albany, 1968. 37pp. Free.

This bibliography on algae includes approximately 540 citations arranged by author. Many of the citations have lengthy annotations. A complete listing of all New York State Museum Bulletins that apply is featured. A limitation is that major taxonomic and ecological monographs are not included.

632.   New York. Agricultural Experiment Station. **Annotated Bibliography on Interpretation of Clouds and Cloudiness by Means of Satellite Photographs, 1965-69.** (By J. P. Ormsby and R. E. Dethier) Ithaca, 1970. 76pp. LC card No. 70-635690.

This pioneering study from the early era of satellite usage for weather purposes includes over three hundred citations on the subject.

633.   New York. Temporary State Commission on Tug Hill. **Annotated Bibliography on Planning in the Tug Hill Area of New York State**. (Prepared by Benjamin P. Coe and Roswell P. Trickey) Watertown, 1982. 73*l*. Free.

The Tug Hill region includes 1.3 million acres of natural area in the southern Adirondack Mountains. This is a comprehensive bibliography divided into eight sections: regional reports, cooperative reports, titles from special regional groups, audiovisual programs, and writings by others than Tug Hill organizations. Annotations and author are included.

634.   New York. State Library. Legislative Service. **Solid Waste Management, Project Plans and Operating Programs: A Selected Annotated Bibliography.** (By Marilyn Gehr) Albany, 1976. 28pp. Price on application.

There are 106 reports with abstracts covering the basics of solid waste management: general works, conferences, federal documents, bibliographies, and serials. Part II reports works on technical projects such as disposal of automobiles, beverage containers, hazardous waste, organics, and recycling. Part III includes projects sponsored by states, localities, and industries.

635.   New York. State Library. Legislative Service. **Solid Waste Management, Technical Information: A Selected Annotated Bibliography**. (By Marilyn Gehr) Albany, 1976. 31pp. Price on application.

This is Part II of a three-part solid waste bibliography. It includes 103 citations on seven categories of technical information. Most are periodical articles or government documents. Most titles are annotated and acquisition information is provided.

636.   New York. State Library. Legislative Service. **Solid Waste Management, the Basics: A Selected Annotated Bibliography**. (By Marilyn Gehr) Albany, 1976. 31pp. Price on application. Bulletin No. 64.

The basics of solid waste management are addressed in 107 citations. Most are government publications and are included in the Legislative Service collection of the State Library. Arrangement is alphabetical by author within each of seven categories.

637.   New York. State Library. Legislative and Governmental Services. **Water Quality**. (By Colin Campbell) Albany, 1983. 4pp. Free. Topic No. 70.

Both general water quality and acid rain are covered in this useful bibliography; all of the citations are annotated.

HEALTH

638. New York. State Education Department. Division of Research. **Anxiety and School Related Interventions: A Selective Review and Synthesis of the Psychological Literature.** (By Beeman N. Philips) Albany, 1971. 138pp. Free. LC card No. 72-611297. Interpretive Study No. 2.

The stated purpose of this document is to "review, synthesize, and interpret literature on anxiety." There are sections on the nature of anxiety, psychological theories, measurement, selective reviews of the literature, and recommendations for the classroom. Over 250 citations are reviewed.

639. New York. Agricultural Experiment Station. **Nutrition Books: A Guide to Their Reliability.** (By Marjorie Burns) Ithaca, 1967. 24pp. Free.

Over one hundred nutrition titles are adequately annotated in this evaluative bibliography.

640. New York. State Education Department. Bureau of School Health Education. **Selected References in the Areas of Teen-Age Pregnancy, Teen-Age Parenting, Prevention of Teen-Age Pregnancy.** Albany, 1976. 12pp. Free.

The emphasis of this collection is on high school students and pregnancy. It consists of forty-six citations from journals, government publications, and the ERIC system, arranged alphabetically by author. Most of the citations have lengthy annotations.

HISTORY

641. New York. State Education Department. Bureau of Secondary Curriculum Development. **American History Bibliography.** Albany, n.d. 112pp. Free.

There are over twenty-seven hundred citations in this bibliography, prepared for use with learning activity handbooks. Citations are divided according to time periods. Within each period are found categories of history, social life, government, enrichment, biography, and fiction.

642. New York. American Revolution Bicentennial Commission. **American Revolution for Young Readers: A Bibliography.** (By Barbara Jean Beharriell) Albany, 1971. 11pp. Free.

"This present annotated list has been designed for students in the fourth through sixth grades although some titles may appeal to junior high readers." The 130 titles are arranged by author with one paragraph annotations for each.

643. New York. American Revolution Bicentennial Commission. **New York in the American Revolution: A Bibliography.** (By Milton M. Klein) Albany, 1974. 197pp. Free.

There are 1,089 citations in this bibliography on New York State in the Revolution. Most citations include one-line annotations. Sections include: general history, biographies, politics, military campaigns, the loyalists, ideology, economy, Indians, religion, women, blacks, historiography, and printed primary sources. There is a combined author-subject index.

644. New York. School of Industrial and Labor Relations. **Representative Bibliography of American Labor History**. (By Maurice F. Neufeld) Ithaca, 1964. 160pp. $4.50. ILR Bibliography No. 6.

This is an inclusive list of materials on American labor history. The more than twenty-three hundred titles include publications dated as early as 1814. Classification is by subject and there is an alphabetical index.

645. New York. Office of State History. **Research and Publications in New York State History**. Albany, 1969- . Annual. Free.

Each annual issue of this bibliography lists research completed or in progress dealing primarily with New York State history. Each volume is divided into thirty-five to forty subject categories. The 1979 edition includes almost two thousand citations, some annotated, of books, scholarly papers, and government documents. Prior to 1969 such research was reported in *Research in Progress in New York State History*. Publisher and periodical indexes are included.

LAWS AND LEGISLATION

646. New York. State Library. **Bail Reform: A Selective Annotated Bibliography**. (Compiled by Roland Barth) Albany, 1973. 24pp. Price not available.

This collection of two hundred citations on bail reform was assembled at a time when there was much emphasis on local action.

647. New York. Division of Human Rights. **Bibliography of Publications by and about New York State Division of Human Rights, 1945-1970**. (By Simon Fediuk) New York, 1971. 41*l*. Free. Special Collection Bibliography No. 5.

Some two hundred historic titles dating from the beginning of the modern human rights movement in New York State are included.

648. New York. State Library. Legislative and Governmental Services. **Computer Crime**. (By Robert Allan Carter) Albany, 1983. 4pp. Free. Topics No. 71.

Thirty-seven current citations to this growing problem are presented here, arranged alphabetically by title. There are short annotations for each.

649. New York. State Library. Legislative Reference Bureau. **History of the Insanity Defense in New York State**. (By Robert Allan Carter) Albany, 1982. 46pp. Price not available. LC card No. 82-623135.

Designed for New York State legislative use, this is a collection of over four hundred current citations on the pros and cons of pleading insanity. Many government publications are included.

650. New York. State Library. Legislative and Governmental Services. **Motorcycle Helmets: Bibliography**. (By Robert Allan Carter) Albany, 1982. 4pp. Price on application.

The ongoing debate about the need for motorcycle helmet laws is the focus of this bibliography.

651. New York. State Library. Legislative and Governmental Services. Cultural Education Center. **New York State—Legislative Intent**. (By Robert Allan Carter) Albany, 1981. 57pp. Price on application. Annotated Bibliography No. S-1.

This is a bibliographic guide to the legislative workings of New York State. There are major sections on sources of legislative intent and on legislative intent of consitutional amendments. This is followed by a general bibliography of seventy-three citations.

652. New York. State Library. Legislative and Governmental Services. **Rural Crime: Bibliography**. (By Owen Jones) Albany, 1983. 4pp. Free. Topic No. 68-3.

There are thirty-eight citations in this current bibliography on rural crime, arranged alphabetically by title. Many of the items cited are government publications, followed by periodicals and several books. All citations are annotated.

653. New York. Division of Human Rights. **Special Collections**. (By Simon Fediuk) Albany, 1972. 3 vols. Free. LC card No. 72-612410.

This excellent bibliography on human rights comprises five sections in three volumes. Part I reviews housing and urban renewal publications, parts II-IV cite education studies, and part V is strictly publications by or about the New York State Division of Human Rights.

LIBRARIES

654. New York. State Library. **Bibliography of Articles Pertaining to Government Documents in Microform**. Albany, 1983. 3*l*. Free.

A very useful bibliography of eighteen citations for document specialists on the management of government publications in microform. Each citations includes a one-paragraph summary.

655. New York. State Library. Legislative and Governmental Services. **Library Research Guides: Where to Begin**. (By Dorothy Holt) Albany, 1982. 13pp. Bibliography No. 82.

This is a selective, annotated guide of business, humanities, science, technology, and social science sources. The 116 titles can all be found in the State Library. They are arranged under forty-one subheadings.

MINORITY GROUPS

656.　New York. State University of New York, Geneseo. Library. **Black Studies and the Negro in the United States.** (By David W. Parish) Geneseo, 1974. 12pp. Free. Collection Descriptive Series No. 10.

General references, civil rights, economic conditions, education, history, medicine, health, politics, and social conditions are the subjects addressed in this bibliography. Federal and state documents, directories, and other bibliographies are included in this work.

657.　New York. State University, Buffalo. University Libraries. Polish Room. **The Polish-American Catholic and His Piety: A Select Bibliography.** (By Manual D. Lopez) Buffalo, 1979. 39pp. Free.

This unique annotated bibliography of books, sections of books, and articles makes an important contribution to literature regarding Polish-American piety and culture. It is divided into sections on the American hierarchy, parishes, orders, Catholic education, and the Polish National Church.

NATIVE PEOPLE

658.　New York. State Department of Education. Native American Education Unit. **Selected Bibliography.** Albany, 1972. 1 vol. Free.

Designed for grades 10 to 12, this title lists general references in the following areas: native American education, the Iroquois, and general information pertaining to native Americans.

NATURAL RESOURCES

659.　New York. Cornell University Water Resources and Marine Sciences Center. **Annotated Bibliography of Limnological and Related Literature Dealing With the Finger Lakes Region.** Ithaca, 1970. 28pp. Free. Publication No. 29.

This bibliography on New York's Finger Lakes includes citations on algae, fisheries, geology, meteorology, physical-chemical water properties, pollution, and the zooplankton. The arrangement is according to author.

660.　New York. Syracuse University, Syracuse. College of Environmental Science and Forestry. **An Annotated Bibliography of Recent Tree Harvesting Literature.** (By William J. Gabriel and James T. Christensen) Syracuse, 1974. 171pp. Free. AFRI Research Report No. 19.

This report is divided into three major parts and twenty-two subdivisions and contains 1,320 references. Part I contains references of a general nature, part II deals with specific phases of tree harvesting, and part III presents the planning and layout aspects of tree harvesting.

661. New York. Syracuse University, Syracuse. Environmental Science and Forestry. **Annotated Bibliography on the Timber Resources and Primary Wood-using Industries of New York State.** Syracuse, 1969. 148pp. Free. LC card No. 72-611816.

This is an important bibliography of over five hundred citations prepared for the New York State Office of Planning Coordination.

662. New York. College of Agriculture and Life Sciences. **Bibliography for Forestland Owners—Forest Products.** Ithaca, 1980. 9pp. $2.00. Conservation Circular Volume 18, No. 9.

Publications that address some popular products and benefits derived from wise forest management are reviewed here. Christmas trees, fuelwood, maple syrup, other food products, recreation and aesthetics, solid wood products, and wildlife enjoyment are addressed in the seventy-five citations.

663. New York. College of Agriculture and Life Sciences. **Bibliography for Forestland Owners—In-Forest Management.** Ithaca, 1980. 12pp. $1.00. Conservation Circular Volume 18, No. 8.

Designed for use by owners of private nonindustrial forestland, this bibliography includes one hundred citations with abstracts on such topics as forest ecology, tree identification, soils, silvics and siviculture, economics, tree selection, forest damage, and harvesting.

664. New York. College of Agriculture and Life Sciences. **Bibliography of Fuelwood Use and Management.** Ithaca, 1982. 12pp. $2.00. Conservation Circular Volume 19, No. 2.

"Most firewood users could benefit from the information presented in this bibliography." The sixty-eight reports and journal articles are divided into the following categories: general works, fuelwood harvesting, use, and miscellaneous. Each citation is thoroughly annotated.

665. New York. Water Resources Commission. **Bibliography of the Ground-Water Resources of New York through 1967 with Subject and Location Cross Reference to the Annotated Bibliography.** (By Robert D. ManNish) Albany, 1969. 186pp. LC card No. 77-631205. Bulletin No. 66.

Approximately seven hundred citations arranged according to author with extensive summaries of the content of each study are offered in this bibliography on ground water. Each citation is keyed to location and subject indexes so that the reader can look under principal subjects related to ground water and find materials related to areas of New York State. All bulletins of the commission are also listed.

POLITICS AND GOVERNMENT

666. New York. Division of the Budget. Planning and Resource Group. Research and Federal Relations Unit. **Selected Source Documents on Public Finance Pertaining to New York State.** (By Harold W. Juhre, Jr., et al.) Albany, 1982. 74*l.* Free.

This heavily annotated listing makes an important contribution in meeting the needs of students of New York State government finances. Reports, studies, and commentaries issued by state and federal agencies, the legislature, Congress, and nongovernmental bodies since 1966, including some classics in the field are cited. Section I is grouped by issues; section II contains distinctive titles grouped in subject categories.

SOCIAL CONDITIONS

667.   New York. State Education Department. Bureau of School Psychological and Social Services. **Child Abuse and Neglect Bibliography**. Albany, 1980. 32pp. Free.
"This bibliography has been prepared to provide educators with an annotated bibliography listing of the Department's resources on child abuse." The 110 citations are divided according to curricular and audiovisual resources, articles, and general studies. Each has a short annotation and all may be borrowed from the bureau.

TRANSPORTATION

668.   New York. Port Authority of New York. **Bibliography, 1921-1968**. New York, 1969. 81pp. Free.
The Port Authority serves varied transportation needs of the New York City metropolitan area. Pertinent resources on its operation, including history, administration, public affairs, facilities, promotion, and the World Trade Center are documented in over fifteen hundred citations.

669.   New York. State University, Albany. Research Foundation. **Traffic Safety Subject Bibliography**. Albany, 1980. 8pp. Free. TSSB 03-1180.
Published in conjunction with the Governor's Alcohol and Highway Safety Task Force, the thirty-six well-annotated citations here are a useful mix on youthful drivers, rural areas, the courts, and the judicial system.

WOMEN

670.   New York. School of Industrial and Labor Relations. **Academic Women and Employment Discrimination: A Critical Annotated Bibliography**. (By Jennie Farley) Ithaca, 1982. 112pp. $8.95. ILR Bibliography No. 16.
Nearly two hundred of the most influential works on the employment troubles of academic women are reviewed in this collection. The annotations provide candid appraisal of the issues—sex bias in hiring, teaching, and tenure decisions, and sexual harassment. The introduction provides a broad view of the status of women in academia.

671. New York. State Library. Legislative Reference Bureau. **Affirmative Action Ideas on the Employment of Women: A Selected Annotated Bibliography**. (Compiled by Marilyn Gehr) Albany, 1975. 13pp. Price not available.

This publication reviews over 150 citations on the employment of women and discrimination against women from the holdings of the State Library.

NORTH CAROLINA

AGRICULTURE

672.   North Carolina. Agricultural Extension Service. **Guide to the Literature on Plants in North Carolina.** (By James W. Hardin and J. D. Skean) Raleigh, 1981. 22pp. Free. LC card No. 82-622109. AG Series No. 124.
This is an important bibliography of over 125 citations on major plants of North Carolina.

673.   North Carolina. Agricultural Experiment Station. **Tobacco Literature: A Bibliography of Publications.** (By Carmen M. Marin) Raleigh, 1970. 303pp. Free. LC card No. 74-633488. Bulletin No. 439.
The 1,128 titles in this tobacco bibliography encompass domestic and foreign books, federal and state documents, periodical articles, monographs, theses, and motion pictures, all found in the Library of Congress. Arrangement is alphabetic by author. There are author and subject indexes.

DISABLED

674.   North Carolina. Whitten Village. Department of Education. **Bibliography of Professional Materials on Mental Retardation and Reference.** (By H. Y. Keng) Clinton, 1980. 27pp. Free.
This is a supplement to an edition issued in 1975 and updates it with over two hundred current citations on retardation.

GEOGRAPHY

675.   North Carolina. University, Chapel Hill. Department of Geography. **Bibliography of Dissertations in Geography: 1901-1969.** (By Clyde E. Browning) Chapel Hill, 1970. 1 vol. $3.00. Studies in Geography No. 1.
This is an annotated listing of fifteen hundred dissertations in the field of geography, arranged in twenty-three categories. Major sections include climatology, cultural geography, economic geography, and population. Arrangement within each category is by author. There is a broad regional index.

MINORITY GROUPS

676.   North Carolina. State University, Raleigh. D. H. Hill Library. **Black Literature: A Classified Bibliography of Newspapers, Periodicals, and Books by
and about the Negro.** (By W. Robert Pollard) Raleigh, 1969. 77*l.* Out-of-
Print.
The 250 titles in this collection of materials from the D. H. Hill Library include
some historic slavery documents.

677.   North Carolina. Central University. Institute on Desegregation. **Desegregation and the White Presence on the Black Campus: A Bibliography for
Researchers.** (By Charles I. Brown and Benjamin F. Speller) Durham,
1980. 46pp. $3.00.
A bibliography of research and related literature from the social and behavioral
sciences dealing with the concerns, issues, problems, and policies of desegregation.
Desegregation in general, black postsecondary education, historically black institutions, and the white presence on black campuses are the issues highlighted. Books,
monographs, research reports, journal articles, theses, and dissertations are
included.

PLANNING

678.   North Carolina. Department of Conservation and Development. **Reports
Published.** Raleigh, 1969. 37*l.* Free.
This listing of over seven hundred titles published to July 1968 covers land analysis,
population, general planning documents, zoning, and studies on education.

WILDLIFE

679.   North Carolina. Department of Natural and Economic Resources. Division
of Commercial and Sports Fisheries. **Annotated Bibliography of
Anadromous Fishes of North Carolina through 1972.** (By Michael W.
Street and Ann Bowman Hall) Raleigh, 1973. 85pp. Free. Special
Scientific Report No. 23.
Annotated references are provided to 238 papers issued from 1846 through 1972
on the American Shad, Hickory Shad, Blueback Herring, Alewife, Striped Bass,
Atlantic Sturgeon, and Shortnose Sturgeon. There is a subject index for each
species.

NORTH DAKOTA

ARTS

680.   North Dakota. State Board for Vocational Education. **Selected Film Bibliography for Graphic Communications Cluster.** (By Clemens Gruen) Bismarck, 1976. 48pp. Free. Research Series No. 52.

This bibliography includes over two hundred films and print resources related to the graphic arts.

DISABLED

681.   North Dakota. State Library Commission. **Books for the Visually Impaired Young Children: An Annotated Bibliography.** (By Beverly Simmons) Bismarck, 1978. 48pp. Free.

This bibliography of almost two hundred citations for use by both parents and teachers provides insights into the visually impaired and their problems.

ENERGY

682.   North Dakota. Governor. Office of Energy Management and Conservation. **Energy Bibliographies on File.** Bismarck, 1978. 20pp. Free.

This bibliography of bibliographies offers several hundred energy lists collected to aid the Office of Energy Management research.

ENVIRONMENT

683.   North Dakota. State Library Commission. **Environmental Science: A Bibliography.** (Edited by Edith P. Siegrist) Bismarck, 1971. 21pp. Free.

This is a basic bibliography of seventy-five to eighty titles on the environment of North Dakota.

GEOLOGY

684. North Dakota. Geological Survey. **Annotated Bibliography of the Geology of North Dakota, 1960-1979.** (By Mary Woods Scott) Grand Forks, 1981. 287pp. LC card No. 82-621010.

This is an important bibliography of over five hundred bulletins, special reports, and maps relating to North Dakota geology.

685. North Dakota. Legislative Council. Regional Environmental Assessment. **Bibliography of North Dakota Geology and Water Resources.** Bismarck, 1977. 7pp. $0.50. REAP Report No. 78-5.

Approximately fifty of the most important North Dakota geological studies are reviewed in this guide.

WETLANDS

686. North Dakota. Agricultural Experiment Station. **Fauna of the Prairie Wetlands: Research Methods and Annotated Bibliography.** (By Louis A. Ogaard) Fargo, 1981. 23pp. Free.

The subjects of waterfowl, nongame birds, mammals, and poikilothermic vertebrates and invertebrates are addressed in this collection of over sixty citations with lengthy annotations.

687. North Dakota. Agricultural Experiment Station. **Prairie Wetland Drainage Regulations: Discussion and Annotated Bibliography.** (By Jay A. Leitch and David M. Saxowsky) Fargo, 1981. 10pp. Free. Research Report No. 73.

An overview of wetland issues precedes this seventy-three-item annotated bibliography. There are summaries of conditions in Minnesota, North Dakota, and South Dakota. Arrangement is alphabetical by author.

688. North Dakota. Agricultural Experiment Station. **Socioeconomic Values of Wetlands: Concepts, Research Methods, and Annotated Bibliography.** (By Jay A. Leitch and Laurence Falk) Fargo, 1981. 42pp. LC card No. 82-623101. Research Report No. 81.

The socioeconomics of wetlands—economics, cash flow, market values, and recreation—are addressed in over five hundred citations. The most important studies are annotated. There is a subject index.

689. North Dakota. Agricultural Experiment Station. **Soils, Microbiology, and Chemistry of Prairie Wetlands: Research Methods and Annotated Bibliography.** (By Louis A. Ogaard) Fargo, 1981. 30pp. Free. North Dakota Research Report No. 84.

"The broad topics of wetland soils, wetland microbiology, and wetland chemistry are briefly discussed" in this selected annotated bibliography detailing some of the contemporary research being pursued in these fields. There are approximately 175 citations. An author index is supplied.

690.　North Dakota. Agricultural Experiment Station. **Wetland Hydrology: State-of-the-Art and Annotated Bibliography.** (By Jay A. Leitch and others) Fargo, 1981. 16pp. Free. North Dakota Research Report No. 82.

Over two hundred citations on wetlands and prairie potholes related to flood control, erosion, sediment entrapment, ground water recharge, and water supply are included in this research report.

691.　North Dakota. Agricultural Experiment Station. **Wetland Vegetation of the Prairie Pothole Region: Research Methods and Annotated Bibliography.** (By Louis A. Ogaard, Jay A. Leitch, and Gary K. Clambey) Fargo, 1981. 50pp. Free.

"Analysis of freshwater vegetation is the focus of this paper." This annotated bibliography confirms the eclectic nature of this field. There are 265 amply annotated citations on primary production, nutrient cycling, and plant distribution. There is an author index.

WILDLIFE

692.　North Dakota. Agricultural Experiment Station. **Selected Annotated Bibliography of Economic Values of Fish and Wildlife and Their Habitats.** (By Jay A. Leitch) Fargo, 1977. 132pp. Free. Miscellaneous Report No. 27.

This selected, annotated bibliography is divided into seven categories: wetland economics, economics of fish and wildlife, evaluation techniques, socioeconomic characteristics, outdoor recreation, water resource economics, and bibliographies.

AGRICULTURE

693. Ohio. Agricultural Research and Development Center. **Annotated Bibliography of the Yellow-Headed Cutworm.** (By Roy W. Rings and Beth A. Johnson) Wooster, 1976. 13pp. Free. Research Circular No. 225.

"The purpose of this circular is to consolidate the abstracted literature on the yellow-headed cutworm, *Apamea amputatrix* (Fitch)." There are seventy-five citations taken from major journals in the field, U.S. Department of Agriculture reports, and Canadian studies. Most citations are thoroughly abstracted. There is a key-word-in-context index.

694. Ohio. Agricultural Research and Development Center. **Annotated Bibliography of Weeds as Reservoirs for Organisms Affecting Crops: Arthropods.** (By Leo E. Bendixen, Kil Ung Kim, Cynthia M. Kozak, and David J. Horn) Wooster, 1981. 117pp. Free. Research Bulletin No. 1125.

This second volume of a bibliography on the aspects of crop protection and crop production associated with weeds emphasizes the key role of weeds and their control. The main part of the bibliography composes 291 amply annotated citations on more than seventy arthropod families. The arrangement is alphabetic by author. The index includes not only authors' names but also key descriptive words and a serial number to the publication.

695. Ohio. Agricultural Research and Development Center. **An Annotated Bibliography of Weeds as Reservoirs for Organisms Affecting Crops: Nematodes.** (By Leo E. Bendixen, Dean A. Reynolds, and R. M. Riedel) Wooster, 1979. 64pp. Free. Research Bulletin No. 1109.

This annotated bibliography brings together literature relating to this neglected aspect of crop protection and crop production with emphasis on nematodes. More than twenty-five families of plants are covered in almost three hundred citations. Over one-quarter of the citations are abstracted; there is a key-word-in-context index.

696. Ohio. State University, Columbus. Department of Agricultural Economics and Rural Sociology. **Annotated Bibliography on Agricultural Credit and Rural Savings: IV.** Columbus, 1980. 160pp. Free.

This valuable bibliography emphasizing credit in developing countries offers 428 well-abstracted citations. Arrangement is alphabetical according to author. There is an organization index.

697.   Ohio. State University, Columbus. Department of Agricultural Economics and Rural Sociology. **Annotated Bibliography on Agricultural Credit and Rural Savings: V.** Columbus, 1980. 60pp. Free.

This bibliography contains 172 citations with lengthy annotations. The emphasis is on South Asia and Central America. The two sections on credit and rural savings are indexed by author-organization and geographical regions.

698.   Ohio. State University, Columbus. Department of Agricultural Economics and Rural Sociology. **Annotated Bibliography on Agricultural Credit and Rural Savings: VI.** Columbus, 1980. 65pp. Free.

This supplement to bibliography IV offers lengthy annotations to 180 citations on agricultural credit and rural savings. Many of the department's papers are included. There are organization, author-organization, and geographic indexes.

699.   Ohio. State University, Columbus. Department of Agricultural Economics and Rural Sociology. **Annotated Bibliography on Agricultural Credit and Rural Savings: VII.** Columbus, 1983. 84pp. Free.

This is the seventh in a series, offering 196 annotated citations on rural credit and savings in India. A majority of the citations are from journals. There are author and organization indexes.

700.   Ohio. Agricultural Research and Development Center. **Bibliography of Terrestrial Slugs.** (By R. K. Lindquist) Wooster, 1977. 59pp. Free. Research Circular No. 232.

Slugs are becoming increasingly important to researchers in North America. This comprehensive bibliography includes over one thousand citations on *Gastropoda: stylommatophera* and *systellommatophora.* The arrangement is alphabetic by author.

701.   Ohio. Agricultural Research and Development Center. **List of References: Maize Virus Diseases and Corn Stunt.** (By R. M. Ritter) Wooster, 1978. 39pp. Free.

This bibliography on corn would be useful to biologists and farmers. Its features include a reference list to over two hundred citations, a key-word-in-context index, and an author index.

702.   Ohio. State Library. **Pesticides: Selected Publications.** Columbus, 1977. 4pp. Free. Selected Publication List No. 53.

There are fifty-six citations on the general problem and wise use of pesticides included in this publications list. Many of these are government publications, including hearings before Congress.

703.   Ohio. Agricultural Research and Development Center. **Worldwide, Annotated Bibliography of the Variegated Cutworm.** (By Preidroma S. Hübner) Wooster, 1976. 126pp. Free. Research Circular No. 219.

This bibliography consolidates the world literature on the variegated cutworm for pest management purposes. Research from important journals and from the *Bibliog-*

raphy of Agriculture are included. There are 810 citations, most with lengthy annotations. There is a thorough key-word-in-context index.

DISABLED

704. Ohio. State Library. **Architectural Barriers and the Handicapped**. Columbus, 1980. 7pp. Free. Selected Publication List No. 69.

Aspects of access for the handicapped in public buildings, the general community, parks, and residences are addressed in this list of ninety-three resources. Some Congressional hearings are included.

705. Ohio. State Library. **Education of the Mentally Handicapped**. Columbus, 1980. 7pp. Free. Selected Publication List No. 4.

Over 150 titles published since 1970 on communication, curriculum planning, educable mentally retarded, mainstreaming, reading, and teaching, are featured in this selected list.

706. Ohio. State Library. **Mentally Handicapped**. Columbus, 1980. 15pp. Free. Selected Publication List No. 48.

This is a revision of the State Library's *Mental Retardation* bibliography. Over 275 titles are divided into eighteen categories. Both books and government publications are included, with basic bibliographic information. Most citations are post-1972. Sexual behavior, deinstitutionalization, and behavior modification are particularly highlighted.

DRUG USE AND ABUSE

707. Ohio. State Library. **Alcoholism**. Columbus, 1980. 11pp. Free. Selected Publication List No. 64.

Over one-half of the sixty-four titles in this collection are government documents, with numerous Congressional hearings cited. The subjects dealt with include general topics, drinking and driving, employment, fetal alcohol syndrome, physiological effects, prevention, special programs, women, youth, and psychological effects.

ECONOMY/ECONOMICS

708. Ohio. Kent State University. College of Business Administration. **An Annotated Bibliography of Business Articles in the Futurist, 1967-1976**. (By Donald F. Mulvihill) Kent, 1976. 48pp. Free. Institute for 21st Century Business Series No. 10.

"This is an annotated bibliography of articles from the *Futurist* and consists of items of interest to businessmen." Besides businessmen, it should be of interest to teachers and libraries as well. Each of the 150 well-annotated articles serves as a starting point for further exploration.

709. Ohio. State Library. **Budgeting**. Columbus, 1978. 7pp. Free. Selected Publication List No. 21.

This collection of 122 sources is divided into sections on general works, planning and programming, state and local government, federal government, and zero-base budgeting.

710.   Ohio. University of Toledo. Business Research Center. College of Business Administration. **Powers and Limitations of Management Science: A Survey With a Selected Bibliography.** (By Sakara T. Jutila and Parvis Esmailzadeh) Toldeo, 1972. 40pp. Free. Papers in Operations Analysis Working Paper No. 9.

The 950 citations in this bibliography are concerned both with forecasting and a historical survey of the powers and limitations of management science. The categories include: the classics, planning and control, decision making, and systems analysis.

711.   Ohio. University of Toledo. Business Research Center. College of Business Administration. **Review of Forecasting: With a Selected Bibliography.** (By Sakara T. Jutila, Parviz Esmailzadeh, and Marvin D. Heller) Toledo, 1972. 43pp. Free. Papers in Operational Analysis Working Paper No. 8.

"Any decision process associates with itself an anticipation of some desirable future results." An analysis of forecasting is offered here, followed by a bibliography of 232 books and journal articles. Arrangement is alphabetical by author.

712.   Ohio. State Library. **Zero-Base Budgeting.** Columbus, 1978. 3pp. Free. Selected Publication List No. 20.

This pamphlet serves as a ready-reference bibliography of forty books, documents, and journal articles on zero-base budgeting.

EDUCATION AND TRAINING

713.   Ohio. State Library. **Adult Education: Selected Publication List.** Columbus, 1979. 9pp. Free. Selected Publication List No. 32.

There are 145 references, many government publications, in this brief bibliography. The material is organized into the following categories: general, basic education, continuing education, financial aid, library services, methods of study, minorities, training, older persons, teaching adults, and vocational guidance.

714.   Ohio. State Library. **The Teaching of Reading.** Columbus, 1977. 8pp. Free. Selected Publication List No. 33.

This bibliography on teaching reading is very useful for school libraries. Its 148 current citations are organized into sections on: general works, elementary schools, preschool, psychology, disabilities, instruction, and secondary schools. Most citations are to books or government documents.

EMPLOYMENT

715.   Ohio. State Library. **Work Simplification: Selected Publications.** Columbus, 1977. 2pp. Free. Selected Publication List No. 49.

This brief document serves as a ready-reference of twenty-six citations on work simplification, management, and systems.

ENERGY

716.   Ohio. Agricultural Research and Development Center. **Annotated Bibliography of Greenhouse Energy Conservation and Management.** (By Hugh A. Poole and Priscilla A. Gresser) Wooster, 1980. 146pp. Free. Research Circular No. 262.

"Energy management for greenhouse operations was traditionally an overlooked concern in technical and research literature until the oil embargo of 1973-74." This annotated bibliography is intended to provide assistance to those interested in greenhouse management and research. A total of 1,373 references are cited and key terms have been assigned for each reference. The review of literature was terminated May 1, 1980 and the scope does not include citations that were found in literature reviews contained in the papers or articles. There is a subject index arranged by fourteen key terms.

717.   Ohio. Department of Energy. **Bibliography of Procurement Documents Relative to Energy Conservation.** Columbus, 1979. 2pp. Free.

This is an assortment of basic titles on a wide range of energy subjects for home use.

718.   Ohio. State Library. **Electric Energy: Selected Publications.** Columbus, 1978. 5pp. Free. Selected Publications List No. 76.

The conservation, consumption, utilization, economics, and environmental aspects of electrical energy are the subjects covered in this seventy-seven-item bibliography of mostly government publications.

719.   Ohio. State Library. **Energy: Conservation, Consumption, and Utilization.** Columbus, 1978. 11pp. Free.

Over two hundred works on agriculture and industry, community and residential buildings, and transportation—many available from the U.S. Government Printing Office or NTIS—comprise this energy bibliography.

720.   Ohio. State Library. **Solar Energy: Services to State Government.** Columbus, 1978. 6pp. Free. Selected Publication List No. 79.

The categories of this ninety-five-title bibliography include: general works, heating and cooling, research, and development. Electric, nuclear, and solar power are addressed.

ENVIRONMENT

721.   Ohio. Agricultural Research and Development Center. **Annotated Bibliography on Slope Stability of Strip Mine Soil Banks.** (By Glenn J. Hoffman, R. Bruce Curry, and Glenn O. Schwab) Wooster, 1964. 92pp. Free. Research Circular No. 130.

This is a "landmark" bibliography on slope stability. The arrangement is alphabetical by author and there is a very detailed subject index.

722.   Ohio. Biological Survey. **Bibliography of Theses and Dissertations on Ohio Floristics and Vegetation in Ohio Colleges and Universities.** (By Marvin L. Roberts and Ronald L. Stuckey) Columbus, 1974. 92pp. $1.50. Information Circular No. 7.

Fifty doctoral dissertations, 344 Master's theses, and twenty-one undergraduate honors studies on Ohio vegetation, arranged according to regions of Ohio are offered in this collection. There are indexes on major topics, plants, and authors.

723.   Ohio. Agricultural Research and Development Center. **Climatic Studies for Ohio: An Annotated Bibliography.** (By Marvin E. Miller and Valerie J. Seidel) Wooster, 1969. 33pp. Free.

The purpose of this publication is to give a listing of Ohio climatic studies so that the existing information will be more readily available. Entries are listed alphabetically by author. There are 231 entries—some are annotated—and a complete subject index.

724.   Ohio. State University, Columbus. Institute of Polar Studies. **List of Publications of the Institute of Polar Studies.** Columbus, 1972. 47pp. Free.

Over four hundred publications issued in six series by the institute are included in this bibliography on Arctic regions. Publications from the *Anarctic Journal of the United States* are included. There is an author index.

725.   Ohio. State Library. **Noise Pollution: Services to State Government.** (By Annette Heffernan) Columbus, 1980. 10pp. Free. Selected Publication List No. 51.

Government publications account for the majority of the 156 citations in this bibliography of sixteen categories of noise studies.

726.   Ohio. State Library. **Water Pollution.** Columbus, 1977. 7pp. Free. Selected Publication List No. 54.

This is an up-to-date reading list of 137 titles on the general problems of water pollution. Economic impact, the Great Lakes, mine drainage, pesticides, pollution control, waste treatment, and water quality are addressed.

GEOLOGY

727.   Ohio. Biological Survey. **Bibliography of Ohio Paleobotany.** (By Robert C. Romans and Patricia S. McCann) Columbus, 1974. 1 vol. $0.50.

There are 232 citations on paleobotany in this publication, subdivided into the following sections: general, Ordovician, Silurian, Devonian, Carboniferous, Permian, and Pleistocene.

HEALTH

728.   Ohio. State Library. **Food and Nutrition**. Columbus, 1979. 7pp. Free. Selected Publication List No. 19.

The emphasis of this 106-item bibliography is on general nutrition. Diets, health, disease, education, policy, vitamins, and the aged are discussed.

729.   Ohio. State Library. **Health Planning and Administration**. (By Annette Heffernan) Columbus, 1980. 8pp. Free. Selected Publication List No. 85.

This is a compilation of 117 citations, mostly government documents, on health facilities, health planning, and medical policy, with an emphasis on the community. Within each category the arrangement is alphabetical according to title.

730.   Ohio. State Library. **Nursing Homes: Selected Publications**. Columbus, 1978. 7pp. Free. Selected Publication List No. 43.

Included in this bibliography are 117 current resources on administration, aging and elderly, medicaid and medicare, nursing homes, and standards.

HISTORY

731.   Ohio. Historical Society. **Union List of Ohio Printed State Documents, 1803-1970**. Columbus, 1970. 688pp. $20.00.

This document offers historical sketches of each state government agency, followed by a listing of eight thousand separate titles and holdings coded to eighteen Ohio libraries.

LAWS AND LEGISLATION

732.   Ohio. State Library. **Copyright**. Columbus, 1979. 13pp. Free. Selected Publication List No. 30.

The subject of copyright is explored in 235 citations on historical perspective, libraries, photocopying, technology, trademarks, arts and performing rights, literary property, software, and book reviews. All of the Library of Congress Copyright Office circulars are included.

733.   Ohio. State Library. **Juvenile Delinquency and Justice: Selected Publications**. Columbus, 1983. 9pp. Free. Selected Publication List No. 56.

This bibliography was prepared as a service to the state government. It consists of 165 books and government documents on child welfare, delinquency, prevention, institutions, courts, justice, problem children, and victims.

MINORITY GROUPS

734.   Ohio. State Library. **Asian Pacific Americans**. Columbus, 1979. 3pp. Free.
        Selected Publication List. No. 64.
Fifty books, documents, and periodical articles on Japanese-Americans, Chinese-Americans, and Filipinos are included in this bibliography on Asian-Americans. Much of the emphasis is on subcultures.

NATURAL RESOURCES

735.   Ohio. Biological Survey. **Guide to the Literature of Ohio's Natural Areas**.
        (By Lynn Edward Elfner, Ronald L. Stuckey, and Ruth W. Melvin)
        Columbus, 1973. $0.50. Information Circular No. 3.
"This guide is a collection of the scattered but important references on Ohio's natural resources." Over 550 citations are included. Arrangement is primarily by county, followed by natural area.

POLITICS AND GOVERNMENT

736.   Ohio. State Library. **Campaigning**. Columbus, 1978. 7pp. Free. Selected
        Publication List No. 80.
This bibliography is comprised of fifty-four books on campaigning generally and campaign management and financing. It is followed by sixty-five periodical articles on recent elections, PAC groups, and financing.

737.   Ohio. State Library. **Government Reform**. Columbus, 1977. 3pp. Free.
        Selected Publication List No. 2.
Title, author, publisher, date, and pagination are given for sixty-five citations on government reform. Many are critical of government practices.

SOCIAL CONDITIONS

738.   Ohio. State Library. **Volunteer Services: Selected Publications**. Columbus,
        1981. 6pp. Free. Selected Publication List No. 67.
This list includes citations since 1977 related to volunteerism with the aged, alcoholics, child abuse, corrections, the handicapped, those receiving social services, and medical care.

TECHNOLOGY

739.   Ohio. State Library. **Electronic Data Processing: Selected Publications**.
        Columbus, 1981. 15pp. Free.
There are 295 current citations in this publication divided into fifteen subject sections. These include business, management, microcomputers, and vocational guidance. Related bibliographies from the State Library include *Systems Analysis, Computers: General,* and *Computer Programming.*

740. Ohio. State Library. **Videorecorders and Recording**. (By Barbara J. Laughon) Columbus, 1979. 5pp. Free.

Equipment selection, the uses of videotape, training, production, troubleshooting, new developments, and copyright are among the topics covered in this current bibliography of seventy-four citations.

WILDLIFE

741. Ohio. State Library. **Wildlife Conservation**. Columbus, 1977. 7pp. Free. Selected Publication No. 23.

This is a useful bibliography for both college and public libraries. Its 166 citations include general works on birds, conservation, endangered species, fish, mammals, reptiles, wilderness, and wildlife.

WOMEN

742. Ohio. State University, Columbus. Center for Vocational and Technical Education. **Implications of Women's Work Patterns for Vocational and Technical Education: An Annotated Bibliography**. Columbus, 1967. 1 vol. Free.

The annotations in this bibliography of books, government publications, and journal articles date primarily from 1964 to 1967. The status of women, education and employment, the labor force, legislation, vocational guidance, bibliographies, and presentations appropriate for students represent the scope of the collection.

GENERAL

743.   Oklahoma. State Department of Education and Cultural Affairs. Library Resources Section. **Sooners, Gushers, and Dusters: Book Reviews K-12.** Oklahoma City, 1980. 46pp. Free.

This is a listing of recommended books for elementary and secondary grades. Oklahoma is the subject of many of the titles.

EDUCATION AND TRAINING

744.   Oklahoma. State Department of Education. **Study Skills: Study Your Way to Success, Kindergarten-6th.** Oklahoma City, 1982. 83pp. Free.

This booklet provides a multicurriculum collection of ideas and activities to enhance study skills and to help parents work with their children. An extensive bibliography of resources is included.

GEOLOGY

745.   Oklahoma. Geological Survey. **Bibliography of Abandoned Coal Mines Lands in Oklahoma.** (By K. S. Johnson, C. M. Kidd, and R. C. Butler) Norman, 1981. 84pp. $3.50. Special Publication No. 81-2.

This valuable 250-item bibliography for geologists and cave explorers is more specialized than the Iowa Geological Suvey bibliography on abandoned mines.

746.   Oklahoma. Geological Survey. **Combined Bibliographies of Oklahoma Geology, 1955-1979.** (By Elizabeth A. Hamm and Christine D. Gay) Norman, 1981. 2 vols. $8.00. LC card No. 82-620651. Special Publication No. 81-5.

This is a basic reference for geology collections. Volume I covers the 1955 to 1970 time period; volume II reports on 1971 to 1979. They are available only as a set.

747.   Oklahoma. Geological Survey. **List of Publications of Oklahoma Geological Survey 1902-1978.** (By Elizabeth A. Hamm and Claren M. Kidd) Norman, 1979. $2.00. Special Publication No. 79-1.

This is a complete listing of Survey publications, indexed by author, commodity, and county.

MINORITY GROUPS

748. Oklahoma. Department of Libraries. **Black Experience Collection: A Bibliography.** Oklahoma City, 1983. 28pp. Free.

Over thirteen hundred books on the contemporary black experience in American life are listed in this bibliography. Arrangement is according to author; a wide range of material is covered.

749. Oklahoma. Department of Libraries. **Hispanic Collection: A Bibliography.** Oklahoma City, 1983. 44pp. Free.

This is a comprehensive bibliography of books in Spanish and about the Hispanic experience found in the Oklahoma Library. Arrangement is first alphabetical by author, followed by Dewey Classification arrangement. Books for all ages are included.

POLITICS AND GOVERNMENT

750. Oklahoma. University, Norman. Bureau of Government Research. **Contracting for City Services: An Annotated Bibliography.** (By Charles B. Williams) Norman, 1980. 36*l*. $3.00. LC card No. 80-623687.

This annotated bibliography of eighty items taken from books and journals covers a twenty-year period. It is divided into four categories: general, public safety, public works, and health. It contains an author index.

751. Oklahoma. University, Norman. Bureau of Government Research. **Ethics and the Public Service: An Annotated Bibliography and Overview Essay.** (By Elizabeth Gunn) Norman, 1980. 47pp. $3.50.

This essay and bibliography of 152 annotated entries provides an introduction to and review of the ethics issue in the field of public administration. Abstracts are taken from leading political science, public administration, and personnel management journals as well as major books in the field.

752. Oklahoma. University, Norman. Bureau of Government Research. **Evaluations of Social Service Programs: An Annotated and Unannotated Bibliography.** (By Donna Lorenson and Wright D. Davis) Norman, 1977. 170pp. $5.50.

Funded originally by a grant from the Oklahoma Department of Institutions, this comprehensive bibliography of over six hundred entries describes the functions, methodology, and limitations of evaluative studies. Special emphasis is given to the social service programs under Title XX of the Social Security Act.

753. Oklahoma. University, Norman. Bureau of Government Research. **Quantitative Research in Public Administration and Policy Analysis: A Methodologically Annotated Bibliography.** (By T. R. Carr, Dwight F. Davis, and Samuel A. Kirkpatrick) Norman, 1977. 97pp. $4.50.

This comprehensive bibliography of 385 entries is drawn from professional journals in political science, sociology, and general policy analysis from 1966 to 1977.

Entries are divided into six substantive categories with annotations which reflect design type, analytic techniques, and general findings.

754.   Oklahoma. University, Norman. Bureau of Government Research. **State and Urban Policy Analysis: An Annotated Bibliography.** (By T. R. Carr and Stephanie Colston) Norman, 1975. 75pp. $3.50.

The citations in this collation are drawn from professional journals in political science, science, sociology, and general policy analysis in the years 1963 to 1975. It presents a brief typology for policy studies and indicates various characteristics of the studies.

WOMEN

755.   Oklahoma. State University, Stillwater. Edmond Low Library. **Women as People: A Finders List.** (Compiled by Elizabeth M. McCorkle, Jill M. Holmes, and Mary Lynn Brown) Stillwater, 1978. 52pp. Free.

The emphasis of these approximately fifty titles is exploring the newest "frontier"—"women as people." Pamphlets, journals, books, audiovisuals, and ERIC materials have been screened. Arrangement is by author and a complete title index is included.

AGRICULTURE

756. Oregon. Agricultural Experiment Station. **A Bibliography of Bitterbrush (*Purshia tridentata*) Annotated from 1967 to 1978.** (By Robert G. Clark and Carlton M. Button) Corvallis, 1979. 18pp. Free. Oregon Experiment Station Bulletin No. 640.

A major literature review study at Oregon State University yielded these approximately 380 citations on bitterbrush. Arrangement is alphabetical by author. Most citations are journal articles. An appendix of almost two hundred additional citations is included.

757. Oregon. Agricultural Experiment Station. **Hydrologic Outputs from Woodland, Shrubland, and Grassland Ecosystems in Relation to Grazing Management Strategies: An Annotated Bibliography.** (By Robert E. Gaither) Corvallis, 1981. 26pp. Free. Special Report No. 640.

This bibliography combines eighty-eight studies on hydrologic output from woodland, shrubland, and grassland ecosystems. Only unique or landmark studies were selected. The main arrangement is alphabetic by author with full bibliographic information and ample annotations. Government publications and journal articles are included.

758. Oregon. Agricultural Experiment Station. **Indexed Bibliography of Nematode Resistance in Plants.** (Compiled by Judith M. Armstrong and Harold J. Jensen) Corvallis, 1978. 256pp. Free. Oregon Experiment Station Bulletin No. 639.

This bulletin includes over five hundred citations arranged according to twenty-one categories of nematode-resistant plants. An adequate explanation is provided for matching plant genera to citations.

EDUCATION AND TRAINING

759. Oregon. University, Eugene. School of Education. **Bibliography for the Professional Book Shelf in School Libraries.** (By Grace Graham) Eugene, 1960. 6pp. Free. Curriculum Bulletin No. 205.

This is a bibliography of 105 easily obtainable sources. The categories are general references, secondary school, junior high, and elementary education.

760. Oregon. State Library. **Career Education Pamphlets: A Library of 1200 Free and Inexpensive Sources.** (By Dale E. Shaffer) Salem, 1976. 65*l.* Free.

This catalog was prepared to assist librarians, teachers, counselors, and educators in obtaining free and inexpensive resources on career education. It reviews a basic collection of occupational booklets. Of the 1,216 items listed, 604 are free. Arrangement is according to almost 240 career headings. Addresses are provided for the sources.

761. Oregon. State University, Corvallis. **Unrequired Reading: An Annotated Bibliography for Teachers and School Administrators.** (By Iris M. Tiedt and Sidney W. Tiedt) Corvallis, 1967. 128pp. $5.00. LC card No. 63-63839.

This book represents many years of research. There are over eight hundred citations on understanding students. Divisions are children under twelve, adolescents, eighteen plus, understanding the teacher, and sixty citations on understanding the administrator. Most citations are annotated. There is a complete author index.

ENERGY

762. Oregon. State University, Corvallis. **Energy: A Scientific, Technical, and SocioEconomic Bibliography.** (By Kitty Hsieh) Corvallis, 1976. 90pp. $4.00. Bibliographic Series No. 12.

This well-rounded bibliography on all aspects of energy conservation would be useful for both academic and public libraries.

GEOLOGY

763. Oregon. Department of Geology and Mineral Industries. **Bibliography of the Geology and Mineral Resources of Oregon, 1976-1979.** (By Debbie Burnetti and Klaus K. E. Nevendorf) Portland, 1981. 68pp. Price on application. LC card No. GS 54-4.

This is the seventh supplement to this bibliography; it covers the 1976-1979 period. It was compiled in cooperation with Geo-Ref Information Systems and the American Geological Institute.

HEALTH

764. Oregon. Southern Oregon State College, Ashland. Library. **Wholeness of Being.** (By Margaret Christean and Clifford Wolfsher) Ashland, 1979. 26pp. Price on application. Bibliographies Volume 9, No. 1.

Over two hundred current citations on mental health and self-realization are collected here, with forty citations on the psychological concept of conjunction of opposites. All entries are lengthy.

NATURAL RESOURCES

765.   Oregon. State University, Corvallis. **Forestry Theses Accepted in the United States, 1900-1952.** (By Katherine W. Hughes, Ray A. Yoder, and William I. West) Corvallis, 1953. 140pp. $3.50.

This was an important pioneering bibliography to over five hundred forestry theses accepted by graduate schools over a fifty-two-year period.

OCEANOGRAPHY

766.   Oregon. State University, Corvallis. Sea Grant College Program. **Publications Received.** Corvallis, 1972- . Irregular. Free.

Each issue of this irregular publication acts as a current bibliography to over 250 sea-grant publications issued nationwide. There are usually at least twenty subject categories with many reports on coastal zone management, marine biology, economics, and ocean resource law.

PLANNING

767.   Oregon. University, Eugene. Municipal Research and Services Bureau. **Community Planning in Oregon: A List of Publications.** Eugene, 1967. 100pp. Price on application.

This is an invaluable bibliography of documents on local and regional planning in Oregon with over four hundred citations.

POLITICS AND GOVERNMENT

768.   Oregon. Legislative Research. **Legislative Research Cumulative Index.** Salem, 1982. 68pp. Free.

The subjects in this publication list and bibliography to Oregon legislative reports number 130. Each citation is accompanied by a short annotation.

RECREATION/TOURISM

769.   Oregon. State University, Corvallis. Cooperative Extension Service. **Selected Recreation References for Recreation and Tourism.** Corvallis, 1970. 8pp. Free.

This is a core list of over fifty titles for specialized recreation collection use.

WILDLIFE

770. Oregon. State Department of Fish and Wildlife. Research and Development Section. **Bobcat Population: A Review of Available Literature.** (By Dale E. Towiell) Portland, 1979. 28*l*. Free. LC card No. 80-622940.
The bobcat is considered a semi-endangered species. This list provides over one hundred citations with an emphasis on habits and management.

WOMEN

771. Oregon. State University, Corvallis. **Oregon Women: A Bio-Bibliography.** (By Evelyn Leasher) Corvallis, 1981. 64pp. $5.00. Bibliographic Series No. 18.
This collection of writings about important women from Oregon presents over three hundred citations. Access to information about these women in 102 books and journals is provided. The arrangement of entries is alphabetical by the last known name of the woman indexed. There is a symbol for denoting the source for further information. There is a useful classified index according to the profession or occupation of the person.

GENERAL

772. Pennsylvania. State Library. Government Publications Section. **List of Basic Pennsylvania State Publications for Depository Libraries.** (Compiled by Elizabeth G. Ellis and Robert C. Stewart) Harrisburg, 1967. 25pp. Free.

This document serves as a guide to historical as well as current basic publications. Over fifty titles are listed with descriptive annotations. There is an appendix of out-of-print titles.

ECONOMY/ECONOMICS

773. Pennsylvania. Pennsylvania State University. College of Business Administration. Center for Research. **Bibliography of Studies on the Economic Development of Pennsylvania and Its Regions.** University Park, 1962. 7pp. Out-of-Print.

This list is comprised of over fifty citations of major works on the economic development of the state.

EDUCATION AND TRAINING

774. Pennsylvania. Office for Aid to Nonpublic Education. **Additional Source References for Aid to Nonpublic Education.** Harrisburg, 1969. 3*l.* Free.

This basic reading list on federal aid to nonpublic education was prepared in the early days of this program.

775. Pennsylvania. Department of Education. **Careers and Career Education in the Performing Arts: An Annotated Bibliography.** (Edited by William L. Waack) Harrisburg, 1981. 54pp. Free.

This publication attempts to bring all the varied performing arts career titles together for purposes of easy reference. There are over three hundred annotated citations including general sources and divided by: Bibliographies/General bibliographies and specific works on dance, media, music, theatre, and writing. There is a section on future study and a name index.

776.   Pennsylvania. State Library. **Free and Inexpensive Learning Materials: A Brief List of Films, General and Special Learning Material Sources.** (By Mary Schmidt) Harrisburg, 1972. 5*l.* Free.

Over fifty items for teachers, many designed for special education and the mentally retarded, are included in this bibliographic list.

EMPLOYMENT

777.   Pennsylvania. State Library. **Collective Bargaining for State and Local Governments: A Selected Bibliography of Recent Materials in the State Library of Pennsylvania.** (By Mirjana Tolmachev) Harrisburg, 1971. 25pp. Free.

These over one hundred basic sources were gathered during a period in which collective public bargaining was expanding.

HEALTH

778.   Pennsylvania. Governor's Commission on Three Mile Island. **Layman's Guide to Radiological Health Information and Resources: A Selected Bibliography.** Harrisburg, 1980. 19pp. Free.

This bibliography offers a good starting point for general researchers and high school students. Most of the monographs, reference works, government documents, and periodical and newspaper articles included were authored in the past ten years.

779.   Pennsylvania. Office of Mental Health. Research Division. **Mental Health Research in Pennsylvania's State Hospitals: Annual Report, 1978.** Harrisburg, 1978. 114pp. Free.

This is a bibliography of some two hundred publications, reports, and proposed research completed during 1978 in Pennsylvania mental hospitals. An appendix lists all projects according to problem categories.

HISTORY

780.   Pennsylvania. Historical and Museum Commission. **Bibliography of Pennsylvania History: A Supplement.** (Edited by Carol Wall) Harrisburg, 1976. 252pp. $8.95.

After fifteen years, this volume brings up to date Wilkinson's *Bibliography of Pennsylvania History.* This scholarly work includes over four thousand citations arranged according to time period. There is a detailed index.

781.   Pennsylvania. Historical and Museum Commission. **Ethnic History in Pennsylvania: A Selected Bibliography.** (By John E. Bodnar) Harrisburg, 1974. 47pp. $1.95.

This useful bibliography of studies of the major ethnic groups in Pennsylvania offers over two hundred citations.

782. Pennsylvania. Historical and Museum Commission. **Pennsylvania Historical Bibliography**. (By John B. B. Trussell) Harrisburg, 1970- . Irregular. Various pricing.

There have been four supplements since 1970 to the basic *Bibliography of Pennsylvania History*. Each supplement contains over three hundred citations. The fourth supplement brought the bibliography up to date through 1979.

MINORITY GROUPS

783. Pennsylvania. Bureau of General and Academic Education. **American Diversity: A Bibliography of Resources on Racial and Ethnic Minorities from Pennsylvania Schools**. Harrisburg, 1969. 237pp.

This major bibliography of over eight hundred citations was designed to help teachers understand minorities in their classroom and their social and educational problems.

POLITICS AND GOVERNMENT

784. Pennsylvania. Department of Community Affairs. **Perspective on Urban Problems and Local Government Finance: A Bibliography of Recent Readings with Selected Annotations**. Harrisburg, 1977. 49pp. Free.

This bibliography cites over 150 citations on urban problems, including the use of revenue-sharing monies.

RECREATION/TOURISM

785. Pennsylvania. Department of Community Affairs. Bureau of Recreation and Conservation. **Resources Available in the Bureau of Recreation and Conservation Library**. Harrisburg, 1981. 12pp. Free. Leisure Tap No. 30.

Outdoor recreation, playgrounds, program administration, and maintenance are the subjects covered in this 53-item selection. Each citation has an ample annotation and all can be borrowed from the bureau library.

PUERTO RICO

GENERAL

786.   Puerto Rico. Office of the Commonwealth. **Puerto Rico, USA.** San Juan,
        1971. 64pp. Free.
This is a selective reference source describing modern Puerto Rico. It includes
reviews of literature on economic development, housing and education since 1957.
A twenty-four entry bibliography is included.

787.   Puerto Rico. Bureau of the Budget. **Reports.** San Juan, 1949/50- . Annual.
        Price on application.
This is an ongoing bibliographic series of reports on surveys, research projects,
investigations, and other organized fact-gathering activities of the government of
Puerto Rico.

SOUTH CAROLINA

GENERAL

788. South Carolina. State Library. **Large Print Books: An Annotated List.** Columbia, 1975. 152pp. Free.

This complete bibliography of over eight hundred large-print books in the State Library is arranged alphabetically by title. The annotations included are also in large print. There is an author index. A supplement was issued in 1976.

DRUG USE AND ABUSE

789. South Carolina. Commission on Alcohol and Drug Abuse. **An Annotated Bibliography on Primary Prevention of Drug Abuse.** Columbia, 1979. 27pp. Free.

This excellent title for all kinds of drug abuse draws on ERIC, *Psychological Abstracts*, and the HEW *Primary Prevention Drug Abuse Guide to the Literature*. It includes journal articles, books, and many government publications. Of particular interest are the citations on the earlier types of drug education materials.

790. South Carolina. Commission on Alcohol and Drug Abuse. **An Annotated Bibliography on Primary Prevention of Drug Abuse.** Columbia, 1981. 31*l.* Free.

This is a well-rounded bibliography of approximately one hundred citations on drug abuse drawn from the ERIC system, *Psychological Abstracts*, and volumes in the library of the South Carolina Commission on Alcohol and Drug Abuse. Most of the citations are post-1978. Most have lengthy annotations. This volume supplements the 1979 bibliography from the commission (above).

ECONOMY/ECONOMICS

791. South Carolina. Agricultural Experiment Station. **A Bibliography of Rural Development: Listings by Topic.** By Carrie G. Parker et al.) Clemson, 1976. 80pp. Free. AE No. 39*l.*

The fifteen hundred briefly annotated citations in this document are organized into the subject areas of agriculture, area development, communities, economic development, human resources, leadership, and rural development.

EDUCATION AND TRAINING

792. South Carolina. Department of Education. Education Products Center. **Annotated List.** Columbia, 1980. 173pp. Free.

The primary purpose of this annotated bibliography to over 250 educational titles from the department is to provide a cataloging system. There are twenty-three categories, including demography, specific subjects, the handicapped, personnel and groups, research, and tests. Brief annotations are supplied.

ENVIRONMENT

793. South Carolina. State Library. **Inherit What Earth: A Selected Booklist on Conservation and the Environment.** Columbia, 1972. 3pp.

Over fifty of the most popular and important environmental books of the early 1970s are featured in this brief bibliography.

HISTORY

794. South Carolina. Tricentennial Commission. **Books and Articles on South Carolina History: A List for Laymen.** (By Lewis P. Jones) Columbia, 1970. 104pp. Price on application. LC card No. 70-133844. Tricentennial Booklet No. 8.

"The basic aim of this work is to suggest titles from which intelligent readers, by their own trial and error, can satisfy their own interests on South Carolina history." Over one hundred citations are divided into twenty-one categories, such as the American Revolution, antebellum society, the Civil War, and Reconstruction.

OCEANOGRAPHY

795. South Carolina. Sea Grant Consortium. **Search and Review of Elementary Marine Education Materials.** (By Jeanne M. Liu and Wendy B. Allen) Charleston, 1982. 86pp. Free. Technical Report No. 1.

This unique bibliography of over three hundred citations would be useful for elementary and middle schools or for pamphlet collections in public libraries.

RECREATION/TOURISM

796. South Carolina. Clemson University. College of Forest and Recreation Resources. Department of Recreation and Park Administration. **Annotated Bibliography of Corporate Philanthropy as It Affects Synergetic Recreation Programming.** (By Brian J. Mihalik) Clemson, 1981. 30pp. Free. RPA 1981/82-No. 1.

This bibliography includes 295 briefly annotated references on a wide variety of subjects, including the importance of recreation in American life, and corporate and philanthropic giving.

797.   South Carolina. Clemson University. College of Forest and Recreation Resources. Department of Recreation and Park Administration. **Annotated Bibliography of the 1980-82 Extension Publications of the Department of Recreation and Park Administration.** Clemson, 1982. 16pp. Free. RPA 82-9.

This is a useful bibliography of recent extension publications on recreation and park use. The thirty-nine studies have adequate annotations. Arrangement is alphabetic by author within each category.

WILDLIFE

798.   South Carolina. Clemson University. College of Forest and Recreation Resources. **Silvicultural Effects on Wildlife Habitat in the South (an Annotated Bibliography) 1953-1979.** (By Richard F. Harlow and David H. Van Lear) Clemson, 1981. 30pp. Free. Forestry Paper No. 14.

Subject categories of this two-hundred-item listing include: pine cuttings, site preparation, fire, integrated practices, fertilization, pine hardwoods, and diversity in forest types. There are author and subject indexes.

SOUTH DAKOTA

EDUCATION AND TRAINING

799.   South Dakota. State Library Commission. **Play and Learn with Toys and Games: A Bibliography of Toys and Games That Teach Institutionalized Children**. Pierre, 1979? 40pp. Free.

Communication skills, concepts, life skills, math readiness, motor skills, music therapy, reading readiness, sensory, and social studies are the categories of this study of four hundred kits and related programs. There is an appendix listing publisher's addresses. This title is authored cooperatively with Redfield State Hospital and School.

800.   South Dakota. State Library Commission. **Selected Children's Materials**. (By Lotsee Smith) Pierre, 1979. 53pp. Free.

This is a selective list of over one hundred citations for elementary age children.

LAWS AND LEGISLATION

801.   South Dakota. University, Vermillion. McKusick Law Library. **Survey of Holdings in Bankruptcy and Related Subject Areas**. Vermillion, 1982. 14pp. Free. USD Law Library Publication Series No. 5.

Current court decisions, general reports and codes, periodicals, looseleaf information services, and bibliographies about bankruptcy, most imprinted since 1975, comprise the 142 items in this reference tool.

802.   South Dakota. University, Vermillion. McKusick Law Library. **Survey of Holdings in Evidence and Related Materials**. Vermillion, 1983. 41pp. Free. USD Law Library Publication No. 23.

Evidence—including rules, cross-examinations, advocacy, recording of testimony, and general principles—is the subject of this survey. The citations are divided by format—books, updating services, bibliographies, periodicals, and classified material.

803.   South Dakota. University, Vermillion. McKusick Law Library. **Survey of Holdings in Family Law and Related Materials**. Vermillion, 1983. 25pp. Free. USD Law Library Publication No. 22.

This bibliography includes comprehensive coverage of resources on family law, listed alphabetically by title under subject headings. There are approximately seventy-five subject headings with two or three citations for each. There are also groupings of periodicals and bibliographies.

804. South Dakota. University, Vermillion. McKusick Law Library. **Survey of Holdings in Legal Medicine and Related Materials.** Vermillion, 1983. 25pp. Free. USD Law Library Publication.

Legal medicine—including dental law, medicaid, medical colleges, jurisprudence, general legislation, malpractice, medicine, nursing law, and the right to die is the subject of these 252 citations (some annotated). Recent acquisitions, looseleaf publications, periodicals, and bibliographies have been reviewed.

805. South Dakota. University, Vermillion. McKusick Law Library. **Survey of Holdings in Taxation and Related Materials.** Vermillion, 1983. 53pp. Free. USD Law Library Publication Series No. 20.

This collection of 482 citations of books, journal articles, documents, and services on taxation is arranged according to format: services, periodicals, classified materials, and handbooks followed by those on specific subjects. Personal income taxes and inheritance taxes are emphasized.

806. South Dakota. University, Vermillion. McKusick Law Library. **Survey of Holdings in Water Law and Related Subject Areas.** Vermillion, 1982. 13pp. Free. USD Law Library Publication Series No. 7.

Books, looseleaf publications, periodicals, bibliographies, classified material, and related natural resources law make up this 156-item bibliography. There is an emphasis on water rights.

MINORITY GROUPS

807. South Dakota. Agricultural Experiment Station. **Hutterite Brethren: An Annotated Bibliography with Special Reference to South Dakota Hutterite Colonies.** (By Marvin P. Riley) Brookings, 1965. 188pp. Free. Bulletin No. 529.

A result of over ten years of accumulated literature as part of a college project, there are 332 well-annotated citations in this bibliography. An author index and a short essay on the Hutterites are other features.

NATIVE PEOPLE

808. South Dakota. Department of Education and Cultural Affairs. **Indian Studies Curriculum Materials: An Annotated Bibliography.** Pierre, 1975. 39pp. Free.

A guide to Indian ethnic heritage studies, this bibliography includes over fifty citations on general Indian culture, history, music, and literature. Audiovisual materials and a list of addresses are also featured.

809. South Dakota. University, Vermillion. McKusick Law Library. **Survey of Holdings in Indian Law and Related Indian Materials.** Vermillion, 1982. 14pp. Free. USD Law Library Publication No. 8.

An excellent resource of 154 citations is offered here for the study of Indian law, including treaties. There is a section classified according to children, claims, courts, government relations, Indian territory, and land transfer. This current bibliography is useful for acquiring a core collection.

POLITICS AND GOVERNMENT

810. South Dakota. Legislative Research Council. **Bibliography of South Dakota Legislative Research Council Publications.** Pierre, 1970. 39pp. Free. LC card No. 68-66805. Staff Memorandum.

This listing of over four hundred legislative studies completed between 1951 and 1970 under twenty-three subject categories offers an excellent picture of South Dakota government. Some of those categories include business, education, health, welfare, Indian affairs, and legislative affairs.

811. South Dakota. State Library Commission. **Bibliography on the Reorgnization of State Government.** Pierre, 1976. 4pp. Free.

The thirty-two citations on constitutional and administrative reform in this brief list consist of government publications and journal articles.

812. South Dakota. State Planning Agency. Office of Policy Information. **Directory of Informational and Statistical Sources.** Pierre, 1971. 97pp. Free.

Published reports and data on computed tapes maintained by state agencies are reported on in this directory. The aim of this bibliography is to "facilitate a coherent flow of information from government officials to decision-making agencies." Arrangement is by agency subdivided by publications. There is a subject index.

WETLANDS

813. South Dakota. Cooperative Wildlife Research Unit. **Hydrology of Prairie Potholes: A Selected Annotated Bibliography.** (By Daniel E. Hubbard) Brookings, 1981. 41pp. Free. Technical Bulletin No. 1.

This bibliography emphasizes the value of hydrologic cycles as part of wetland values. This is a unique title with ninety-five citations arranged according to author. Most of the entries are government documents or journal articles. There is an author-subject index.

814. South Dakota. Cooperative Wildlife Research Unit. **Wildlife Use of Man-made Wetlands in the Prairie Pothole Region: A Selected Annotated Bibliography.** (By Beth Giron) Brookings, 1981. 23pp. Free. Technical Bulletin No. 2.

A great impact on wetlands has been loss through drainage from agricultural and construction activities so that man-made modifications become more important. This is a forty-six-citation bibliography on the subject with extensive annotations. There is an author-subject index.

WILDLIFE

815.　South Dakota. Cooperative Wildlife Research Unit. **Review of the Biology, Ecology, and Management of the Rails Common to the Prairie Wetlands.** (By Michael R. Broschart) Brookings, 1982. 47pp. Free. Technical Bulletin No. 4.

This is a bibliography of 109 citations on rails; there are four species on the Great Plains. There has been very little research, so this is a pioneer reference work. Arrangement is alphabetical by title. Ample annotations are provided and there is an author-title index.

816.　South Dakota. Cooperative Wildlife Research Unit. **Selected Annotated Bibliography of Mink Behavior and Ecology.** (By Gary W. Pendleton) Brookings, 1982. 33pp. Free. Technical Bulletin No. 3.

The mink is represented here in eighty-four annotated citations. This bibliography is composed mainly of journal articles. It would be useful for wildlife managers and biological researchers. There is an author-subject index.

WOMEN

817.　South Dakota. Commission on the Status of Women. **South Dakota Women, 1850-1919: A Bibliography.** Pierre, 1975. 1 vol. Free.

A short list of bibliographies on South Dakota women is followed by longer listings on fiction and nonfiction. Publication dates for the books and pamphlets range from the mid-1800s to the present. Short annotations provide a sketchy idea of the contents. Locations in at least one library are given.

AREA STUDIES

818. Tennessee. Memphis State University. J. W. Brister Library. **A Researcher's Guide to African Materials.** (By Dalvan M. Coger) Memphis, 1972. 204pp. Price on application.

This bibliography consists of copies of cards reproduced from the library file of African holdings. All periodicals related to African studies are listed separately. There are over six hundred citations with a very thorough index.

ARTS

819. Tennessee. Memphis State University. J. W. Brister Library. **Ann Godwin Winslow: An Annotated Check List of Her Published Works and of Her Papers.** Memphis, 1969. 57pp. Free. MVC Bulletin No. 2.

This is a bibliography about the works of this Memphis author, a registry of her writings, and a collection of citations about her reviews.

820. Tennessee. Memphis State University. J. W. Brister Library. **Bibliography of Lillian Smith and Paula Snelling.** (By Margaret Sullivan) Memphis, 1971. 118pp. Free. MVC Bulletin No. 4.

This useful bibliography on author and artist Lillian Smith offers over five hundred citations to her writings and literary criticism about them. Citations gathered by the Paula Snelling project are included.

821. Tennessee. Memphis State University. J. W. Brister Library. **Jesse Hill Ford: An Annotated Checklist of His Published Works and His Papers.** (By Helen White) Memphis, 1974. 55pp. Free. MVC Report No. 7. LC card No. 74-623241.

This landmark bibliography on the noted writer about Southern life, Jesse Hill Ford, includes a register of his sixty-two works followed by a list of manuscripts, correspondence, and criticism articles.

EMPLOYMENT

822. Tennessee. University, Knoxville. Institute for Public Service. Municipal Technical Advisory Service. **Sources of Assistance for Public Employer-Employee Relations.** (By Jeffrey Crawford) Knoxville, 1979. 10pp. Free. Report No. 23.

This title is a selective bibliography of over fifty titles designed to aid negotiators in collective bargaining. It would also be useful for various types of public employee organizations. Major sources are divided among journals, books, and government documents. Acquisition addresses are provided.

GEOLOGY

823. Tennessee. Division of Geology. **Annotated Bibliography of the Geology of Tennessee through December 1950.** (By C. W. Wilson, Jr.) Nashville, 1953. 308pp. $4.00. Bulletin No. 59.

This is a listing of all publications and articles published on the geology of Tennessee, regardless of source. Subject, author, and regional indexes are supplied.

824. Tennessee. Division of Geology. **Annotated Bibliography of the Geology of Tennessee, January 1951 through December 1960.** (By C. W. Wilson, Jr.) Nashville, 1965. 99pp. $2.00. Bulletin No. 67.

This supplement to an initial 1953 study offers a subject index to that study followed by Tennessee geologic publications for the ten-year-period following. There are over four hundred citations and both subject and author indexes.

825. Tennessee. Division of Geology. **Annotated Bibliography of the Geology of Tennessee, January 1961 through December 1970.** (By C. W. Wilson, Jr.) Nashville, 1973. 141pp. $5.00. Bulletin No. 71.

This 1973 bibliography on Tennessee geology supplements 1953 and 1965 studies, and brings them up to date through 1970. This bibliography is actually three separate bibliographies: general, geologic map series, and mineral resources. Each has both author and subject indexes.

826. Tennessee. Division of Geology. **State Geological Surveys and State Geologists of Tennessee.** (By C. W. Wilson, Jr.) Nashville, 1981. 41pp. $6.00. Bulletin No. 81.

This is both a bibliography of publications from 1971 to 1981 and a review of the organization of the division during its first 150 years. A listing of all state geologists is included.

HISTORY

827. Tennessee. Memphis State University. J. W. Brister Library. **Bulletin Devoted to Bibliography and Original Source Material.** Memphis, 1976. 82pp. Free. MVS Bulletin No. 9.

This reference work is a bibliographic conversation between Reynolds Price and William Ray on the use and building of oral history collections. Approximately 125 books, reviews, and poems as examples are provided.

828. Tennessee. State Library and Archives. Manuscript Division. **Highlander Folk School Manuscript Collection.** Nashville, 1968. 21pp. $3.75. Register No. 9.

The Highlander Folk School was a meeting place for southern liberals for three decades. This bibliography lists some forty-eight hundred items copied from the school's original records. A concise history of the school is also included.

829. Tennessee. State Library and Archives. **Writings on Tennessee Counties.** Nashville, 1971. 45pp. Free.

Tennessee counties generally and specific counties are the subjects of this fifteen-hundred-item bibliography. Census records are interpreted for research use. Documents, periodicals, and books are cited. All material is available from the Tennessee State Library.

POLITICS AND GOVERNMENT

830. Tennessee. State Planning Commission. **Directory of State Statistics for Local Areas in Tennessee: A Guide to Sources.** Nashville, 1972. 1 vol. Free. Publication No. 381.

This bibliography is intended as a guide to current sources of Tennessee published statistics for SMSAs, counties, and cities. (SMSAs—Standard Metropolitan Statistical Areas—are defined by the U.S. Census Bureau as central cities of 50,000 with dependent counties.) There are sixteen subject categories for the 111 annotated sources.

GENERAL

831.   Texas. Texas Tech University, Lubbock. Library. **Bold Land: A Bibliog-
       raphy.** (By Lola Beth Green and Dahlia Terrell) Lubbock, 1970. 47pp.
       Price on application. Library Bulletin No. 8.

Listed in this bibliography are 140 books and 331 articles and reviews along with
236 poems on the general area of the Southwest. The thirty-three authors are
either current or former Texas Tech staff members. There is an index of "books
included."

832.   Texas. Legislature. Legislative Reference Library. **Legislative Library
       Resources: A Guide to Periodicals, Newspapers, Looseleaf Sources, and
       Selected Legal Reference Materials in the Texas Legislative Reference
       Library.** (By Kathy Luscombe and Malinda Allison) Austin, 1973. 25pp.
       Free.

This bibliography of over 250 citations is arranged alphabetically by the type of
material.

833.   Texas. University, Austin. Bureau of Business Research. **Texas Sources:
       A Bibliography.** (By Rita J. Wright, et al.) Austin, 1976. 67pp. $4.00.
       LC card No. 76-358228. Bibliographical Series No. 17.

This is a collection of sources of information about subjects such as agriculture,
construction, mineral resources, population and tourism.

834.   Texas. Texas Tech University, Lubbock. Library. **Theses and Dissertations
       Accepted by Texas Tech University, 1974-1980.** (Compiled by Charlotte
       Ann Martin Hickson) Lubbock, 1982. 142pp. Free. LC card No. 82-
       622112. Library Bulletin No. 12.

This is a wide-ranging bibliography on various social and economic theses related
to Texas.

835.   Texas. University, Austin. General Libraries. **U.S. Government Publica-
       tions.** (By Barbara Turman and Katherine McIver) Austin, 1982. 19pp.
       Free. Selected Reference Source No. 13.

This is a guide to some two hundred document reference materials, including
indexes, abstracts, directories, congressional information, statistics, laws, and series
on microfiche. Many relate to Texas.

AGRICULTURE

836.   Texas. Agricultural Experiment Station. **Bibliography of Glyphosphate.**
        (By P. B. Chykaliuk, J. R. Abernathy, and J. R. Gipson) College Station,
        1978. 87pp. Free. Bulletin No. 1443.
Glyphosphate or Roundup–the herbicide formula of isopropylamine–is the subject
of this bibliography. The 1,026 citations are arranged by author; there is a subject
index.

837.   Texas. Agricultural Experiment Station. **Selected Bibliography of Insect
        Pests of Sunflowers.** (By Charles E. Rogers) College Station, 1979. 41pp.
        Free. LC card No. 80-621131. Miscellaneous Publication No. 1439.
There are 564 citations in this bibliography that attempts to collect "the most
pertinent literature on economically important plant pests." The arrangement is
alphabetical by author.

838.   Texas. Agricultural Experiment Station. **Selected Bibliography of the
        Phenoxy Herbicides, IV: Ecological Effects.** (By R. W. Bovey and J. D.
        Diaz-Colon) College Station, 1978. 28pp. Free. LC card No. NUC 79-
        602295. Miscellaneous Publication No. 1360.
"Ecological changes and population shifts of organic herbicides in the treated
environment as a result of phenoxy herbicide use are of widespread concern."
The 196 citations here are arranged according to senior author's name. A subject
index, consisting of seven sections, is provided. Each section represents a phenoxy
herbicide and the ecosystem affected. These include terrestrial, aquatic, and
miscellaneous.

839.   Texas. Agricultural Experiment Station. **Selected Bibliography of the
        Phenoxy Herbicides, VIII: Effects on Higher Plants.** (By R. W. Bovey
        and J. D. Diaz-Colon) College Station, 1978. 59pp. Free. Miscellaneous
        Publication No. 1338.
This document's 526 citations concentrate on physiological research on higher
plants. Section I comprises research papers dealing with plant responses to herbi-
cides. Section II consists of reviews dealing with aspects covered in Section I.
A separate list of common and chemical names of herbicides is also included.
Most citations are of journal articles or agricultural experiment station reports.

840.   Texas. Agricultural Experiment Station. **Selected Bibliography of the
        Phenoxy Herbicides, V: Interrelations With Microorganisms.** (By J. D.
        Diaz-Colon and R. W. Bovey) College Station, 1978. 87pp. Free.
        Miscellaneous Publication No. 1379.
This 510-item bibliography deals with both herbicide effects on microorganisms
and effects of microorganisms on herbicides. The two parts consist of references
listed in alphabetical order according to the senior author's name. A subject numer-
ical index, consisting of three sections, is provided for each part.

841. Texas. Agricultural Experiment Station. **Selected Bibliography of the Phenox Herbicides, VI: Methods of Extraction and Analysis.** (By R. W. Bovey and J. D. Diaz-Colon) College Station, 1978. 33pp. Free. Miscellaneous Publication No. 1381.

"Acceptabe extraction and analytical methods are required to monitor phenoxy herbicides." There are 242 citations on this subject, listed by the senior author, in this bibliography.

842. Texas. Agricultural Experiment Station. **Selected Bibliography of the Phenoxy Herbicides, VII: Military Use.** (By J. D. Diaz-Colon and R. W. Bovey) College Station, 1978. 25pp. Free. Miscellaneous Publication No. 1387.

This bibliography is particularly useful for its citations on Agent Orange. The 269 citations are arranged by author. If English abstracts were available in the original study, they are included. Many of the citations were obtained from *Chemical Abstracts*.

843. Texas. Agricultural Experiment Station. **Six Decades of Rice Research in Texas.** College Station, 1975. 136pp. Free. Research Monograph No. 4.

"The history of rice research and production in Texas is a story of problems and man's ingenuity in solving them." There are over 750 citations in this monograph. They are organized into fifteen subdivisions, such as soil, weed control, diseases, and storage, and introduced by progress reviews.

844. Texas. Agricultural Experiment Station. **Turfgrass Research in Texas.** College Station, 1976. 19pp. Free. Consolidated Reports 336-337.

This specialized bibliography of thirteen recent research papers on turfgrass supplies a lengthy abstract and information on acquisition for each.

AREA STUDIES

845. Texas. University, Austin. Institute of Latin American Studies. **Latin American Research and Publications at the University of Texas at Austin, 1893-1969.** Austin, 1972. 245pp. $3.75.

This is a valuable bibliography of over one thousand citations prepared by this center for Latin American studies.

ARID LANDS

846. Texas. Texas Tech University, Lubbock. International Center for Arid and Semi-Arid Land Studies. **An Annotated Bibliography of Juniper (*Juniperus*) of the Western United States.** (By Michael A. Smith and Joseph Schuster) Lubbock, 1975. 37pp. Free. LC card No. NUC 77-48884. ICASALS No. 75-2.

This collection of current references that deal wholly or in part with juniper is restricted generally to those articles dealing with the geographic area west of 96° meridian. There are 168 annotated studies and a short subject index.

847.   Texas. Texas Tech University, Lubbock. International Center for Arid and Semi-Arid Land Studies. **Graduate Research in Arid and Semi-Arid Lands at the Texas Tech University, 1928-1972.** (Compiled by Grace Eaton Lee) Lubbock, 1974. 186pp. Free. LC card No. 75-622194. ICASALS No. 74-2.

Each thesis pertaining to arid and semi-arid land studies at the center is provided an annotation and description of contents in this compilation. Major categories include: agriculture, anthropology, biology, business administration, chemistry, engineering, geosciences, home economics, park administration, and general studies. This work represents an extension and expansion of ICASALS No. 2, published in 1967.

ARTS

848.   Texas. University, Austin. Tarleton Law Library. **Art and the Law: An Exhibit and Publication in Celebration of the Centennial of the University of Texas.** Austin, 1983. 40pp. $15.00. Legal Bibliography Series No. 26.

The sections in this study that contain bibliographies include: museums and the law, protection of design elements, copyright protection of choreography, national treasures, art and antiquities, legal assistance for the arts, musicians, labor law, moral and contractual rights, architecture, taxes, sculpture, and art.

849.   Texas. University, Austin. Humanities Research Center. **A Bibliography of Edward Dahlberg.** (By Harold Billings) Austin, 1971. 122pp. Price on application. LC card No. 75-633117. Tower Bibliographical Series No. 8.

This bibliography, which offers over five hundred citations on Dahlberg, was offered for sale through the University of Texas Press.

850.   Texas. University, Austin. Tarleton Law Library. **Legal Novels: An Annotated Bibliography.** (By Karen L. Ketschman and Judith Helburn) Austin, 1979. 31pp. $10.00. Legal Bibliography Series No. 13a.

This valuable reference includes one hundred of the best legal novels retaining importance as examples of law and literature. "Each entry in some way reflects important legal aspects as trials, lawyer traits, prosecution or plot revolving around a point of law." It would be useful for laypersons as well as lawyers.

ECONOMY/ECONOMICS

851.   Texas. Department of Education. Coordinating Information for Texas Educators. **Resource Bibliography on Free Enterprise.** Austin, 1981. 4pp. Free. Bibliography No. 39.

This is a short bibliography of twenty-seven current sources on free economic enterprise for use by educators.

852. Texas. University, Austin. Bureau of Business Research. **A Selected and Annotated Bibliography of Marketing Theory.** (By Ralph B. Thompson and John H. Farley) Austin, 1976. 86pp. $3.00. LC card No. 76-24775. The Bureau of Business Bibliography Series No. 18.

The arrangement of this 330-item bibliography is according to the subject matter of the theory rather than the particular discipline from which it originates.

EDUCATION AND TRAINING

853. Texas. Department of Education. **Case Management and Family Counseling: A Catalog of Continuing Education Materials.** Austin, 1982. 75pp. Free.

These titles pertain to problems and topics of concern frequently encountered in working with parents and young chidren with developmental handicaps. There are seventy-four citations concerned with awareness, teacher-parent relations, working with parents, and behavior management. Books, pamphlets, and cassettes are included.

854. Texas. Department of Education. **Child Development and Learning: A Catalog of Continuing Education Materials.** Austin, 1982. 46pp. Free.

This is a guide to sources on both handicapped and normal child development. An outline of a training session is followed by descriptions of primary sources, activity guides with annotations, and an annotated bibliography of books. Prices are included for all titles.

855. Texas. Department of Education. **Classroom Management—Behavioral, Medical: A Catalog of Continuing Education Materials.** Austin, 1982. 74pp. Price on application.

Issued as part of the Early Childhood Intervention Program, this collection of seventy-five citations looks at medical issues, behavioral issues, emotionally disturbed, and exploring feelings. Availability information is provided for these books and multimedia materials.

856. Texas. Department of Education. **Developmental Therapy Intervention Strategies: A Catalog of Continuing Education Materials.** Austin, 1982. 164pp. Free.

This volume highlights various models and developmental strategies for the following conditions: visually or hearing impaired, Down's Syndrome, mental retardation, and cerebral palsy. Strategies for specific activities are listed, including developing sensory skills and motor development. There are over 150 well-annotated sources.

857. Texas. Department of Education. **Differences in Language and Cognitive Development: A Catalog of Continuing Education Materials.** Austin, 1982. 60pp. Free.

This bibliography and module is written for teachers, supervisors, and other professionals who work with young handicapped children. Approximately sixty books, documents, and kits are reviewed with cost and source noted. There are separate sections on activity guides, annotated bibliographies, and references.

858.   Texas. Department of Community Affairs. Children and Youth Services
        Division. **In the Interest of Children: Discipline, an Annotated Bibliog-
        raphy for Parents and Children**. Austin, 1981. 6*l*. Free.
This is a ready-reference to books outlining a number of philosophies of and
approaches to discipline. Publishers, prices, and annotations are supplied.

859.   Texas. Department of Education. **Listing of Active Publications**. Austin,
        1983. 67pp. Free.
Texas has one of the largest state education departments in the nation. This listing
is a valuable bibliography to over six hundred citations. There are sixty-three
subject categories with many valuable education reports and teaching guides under
curriculum development, bilingual education, education, assessment, and special
education. Most of the citations are available from the department.

860.   Texas. Department of Education. **Materials and Equipment: A Catalog of
        Continuing Education Materials**. Austin, 1982. 88pp. Free.
This bibliographic module is designed to provide information on equipment, materials, and activities for use with young handicapped children. There are over three
hundred citations to toys, playgrounds, manipulative equipment, and instructional
activity books. All are well annotated. Sources for acquisition are noted.

861.   Texas. Department of Education. **Parenting for the Handicapped: A Cata-
        log of Continuing Education Materials**. Austin, 1982. 97pp. Free.
Over two hundred citations for selecting materials for parent-lending libraries
and for making parent bibliographies are listed here. There are sections on child
development, activities and toys, self-concept, health and safety, and behavior.
There is a special section of books for children. All citations are well annotated
and prices are provided.

862.   Texas. Department of Education. **Programs and Curriculums: A Catalog
        of Continuing Education Materials**. Austin, 1982. 117pp. Free.
This report acts as a bibliographic module for teachers, supervisors, and
administrators. There are approximately seventy citations for books, and curriculum guides with purpose, level, and special features noted.

863.   Texas. Department of Education. Coordinating Information for Texas
        Educators. **Resource Bibliography on Disadvantaged and Handicapped
        Gifted**. Austin, 1981. 5pp. Free. Bibliography No. 7.
This is a unique bibliography of forty-three citations on children that are both
physically handicapped and intellectually gifted. Emphasis is on identification and
programs.

864.   Texas. Department of Education. Coordinating Information for Texas
        Educators. **Resource Bibliography on Dropout Prevention**. Austin, 1981.
        4pp. Free. Bibliography No. 14.
The high school dropout rate continues to be a national problem. These thirty-two
citations—most published since 1978—highlight research, principles, and programs.

865. Texas. Department of Education. Coordinating Information for Texas Educators. **Resource Bibliography on Evaluation of Written Composition.** Austin, 1982. 5pp. Free.

Books, ERIC titles, and journal articles centering on the teaching of writing skills and effective evaluation comprise this bibliography. Most examine specific methods.

866. Texas. Department of Education. Coordinating Information for Texas Educators. **Resource Bibliography on Improving Attendance.** Austin, 1981. 3pp. Free. Bibliography No. 3.

There are thirty-two citations on recording truancy, school discipline, and making the school program exciting.

867. Texas. Department of Education. Coordinating Information for Texas Educators. **Resource Bibliography on Mainstreaming.** Austin, 1981, 13pp. Free. Bibliography No. 34.

Mainstreaming into the regular classroom has become an important educational movement in recent years. This bibliography cites 113 current resources on mainstreaming, primarily of the mentally retarded. The bibliography is divided according to the state of the art, research, theory, methods and practices, program descriptions, and other bibliographies.

868. Texas. Department of Education. Coordinating Information for Texas Educators. **Resource Bibliography on Parental Involvement.** Austin, 1981. 5pp. Free. Bibliography No. 13.

Parents' involvement in the schools and as teachers at home is becoming more important. This is a bibliography of forty-eight citations for teachers on how parents can be positively involved. There are sections on the state of the art, research, methods, practices, and bibliographies.

869. Texas. Department of Education. Coordinating Information for Texas Educators. **Resource Bibliography on Prevention of Violence and Vandalism.** Austin, 1981. 6pp. Free. Bibliography No. 16.

The forty-nine current citations on juvenile delinquency and violence in this collection are divided according to the state of the art, research, methods and practices, program descriptions, and bibliographies.

870. Texas. Department of Education. Coordinating Information for Texas Educators. **Resource Bibliography on Sex Education for the Handicapped.** Austin, 1981. 5pp. Free.

This is a useful bibliography of current citations for special educators. Its thirty-five citations include many program descriptions.

871. Texas. Department of Education. Coordinating Information for Texas Educators. **Resource Bibliography on Teaching Citizenship Skills, K-12.** Austin, 1981. 4pp. Free.

Here are thirty-eight recent citations on general teaching of social studies and citizenship education. There are sections on research, methods, and programs.

872.   Texas. Department of Education. Coordinating Information for Texas
        Educators. **Resource Bibliography on Teaching Reading in the Content
        Areas.** Austin, 1981. 6pp. Free. Bibliography No. 8.
Fifty-four current articles integrate the teaching of reading in content areas; sym-
bols indicate the type of material included. Divisions include: state of the art,
methods, principles and practices, and program descriptions.

873.   Texas. Department of Education. Coordinating Information for Texas
        Educators. **Resource Bibliography on Teaching Spelling.** Austin, 1982.
        8pp. Free. Bibliography No. 20.
Spelling is always a challenge for teachers to integrate with subject areas. This bibliography lists eighty-one current citations on the state of the art, research, principles, methods, curriculum guides, and descriptions of programs.

874.   Texas. Department of Education. Coordinating Information for Texas
        Educators. **Resource Bibliography on Teaching the Disadvantaged Student.**
        Austin, 1981. 7pp. Free. Bibliography No. 12.
The fifty-four citations in this collection emphasize the methods and practices
of teaching. Sections include the state of the art, research, programs, curriculum
guides, and bibliographies.

875.   Texas. Department of Community Affairs. Children and Youth Services
        Division. **Toddlers: An Annotated Bibliography for Parents and Teachers.**
        Austin, 1981. 6pp. Free.
This short bibliography lists books that increase understanding of the physical,
emotional, sensory, and intellectual development of children from eighteen months
to three years. Many of the books describe games. Lengthy annotations and full
bibliographic information are provided for each title.

876.   Texas. Department of Education. **Working With Adults: A Catalog of
        Continuing Education Materials.** Austin, 1982. 66pp. Free.
The first section of this bibliography is concerned with adults as learners; the
second is concerned with working with parents. There are sixty citations from
books and journal articles; titles, authors, publishers, and short annotations are
provided.

EMPLOYMENT

877.   Texas. University, Austin. Bureau of Business Research. **Compensation
        of Professionals: A Selected and Annotated Bibliography.** (By Carroll
        N. Mohn) Austin, 1972. 90pp. $4.00. Bibliographic Series No. 16.
Conclusions and impressions contained in the literature of professional compensation are assessed in part I of this bibliography; part II is an annotated bibliography
of materials on compensation.

ENERGY

878. Texas. University, Austin. Bureau of Business Research. **Economics of Natural Gas.** (By Richard C. Henshaw, Jr.) Austin, 1954. 61pp. $1.50. Bibliography No. 11.

This is an important reference volume for material on every aspect of the natural gas industry, from the economic aspects to competitive fuels. It is useful for historical research.

ENVIRONMENT

879. Texas. Texas A and M University. Sea Grant Program. **Computer-Accessible Annotated Bibliography of the Corpus Christi Bay Estuary.** (By R. W. Flint) College Station, 1983. 280pp. $5.00. TAMU-SG-83-605.

The Bay Estuary, including its pollution problems, is the subject of this five hundred-item bibliography.

880. Texas. Texas A and M University. Transportation Institute. **Development of Traffic Information for Estimation of Mobile Source Emissions for Air Quality Modeling, Volume I: Annotated Bibliography.** (By George B. Dresser and Ann M. Horton) College Station, 1981. 137pp. Free. Research Report No. 218-1.

This report provides annotations of over 90 publications that were relevant to the objectives of a research study on the development of traffic information for estimating mobile source emissions. Annotations are categorized and presented in the following areas: air quality and mobil source emissions, models, air quality impacts of transportation, system management, peak periods, and related oxidant studies.

881. Texas. Agricultural Experiment Station. **Natural Vegetation of Texas and Adjacent Areas, 1675-1975: A Bibliography.** (By Fred E. Smeins and Robert B. Shaw) College Station, 1978. 35pp. Free. Miscellaneous Publication No. 1399.

No comprehensive treatment of the vegetation in Texas existed until this bibliography. There are 458 citations taken mainly from *American Forests, Ecology,* ten other important ecological journals, and Texas Agricultural Experiment Station bulletins. Arrangement is alphabetical by author.

GEOLOGY

882. Texas. University, Austin. Bureau of Economic Geology. **List of Publications, 1983.** Austin, 1983. 38pp. Free.

This is a publication list that doubles as a bibliography. It consists of over two hundred geologic studies and maps issued by the bureau. An index is appended.

HEALTH

883. Texas. Department of Community Affairs. Children and Youth Services Division. **Emotions: An Annotated Bibliography for Parents and Professionals.** Austin, 1981. 6*l*. Free.

This is a basic reading list of books on emotions, with full citations and ordering information. Most of the citations are appropriate for use with young children.

884. Texas. Department of Community Affairs. Children and Youth Services Division. **Fears: An Annotated Bibliography for Parents and Professionals.** Austin, 1981. 6*l*. Free.

Most of the annotated citations in this collection are designed for working with young children. Fear of the unexpected is emphasized.

885. Texas. Department of Education. Coordinating Information for Texas Educators. **Resource Bibliography on Hyperactivity.** Austin, 1982. 6pp. Free. Bibliography No. 44.

The fifty-nine citations gathered here are organized according to the state of the art, research, principals and theories, methods and practices, and bibliographies. Chapters from books are included. Many of the citations are from the ERIC system.

HISTORY

886. Texas. Texas A and M University. Sea Grant Program. **Bibliography of Maritime and Naval History Periodical Articles Published 1976-1977.** (By Charles R. Schultz) College Station, 1979. 90pp. Price on application. LC card No. 79-624012. TAMU 79-607.

This is an excellent bibliography of over six hundred citations covering general works, exploration, merchant sail and general shipping, seaports, maritime law, fisheries, marine art, naval to 1939, World War II, pleasure boating, and yacht racing.

887. Texas. East Texas State College, Commerce. Gee Library. **Texas Educational History: A Bibliography.** (Compiled by James H. Conrad) Commerce, 1979. 109pp. $3.00.

The stated purpose of this volume is "to provide a comprehensive and systematic check list to the literature of Texas educational history." Much of this material has never been indexed in other places. It is divided by: general aspects, historic, minorities, religious education, education in the counties, public education, and higher levels. There are 1,086 citations arranged by author; minimal bibliographic information is provided. An author index and a listing of both past and present Texas colleges are other features.

LAWS AND LEGISLATION

888. Texas. University, Austin. Tarleton Law Library. **Bankruptcy Reform Act of 1978: Analysis, Legislative History, and Selected Bibliography.** (By Mickie A. Voges and Kathy E. Shimpock) Austin, 1981. 60pp. $15.00. Legal Bibliography No. 23.

This bibliography provides a legislative history of the Act and a selected bibliography of literature about it through the end of 1980. It is especially recommended for law firm libraries.

889. Texas. Legislature. Legislative Reference Library. **Constitutional Revision Materials Available in the Legislative Reference Library.** (Compiled by Malinda Allison and Brenda Shelton) Austin, 1973. 74pp. Free. LC card No. NUC 74-93288.

This bibliography presents over eleven hundred citations divided into two sections. The first addresses state constitutional revision in general and the second deals with the Texas Constitution specifically. The general works in the first part are divided according to various states.

890. Texas. University, Austin. Tarleton Law Library. **Freedom of Information Act: A Comprehensive Bibliography of Law Related Material.** (By Frank Houdek) Austin, 1981. 61pp. $15.00. Legal Bibliography No. 22.

This bibliography contains a structuring of the commentary and Congressional documents relating to the Act which had been published through the end of 1980. It includes a legislative history and relevant legal materials; there are many subject headings.

891. Texas. University, Austin. Tarleton Law Library. **Julius Stone: A Bio-Bibliography Including Trends in Jurisprudence in the Second Half Century.** (By Barbara Drexler Hathaway) Austin, 1980. 51pp. $15.00. LC card No. 80-622279.

This publication includes a list of Professor Stone's books, articles, speeches, and book reviews as well as a short biographical sketch.

892. Texas. University, Austin. Tarleton Law Library. **Right of Privacy—Its Constitutional and Social Dimensions: A Comprehensive Bibliography.** (By David M. O'Brien) Austin, 1980. 55pp. $15.00. LC card No. 80-622796. Legal Bibliography No. 21.

This bibliography traces the privacy defense from Samuel Warren to Louis Brandeis and then from *Griswold* v. *Connecticut* to the present. Books, articles, government documents, and Supreme Court cases are covered.

893. Texas. University, Austin. Tarleton Law Library. **Selected Bibliography on Child Abuse and Neglect.** Austin, 1976. 1 vol. $10.00. Law Library Bibliography No. 12.

Several hundred timely citations on the legal aspects of child abuse and cruelty to children are included in this study.

894.   Texas. University, Austin. Tarleton Law Library. **Texas Supreme Court:
        An Index of Selected Sources on the Court and Its Members.** (Compiled
        by Linda Gardner) Austin, 1983. 142pp. $15.00.
This bibliography lists sources on all members of the Texas Supreme Court from its
beginning to 1981. A historical postscript by former Texas Supreme Court Judge
Joe R. Greenhill is included.

MINORITY GROUPS

895.   Texas. University of Houston. Libraries. Office of the Assistant Director
        for Collection Development. **Mexican-Americans: A Selected Bibliography.**
        Houston, 1974. 151pp. $4.00.
This guide to library holdings presents over twenty-three hundred citations. There
are fourteen categorical headings including politics, employment, education, fine
arts, biography, journals and newspapers, and bibliographies. There is an author-
main entry index. Many of the citations are to government publications.

NATURAL RESOURCES

896.   Texas. University, Austin. Center for Research in Water Resources. **Bib-
        liography of Water-Related Theses and Dissertations Written at the Uni-
        versity of Texas at Austin, 1897-1970.** (Compiled by C. Stanley Ferguson)
        Austin, 1970. 54*l*. Free. LC card No. 78-634478.
Water-related theses and dissertations from the University of Texas at Austin
are chronologically listed under the department conferring the degree.

897.   Texas. University, Austin. Center for Research in Water Resources. **Inven-
        tory of Water Sources in the Coastal Zone.** Austin, 1970. 1 vol. Price on
        application.
This inventory summarizes and lists the available data which characterize the
environmental quality of the Texas coastal zone.

PLANNING

898.   Texas. University, Austin. Bureau of Business Research. **Planned Suburban
        Shopping Center.** (By Jack D. L. Holmes) Austin, 1960. 55pp. $0.50.
        Bibliography No. 13.
The problems of design, traffic, and finance involved in the successful operation
and construction of shopping centers and the effects of shopping centers on down-
town business districts are the subjects of this bibliography.

RECREATION/TOURISM

899.   Texas. Department of Parks and Wildlife. **A Partial List of Texas State Agency Programs and Services Which Import Outdoor Education, 1979.** (By James C. Riggs and John E. Emerson) Austin, 1980. 20pp. Free.
This document is designed to assist agencies, individuals, and organizations in the provision of various recreational opportunities. Over two hundred programs are described for applicability; the contact agency and address are provided. A wide range of topics is discussed.

SOCIAL CONDITIONS

900.   Texas. University, Austin. Institute for Constructive Capitalism. **Lifestyle: A Critical Review.** (By W. Thomas Anderson, Jr. and Linda L. Golden) Austin, 1981. 39pp. Price on application. Survey Series No. 5.
This critical bibliography offers 120 sources on lifestyle subdivided by historical basis, psychographics, definition, cognitive style, and summary.

901.   Texas. Agricultural Experiment Station. Department of Agricultural Economics and Rural Sociology. **Occupational Aspirations and Expectations of Youth: A Bibliography of Research Literature, I.** (By William P. Kuvlesky and David H. Reynolds) College Station, 1970. 70*l.* LC card No. 71-636205.
This is a valuable bibliography for interpreting the values of urban and rural youth during the social changes of the sixties and seventies. There are approximately two hundred citations. A forty-three-page supplement is appended.

902.   Texas. Department of Community Affairs. Children and Youth Services Division. **Stepparenting: An Annotated Bibliography for Parents and Professionals.** Austin, 1981. 6pp. Free.
The citations in this collection are written for stepparents, by stepparents. Most have short annotations with full bibliographic information and cost.

TRANSPORTATION

903.   Texas. Department of Highways and Public Transportation. **Listing of Research Studies and Reports.** Austin, 1981. 151pp. Free.
This bibliography documents all research and technical studies performed under the Highway Department Cooperative Research Program. Many studies were authored cooperatively with the Texas Transportation Institute. Approximately 1,000 studies are listed by document number followed by technical studies performed with the Urban Mass Transportation Administration. Experimental studies and those without numbers are also separate. Finally there are subject and author indexes. Computer programs are also noted.
        Most of the studies refer to pavement research although some cover the socioeconomic effects of highway relocation.

904.   Texas. Department of Highways and Public Transportation. **State of the Art Related to Safety Criteria for Highway Curve Design: Summary Report.** (By John C. Glennon) Austin, 1969. 6pp. Free.
This is a review of over one hundred pertinent studies on construction of highway curves; all reports are fully cited.

WILDLIFE

905.   Texas. Department of Parks and Wildlife. **An Annotated Bibliography for Sand Seatrout,** *Cynoscion arenarius.* (By A. W. Moffett, L. W. McEarchron, and J. G. Key) Austin, 1979. 13pp. Free. Bulletin No. 3000-71.
This collection of some 150 basic sources was issued cooperatively with the Seabrook Marine Laboratory.

906.   Texas. University, Austin. Texas Memorial Museum. **Bibliography of the Recent Mammals of Texas.** (By G. G. Raun) Austin, 1962. 81pp. $4.00.
This is an important bibliography with over two hundred citations to all types of important Texas wildlife.

907.   Texas. University, Austin. Texas Memorial Museum. **Checklist and Bibliography of the Japygoidea (Insects:** *Diptura***) of North America, Central America, and the West Indies.** (By James R. Reddell) Austin, 1983. 43pp. Free. Pearce Seelards Series No. 37.
Over 150 citations are arranged according to subfamily and by locality. There are no indexes.

WOMEN

908.   Texas. University, Austin. School of Social Work. Center for Social Work Research. **Women in Management: A Bibliography.** (By Martha Williams, June Oliver, and Meg Gerrard) Austin, 1977. 64pp. Free. Human Services Monograph Series.
Twelve hundred citations, mostly from the 1970s, are divided according to: women in the work force, legal issues, personal-work roles, women as leaders, organizational factors, and personal change strategies. Arrangement is alphabetical by author within each section.

AGRICULTURE

909.   Utah. Agricultural Experiment Station. **Aphids of Utah.** (By George F. Knowlton) Salt Lake City, 1983. 155pp. Free. Research Bulletin No. 509.
This document reports on aphids, their host plants, their known distribution, and some dates of collection in Utah. There are some six hundred collection records on aphids listed. For each scientist credited there are lists provided of their research papers and other written contributions.

EMPLOYMENT

910.   Utah. Department of Employment Security. Research and Analysis Section. **Occupational Information in Utah: A Bibliography.** (By Diane C. Burks) Salt Lake City, 1980. 84pp. Free.
Issued in cooperation with the State Occupational Information Coordinating Committee, over two hundred citations on a wide variety of common occupations in Utah are offered.

GEOLOGY

911.   Utah. Geological Survey. **List of Geological Survey Geologic and Water-Supply Reports and Maps for Utah.** Salt Lake City, 1980. 67pp. Free.
This list, authored with the aid of the U.S. Geological Survey, contains approximately twelve hundred reports and maps of the Geological Survey related to the geology and minerals of Utah.

HEALTH

912.   Utah. University, Salt Lake City. Regional Rehabilitation Institute. **Interpersonal Relationships in Rehabilitation Counseling: A Literature Review.** (By Gary O. Jongersen and others) Salt Lake City, 1967. 56pp. Free.
This bibliography is useful for social workers, family courts personnel, and all types of counselors. Selected reviews of 120 sources on interpersonal counseling and rehabilitation are included.

MINORITY GROUPS

913.   Utah. University, Salt Lake City. Marriott Library. **Black Bibliography**. Salt Lake City, 1974. 825pp. Price on application. Marriott Library Bibliographic Series No. 2.

This is a major bibliography with over five thousand journal articles, books, and government documents on forty-five subjects. It is indexed by author and contains a separate index for bibliographies. There is a valuable section on the Mormon Church and blacks as well as a selective ERIC document listing.

914.   Utah. University, Salt Lake City. Marriott Library. **Black Bibliography, Supplement**. Salt Lake City, 1977. 458pp. Price on application (approx. $20.00). Bibliographic Series No. 3.

This bibliography is a supplement to the *Black Bibliography* (No. 913). It includes materials about the history of Afro-Americans and their experience in America from 1619 to 1976. There is emphasis on slavery, abolitionists, and Afro-Americans in the twentieth century.

915.   Utah. University, Salt Lake City. Libraries. **Black Bibliography Prepared by the Departments of Literature and Social Sciences**. Salt Lake City, 1970. 20pp. Out-of-Print.

This is a listing of over one hundred books from the social sciences and literature related to black Americans.

NATIVE PEOPLE

916.   Utah. University, Salt Lake City. American West Center. **An Essay on the Historiography of the Indians of the Americas**. (By S. Lyman Tyler) Salt Lake City, 1977. 145*l*. Price on application. American West Center Occasional Paper.

This basic bibliographic guide to research on American Indians is organized into twenty-three categories, including accounts of exploration, general works, divisions according to time periods, and government documents. There is also a useful explanation of the Human Relations Area Files. Most of the sources have at least a paragraph of description.

NATURAL RESOURCES

917.   Utah. State University. College of Engineering. Utah Water Research Laboratory. **Publications, 1965-1977**. Logan, 1978. 12pp. Free.

Besides a publication list, this serves as a bibliography to water research in the West and particularly to the Salt Lake area. There are sections on hydraulics, water resource planning, water quality, atmospheric water resources, and general studies.

VERMONT

GENERAL

918.   Vermont. Historical Society. **Books about Vermont.** Montpelier, 1973.
        25pp. Free.
Over 250 books, posters, and maps on Vermont, most available from the State
Historical Society, comprise this bibliography. Subject headings include biography,
geneology, history, juvenile works, town histories, railroad books, and covered
bridges.

GENERAL

919. Virgin Islands. College of the Virgin Islands. Caribbean Research Institute. **A Bibliography of Articles on the Danish West Indies and the United States Virgin Islands in the New York Times 1867-1975.** (By Arnold R. Highfield and Max Bumgarner) Gainesville, Florida, University of Florida Press, 1978. 209pp. Price on application. Institute Occasional Paper No. 1.

A carefully worked bibliography of 1,054 citations limited to the *Times.* The work "provides a running commentary on the major events on the Islands." The articles are arranged chronologically from 1967 to 1975; the article title and date are given. The study serves as a historical outline to the Virgin Islands.

920. Virgin Islands. College of the Virgin Islands. Caribbean Research Institute. **Selected, Annotated Bibliography of Caribbean Bibliographies in English.** (By Henry C. Chang) St. Thomas, 1975. 54pp. Free. LC card No. 77-621905.

This pioneer work of titles is designed to lead scholars to more comprehensive works. It is limited to English-language works. Short descriptive annotations are provided. The 101 titles are arranged primarily by author; there are title and subject-key word indexes.

LANGUAGE AND LINGUISTICS

921. Virgin Islands. Bureau of Libraries, Museums, and Archaeological Services. **Selected Bibliography of Materials on Language Varieties Spoken in the Virgin Islands.** (Compiled by Robin Sabino) Charlotte-Amalie, 1980. 8pp. Free. Occasional Paper Series No. 6.

"The purpose of this bibliography is to provide a listing of works available in the Virgin Islands on the Dutch, English, and French languages spoken there." The fifty-two citations include both books and journals.

MINORITY GROUPS

922. Virgin Islands. Bureau of Libraries, Museums, and Archaeological Services. **Black Experience in Children's Literature**. Charlotte-Amalie, 1975. 1 vol. Free.

This bibliography on the black experience is oriented toward Caribbean children.

VIRGINIA

ENVIRONMENT

923. Virginia. Virginia Polytechnic Institute and State University. Research Division. **Mycoplasmataceae: A Bibliography and Index, 1852-1970.** (By C. H. Domermuth and J. G. Rittenhouse) Blacksburg, 1971. 136pp. Free. LC card No. NUC 73-78180. Research Division Bulletin No. 61.

This bibliography lists titles of much of the research literature which has been published on the mycoplasmataceae. There are 3,519 citations included. When possible, references are indexed by species only and are not cross listed. "This bibliography includes a variety of case reports and non-research reviews; however an attempt has been made to avoid excessive inclusion of such articles." There is a detailed subject index.

924. Virginia. Virginia Polytechnic Institute and State University. Research Division. **Mycoplasmatales: A Bibliography and Index, 1970-1972.** (By C. H. Domermuth and J. G. Rittenhouse) Blacksburg, 1973. 84pp. Free. Research Division Bulletin No. 84.

This bibliography lists the titles of the most recent literature which deals primarily with mycoplasmatales. The 1,993 references have been indexed both by species and by subject matter whenever possible.

925. Virginia. Virginia Polytechnic Institute and State University. Research Division. **The Mycoplasmas: A Bibliography and Index, 1973-1975.** (By C. H. Domermuth and J. G. Rittenhouse) Blacksburg, 1976. 71pp. Free. Research Division Bulletin No. 114.

This collection of 1,612 writings dating from 1973 to 1975 is designed to be used with the volumes on mycoplasmatales (No. 84) and mycoplasmataceae (No. 61).

GEOLOGY

926. Virginia. Division of Mineral Resources. **Bibliography of Published Measured Sections West of the Blue Ridge in Virginia.** (By Harry W. Webb, Jr. and Edward Nunan) Charlottesville, 1972. 219pp. LC card No. 72-612416. Information Circular No. 18.

"Measured stratigraphic sections provide detailed information on the thickness, lithography, paleontologic content of rocks at specific localities." This bibliography of over one thousand citations provides such information for twenty counties of Virginia.

927.   Virginia. Division of Mineral Resources. **Bibliography of Virginia Geology and Mineral Resources, 1941-1949.** (By F. B. Hoffer) Charlottesville, 1968. 58pp. Free. Information Circular No. 14.

Over five hundred journal articles, government publications, theses, and open-file reports on all aspects of Virginia geology, arranged by author, comprise this bibliography.

928.   Virginia. Division of Mineral Resources. **Bibliography of Virginia Geology and Mineral Resources, 1950-1959.** (By F. B. Hoffer) Charlottesville, 1972. 103pp. Free. LC card No. 72-612415. Information Circular No. 19.

This present bibliography is patterned after the *Bibliography of North American Geology.* It lists literature on Virginia geology and mineral resources from 1950 through 1959. There are approximately 650 citations included, with all works by an author in one place. There is a detailed subject index.

NATURAL RESOURCES

929.   Virginia. Division of Mineral Resources. **Bibliography of Virginia Coal.** (By G. P. Wilkes and James A. Henderson, Jr.) Charlottesville, 1983. 18pp. Free. Resources Publication No. 39.

"Coal has been produced in Virginia for over 200 years with a tremendous amount of information produced." This document lists approximately nine hundred citations arranged according to author, with coauthors listed in parentheses. There is an index including stratigraphic, subject, and locality citations.

930.   Virginia. Virginia Polytechnic Institute and State University. Water Resources Research Center. **Water Resources Research in Virginia, 1969-1971.** (By William R. Walker and T. W. Johnson) Blacksburg, 1972. 125pp. Free. Bulletin No. 49.

This bibliographic guide to over one hundred water-related studies arranged according to twelve research centers supplies information on title, sponsor, funding, objectives, conclusions, and relevance for each study. Most studies relate to cities and towns, fauna, lakes, nutrients, pesticides, rivers, creeks, and water treatment. There are sponsor and subject indexes.

ARTS

931. Washington. State Library. **Washington State Authors, 1982.** Olympia, 1983. 24pp. Free.

This bibliography also serves as a report on the year's acquisitions of the Washington State Author Collection. It includes 243 citations—many of poetry and fiction—arranged alphabetically by author. There is also a list of publications under "All My Somedays"—a living history project.

DISABLED

932. Washington. State Library. **Multihandicapped.** (By George R. Trammell) Olympia, 1976. 65pp. Free.

Mostly onprint materials are included in this bibliography of some three hundred citations. These materials are thought to be of interest to staff persons working in the special education field. Most of the citations are amply annotated.

EDUCATION AND TRAINING

933. Washington. Superintendent of Public Instruction. **A Selected Bibliography of Sex Fair Materials, Grades K-12.** (Edited by Nancy Motomatsu) Olympia, 1977. 50pp. Free.

This is a bibliographic guide to both textbooks and library books evaluated as nonprejudiced for children.

934. Washington. Superintendent of Public Instruction. **Washington State Materials on School Discipline.** Olympia, 1982. 73pp. Free.

This is an excellent guide to over two hundred citations on school discipline. Books, professional articles, general research, and the ERIC microfiche collection are cited. The ERIC documents have lengthy annotations. Almost all sources are post-1975.

ENVIRONMENT

935.   Washington. Department of Ecology. **Palouse-Lower Snake River Basin Bibliography.** Olympia, 1973. 10pp. Free. Basin Bibliography No. 14.

Studies and reports related to the Palouse Basin comprise the eighty-six citations in this collection. The arrangement is alphabetical by author.

936.   Washington. Department of Ecology. **Social Impact Assessment: An Annotated Bibliography.** (By Mary A. Kogut) Olympia, 1976. 30pp. Free. WRIS Information Bulletin No. 31.

"A water resources development project is not created in a vacuum. It certainly has some sort of impact on the lives of people." The eighty-nine thoroughly annotated citations in this bibliography serve as an aid in measuring changes of lifestyle.

937.   Washington. Department of Ecology. **Yakima River Basin Bibliography.** Olympia, 1977. 57pp. Free. Basin Bibliography No. 3.

This is a bibliography of over 350 reports available in the Water Resources Information Library. Full bibliographic information is supplied and some of the titles are abstracted.

GEOLOGY

938.   Washington. Department of Natural Resources. Division of Geology and Earth Resources. **Annotated Guide to Sources of Information on the Geology, Minerals, and Ground-Water Resources of the Puget Sound Region, Washington, King County Section.** (By William H. Reichert) Olympia, 1978. 63pp. Free. Information Circular No. 61.

"Local and regional planning agencies are faced with an almost continual expansion of urban encroachment into suburban and rural areas in the Puget Sound region." For this reason, knowledge of the geologic and mineral conditions is necessary. Over two hundred studies supplying such knowledge are amply annotated here.

939.   Washington. Department of Natural Resources. Division of Geology and Earth Resources. **Theses on Washington Geology: A Comprehensive Bibliography, 1901-1979.** (By Connie Manson) Olympia, 1980. 212pp. $5.50. Information Circular No. 70.

Citations to over eight hundred Washington State geologic studies are included in this first comprehensive index of doctoral, master's and selected undergraduate theses. The index is arranged in four sections: author, subject, geologic map index, and university index.

HEALTH

940.   Washington. State Library. Institutional Library Services. **Group Psychotherapy for Geriatric Patients Bibliography.** (By Justina Costales) Olympia, 1970. 3*l.* Out-of-Print.

This bibliography of forty-five principal sources—mostly from professional journals—is designed for use by professionals working with geriatric patients.

MINORITY GROUPS

941.　Washington. State Library. **Selected Bibliography for Spanish Speaking Americans**. Olympia, 1971. 18pp. Free.

Most of the 290 citations in this collection are designed as information sources for initiating programs. There are sections on bibliographies, indexes, books in English, Washington State documents, and federal documents. Arrangement is by author within each section.

NATIVE PEOPLE

942.　Washington. Center for the Study of Migrant and Indian Education. **Indian Education Bibliography**. Toppenish, 1971. 72pp. Free. LC card No. 72-611404.

This is a bibliography of approximately two hundred studies and articles on the challenges of Indian education.

NATURAL RESOURCES

943.　Washington. Department of Ecology. **Bibliography of Bibliographies on Water Resources**. Olympia, 1973. 18*l*. Free. Water Resources Information System No. 9.

The 159 citations are most useful for scientists and environmental groups, They "attempt to list by subject, selected reference tools which are useful in initial searches for materials on water resources." Subject headings include legal aspects, water resource quality, oil pollution, biological aspects, marine sciences, estuaries, and general problems.

944.　Washington. Department of Natural Resources. **Bibliography of DNR Publications**. Olympia, 1982. 86pp. Free.

This is a bibliography to over five hundred reports authored by the department. Arrangement is primarily by title and then by series. Most are for sale through the DNR.

945.　Washington. Department of Natural Resources. Division of Geology and Earth Resources. **Mount Saint Helens: Annotated Index to Video Archives**. (By Robert Logan and Connie J. Manson) Olympia, 1983. 51pp. Free. Information Circular No. 76.

The reawakening of Mount Saint Helens in 1980 shocked and fascinated Pacific Northwest residents. This is a unique bibliographic reference to over one thousand video records preserved by the division.

OCEANOGRAPHY

946.　Washington. University, Seattle. Sea Grant Program. **Bibliography of Literature: Puget Sound Marine Environment.** (By E. E. Collias and A. C. Duxbury) Seattle, 1971. 401pp. Free. WSG Report No. 71-6.

This core bibliography for the study of Puget Sound offers over one thousand citations.

947.　Washington. Department of Ecology. **Central Sound Basin Bibliography.** Olympia, 1973. 26pp. Free. Basin Bibliography No. 20.

In this bibliography covering the water-related aspects of the Puget Sound, there has been no attempt to be comprehensive. The 293 citations are arranged alphabetically by author. Most of them are government publications.

948.　Washington. University, Seattle. Department of Oceanography. **Index to Physical and Chemical Oceanographic Data of Puget Sound and Its Approaches, 1932-1966.** (By Eugene E. Collias) Seattle, 1977. 832pp. Price on application. Special Report No. 43.

This resource of twenty-five hundred citations is considered a landmark bibliography on Puget Sound.

949.　Washington. Department of Ecology. **West Sound Basin Bibliography.** Olympia, 1973. 16pp. Free. Basin Bibliography No. 18.

The majority of the 144 citations in this document are government publications, proceedings, and open-file reports.

POLITICS AND GOVERNMENT

950.　Washington. State Library. **Washington State Government and Politics, 1845-1971: A Bibliography.** Olympia, 1971. 34pp. Free. LC card No. 72-611414.

This important guide to Washington State politics and government includes among its two hundred titles some of the most important titles needed by a core historical collection.

SOCIAL CONDITIONS

951.　Washington. State Library. **Runaways: A Selective Bibliography.** Olympia, 1973. 6*l*. Free.

This is a general bibliography on the causation and problems of runaways. Its 110 citations are drawn from journals, newspapers, and books.

WILDLIFE

952.   Washington. Department of Game. **Working Bibliography of the Peregrine Falcon** (*Falco peregrinus*) **in Washington State.** (By Richard L. Knight, Leroy E. Stream, and Roger H. Harkins) Olympia, 1979. 25*l.* Free.

This is a valuable bibliography to the habits of these rare birds in Washington State.

WOMEN

953.   Washington. State Library. **Women—Their Struggle for Equality: A Selected Bibliography.** (By Mildred Roberts) Olympia, 1977. 18pp. Free.

This is a well-balanced bibliography for use by those researching economic and social equality for women. Over 170 citations, several of which are annotated, are divided by subject sections on economics and legal matters, sex discrimination in education, and women in government.

WEST VIRGINIA

GENERAL

954. West Virginia. University, Morgantown. Library. **Appalachian Books and Media for Public and College Libraries**. (By George E. Bennett) Morgantown, 1975. 85pp.

This is a bibliography of and purchase guide to in-print available Appalachian materials. There are 375 citations in the following categories: history, social structure, coal mines and mining, religion, picture books, recreation, nature, folklore and music, and belle lettres. There is a separate section for media. Short annotations are included.

955. West Virginia. University, Morgantown. **The Wheeling Area: An Annotated Bibliography**. (By Kenneth R. Nodyne and Dennis E. Lawther) Morgantown, 1981. 54pp. $3.00.

This two-hundred-item guide is divided into five sections: general histories and memoirs of the Upper Ohio Valley, topical histories of regions, the Upper Ohio Valley from prehistory to the Civil War, Civil War and creation of the state, and post-Civil War West Virginia.

ARTS

956. West Virginia. University, Morgantown. Library. **West Virginia Authors: A Biobibliography**. (By Vito J. Brenni and Joyce Binder) Morgantown, 1968. 103pp. $2.50.

Very brief bibliographies and representative works of West Virginia authors are provided. Sources for more detailed information are indicated.

ECONOMY/ECONOMICS

957. West Virginia. Cooperative Extension Service. **Selected Bibliography Related to Safety for the Logging and Lumber Industry**. Morgantown, 1983. 8pp. $1.00. WV-OSH No. 5.

This is a list of over fifty practical titles to promote logging safety. Subject matter areas include: logging, lumbering, chain saws, regulations, injuries and accident statistics, health, safety, and general. Available posters, pay envelope stuffers, and audiovisual aids are reviewed in separate sections.

958. West Virginia. University, Morgantown. **Strip Mining: An Annotated Bibliography.** (By Robert F. Munn) Morgantown, 1973. 110pp. $4.00.
"Strip mining of coal has become a major economic, political, and social problem in the United States." This bibliography aids those interested in the history, development, present practices, and future prospects of strip mining. It includes sections on history, government regulations, environmental effects, and reclamation.

ENERGY

959. West Virginia. Cooperative Extension Service. **Catalog of Visual Aids: Safety-Energy.** Morgantown, 1982. 22pp. Free. P-534; WV-OSH-6.
Over 250 publications, slide programs, films, transparencies, kits, and displays are subdivided by three categories: energy, wood industry safety, and farm-home safety.

960. West Virginia. University, Morgantown. **Coal Industry in America: A Bibliography and Guide to Studies.** (By Robert F. Munn) Morgantown, 1977. 351pp. $16.00.
This annotated bibliography on the development of one of the nation's basic industries includes three thousand references and a complete author-subject index.

GEOLOGY

961. West Virginia. University, Morgantown. **West Virginia Geology, Archeology, and Pedology: A Bibliography and Index.** (By William H. Gillespie and John A. Clendening) Morgantown, 1964. 241pp. $4.00.
More than thirty-one hundred references and a detailed subject index to detailed geologic and pedologic subjects are included in this older study.

GENERAL

962. Wisconsin. University, Madison. Department of Rural Sociology. **Wisconsin Upper Great Lakes Region: A Descriptive Bibliography 1935-1968.** (By N. Candia Welch and Douglas G. Marshall) Madison, 1968. 120pp. Free.

This is a collection of in-depth reviews of over six hundred studies related to the Upper Great Lakes region. The subdivisions include: natural resources, general resources, land use, transportation, industry, recreation, farmers, demographics, social services, community development, and Wisconsin Indians. There are indexes according to upper Wisconsin counties and individual authors.

AGRICULTURE

963. Wisconsin. University, Madison. College of Agriculture and Life Sciences. **Newly Discovered Prokaryotic Plant Pathogens: A Bibliography.** (By Eleanor Elmendorf) Madison, 1977. 85pp. Free. Research Bulletin No. 2901.

"This bibliography is an attempt to bring together literature on a subject which has no current concise name." It concerns plant pathogens, formerly considered viruses, usually transmitted by Homoptera. Over eighteen hundred citations to journal articles are followed by detailed subject and author indexes. Most of the citations are for years since 1965.

964. Wisconsin. University, Madison. College of Agriculture and Life Sciences. **Newly Discovered Prokaryotic Plant Pathogens: A Bibliography Supplement to RB2901.** (By Eleanor Elmendorf) Madison, 1981. 192pp. Free. Research Bulletin No. 2901-1.

The bibliographic supplement adds 2,515 citations to Elmendorf's original 1977 bibliography on plant pathogens. Most of the citations are from the 1970s. There are subject and author indexes.

AREA STUDIES

965. Wisconsin. University, Madison. Land Tenure Center. **Agrarian Reform in Brazil, a Bibliography, Part I: A Bibliography of Materials Dealing with Brazil in the Land Tenure Center Library.** Madison, 1972. 91pp. Free. LC card No. 72-611461. Training and Methods Series No. 19.

Over one thousand studies, many written in Spanish, comprise this agrarian reform bibliography. Arrangement is alphabetical by author.

966. Wisconsin. University, Madison. Land Tenure Center. **Agrarian Reform in Brazil, a Bibliography, Part II: Regional Development.** Madison, 1978. 46pp. Free. Training and Methods Series No. 19, Supplement.

The arrangement of the six hundred citations in this volume is according to thirty-two main regions of Brazil. Many of the citations are articles in Spanish or Brazilian government publications.

967. Wisconsin. University, Madison. Land Tenure Center. **Agriculture in the Economy of the Caribbean: A Bibliography.** Madison, 1974. 84pp. Free. Training and Methods Series No. 24.

There are approximately twelve hundred citations for forty countries and the Caribbean in general in this collection, divided by agriculture, economy, politics, and society. Many of the citations are government publications.

968. Wisconsin. University, Madison. Land Tenure Center. **Bolivia, Agricultura, Economica: A Bibliography.** (By Teresa J. Anderson) Madison, 1968. 21pp. Free. Training and Methods Series No. 7.

All of the 220 titles on the agriculture, economics, and politics of Bolivia cited in this compilation can be found in the Land Tenure Center Library.

969. Wisconsin. University, Madison. Land Tenure Center. **Central American Agrarian Economy: A Bibliography, Part I.** Madison, 1975. 97pp. Free. Training and Methods Series No. 26.

The wealth of materials in this bibliography represent holdings in the Land Tenure Center Library. There are over twelve hundred citations on Belize, Costa Rica, El Salvador, and the general Central American region. Subheadings for each country include agriculture, colonization, commerce, economic affairs, human resources, land, money, politics, and statistics.

970. Wisconsin. University, Madison. Land Tenure Center. **Central American Agrarian Economy: A Bibliography, Part II: Guatemala, Honduras, Nicaragua, Panama.** Madison, 1978. 98pp. Free. Training and Methods Series No. 27.

This comprehensive bibliography of over eighteen hundred citations offers over five hundred on Guatemala, four hundred on Honduras, four hundred on Nicaragua, and the remainder on Panama. There is a balance between older and current citations. Divisions within each country include: agriculture, commerce, economy, human resources, Indians, land tenure, money, politics, social affairs, and statistics.

971. Wisconsin. University, Madison. Land Tenure Center. **Chile's Agricultural Economy: A Bibliography**. (By the staff) Madison, 1970. 65pp. Free. Training and Methods Series No. 12.

There are over twelve hundred citations arranged by the subject categories of agriculture, economics, politics, society, and general in this bibliography. A supplement to this basic volume appeared in 1971.

972. Wisconsin. University, Madison. Land Tenure Center. **Colombia: Background and Trends: A Bibliography**. Madison, 1969. 34pp. Free.

Agriculture, the economy, politics, society, agrarian reform, finance, taxation, education, and violence are among the subjects covered in the approximately one thousand citations in this volume. At least half are in the Spanish language.

973. Wisconsin. University, Madison. Land Tenure Center. **Colombia, Background and Trends: A Bibliography, Supplement 2**. Madison, 1973. 33pp. Free. Training and Land Tenure Center No. 9, Supplement No. 2.

This is a supplement to an original 1970 bibliography. There are 620 citations on general subjects, agriculture, agrarian reform, economy, politics, society, and education. Arrangement is by author.

974. Wisconsin. University, Madison. Land Tenure Center. **Cuban Agrarian Economy: A Bibliography**. (By Teresa Anderson) Madison, 1974. 47pp. Free. Training and Methods Series No. 23.

The approximately one thousand citations in this study are arranged according to author in the major subject categories of: agriculture, economic conditions, politics and government, and social conditions. Many of the citations are in the Spanish language.

975. Wisconsin. University, Madison. Land Tenure Center. **East and Southeast Asia: A Bibliography**. Madison, 1971. 88pp. Free. Training and Methods Series No. 14.

Twenty-one countries are represented in this bibliography. Many of the citations are official documents from the nations.

976. Wisconsin. University, Madison. Land Tenure Center. **East and Southeast Asia: A Bibliography, Supplement 1**. Madison, 1972. 46pp. Free. Training and Methods Series No. 14, Supplement No. 1.

This collection of 750 citations updates the center's 1971 bibliography. Many of the entries in this supplement date from the Vietnam War era. Twenty-one countries are again represented. Arrangement is alphabetical by author and a list of journal abbreviations is provided.

977. Wisconsin. University, Madison. Land Tenure Center. **East and Southeast Asia: A Bibliography, Supplement 2**. Madison, 1979. 119pp. Free. Training and Methods Series No. 14, Supplement 2.

The approximately two thousand entries in this supplement are organized into major geographic divisions: Asia, Central Asia, East Asia, China, Hong Kong, Japan, Korea, Korean People's Republic, Macao, and Taiwan. Most citations are articles written in the 1970s.

978.   Wisconsin. University, Madison. Land Tenure Center. **Land Tenure and Agrarian Reform in Mexico: A Bibliography.** Madison, 1969. 51pp. Free. Training and Methods Series No. 10.

This bibliography of land tenure and agrarian reform in Mexico reviews almost one thousand citations in the areas of agriculture, economy, politics and law, and society.

979.   Wisconsin. University, Madison. Land Tenure Center. **Land Tenure and Agrarian Reform in Mexico: A Bibliography, Supplement 2.** Madison, 1976. 67pp. Free. Training and Methods Series No. 10, Supplement 2.

The supplement updates the 1969 bibliography with citations—most from the early 1970s. There is emphasis on agrarian reform, history, Indians, and social conditions. The arrangement is by author; there is a broad subject index provided.

980.   Wisconsin. University, Madison. Land Tenure Center. **Lesotho Land Tenure: An Analysis and Annotated Bibliography.** (Compiled by Jerry Eckert) Madison, 1980. 54pp. Free. Special Bibliography No. 2.

Approximately sixty citations are reviewed herein in sections on land tenure issues, work on the land, legal framework, and land tenure references for southern Africa excluding Lesotho.

981.   Wisconsin. University, Madison. Land Tenure Center. **Near East and South Asia: A Bibliography.** Madison, 1971. 74pp. Free. Training and Methods Series No. 13.

Arabia, Iraq, Israel, Lebanon, Syria, Turkey, Afghanistan, Bhutan, Ceylon, Turkey, and Pakistan are the subjects of this eight-hundred-item bibliography. The arrangement is alphabetical by author.

982.   Wisconsin. University, Madison. Land Tenure Center. **Near East and South Asia: A Bibliography, Supplement 1.** Madison, 1976. 99pp. Free. Training and Methods Series No. 13, Supplement 3.

This supplement to the original 1971 bibliography cites almost one thousand additional sources. There are citations for nine countries with the majority on India. Subclassifications include agriculture, cooperatives, economy, food, irrigation, marketing, population, and technological change.

983.   Wisconsin. University, Madison. Land Tenure Center. **Near East and South Asia: A Bibliography, Supplement 2.** Madison, 1976. 60pp. Free.

This supplement to the 1971 bibliography on this subject offers 1,026 citations divided by: Near East in general, Arabian Peninsula, Cyprus, Iran, Iraq, Israel, Jordan, Kuwait, Lebanon, Saudi Arabia, Syria, and Turkey. Many of the citations are government documents or scholarly research.

984. Wisconsin. University, Madison. Land Tenure Center. **Rural Development in Africa: A Bibliography, Part II, North, South, West.** (By the staff) Madison, 1971. 86pp. Free. LC card No. 72-611460. Training and Methods Series No. 17.

The seventeen hundred citations in this study document rural development in northern, southern, and western Africa.

985. Wisconsin. University, Madison. Land Tenure Center. **Sources for Legal and Social Science Research on Latin America: Land Tenure and Agrarian Reform.** (By Teresa J. Anderson) Madison, 1970. 34pp. Free. Training and Methods Series No. 11.

"In Latin America as in most of the developing areas of the world, the land is the principal source of wealth." A discussion of the subject is followed by two hundred important citations reviewed in depth.

986. Wisconsin. University, Madison. Land Tenure Center. **Sources for the Development Statistics: A Bibliography.** (By Charlotte Lott) Madison, 1974. 136pp. Free. Training and Methods Series No. 25.

The major statistical works, current and retrospective, available at the center, are referenced here. General statistical works are followed by those for over 120 countries arranged within continents. There are some short annotations and a broad subject index.

987. Wisconsin. University, Madison. Land Tenure Center. **Women in Rural Development.** (By Beverly Phillips) Madison, 1982. 45pp. Free. Training and Methods Series No. 29.

This title deals with women in developing lands and consists mainly of material found in the Land Tenure Center Library. Women in the United States are discussed. Many of the citations center on the subject of division of work.

DISABLED

988. Wisconsin. University, Madison. Wisconsin Vocational Studies Center. **Bibliography of Materials for Handicapped and Special Education.** (By Lloyd W. Tindall et al.) Madison, 1978. 110pp. Price on application.

This bibliography of over five hundred citations "includes materials on mentally, physically, and socially handicapped students."

989. Wisconsin. University, Madison. Wisconsin Vocational Studies Center. **Vocational Education Resource Materials: A Bibliography of Materials for Handicapped and Special Education.** (By Lloyd W. Tindall et al.) Madison, 1978. 109pp. Free.

This bibliography presents a wealth of curriculum guides, books, and studies on vocational rehabilitation of the handicapped. The sources are arranged according to the following classifications: general, visually impaired, hearing impaired, physical disabilities, mentally retarded, emotionally disturbed, language disabled, learning disabled, and multiply handicapped. Basic bibliographic information is included.

DRUG USE AND ABUSE

990.   Wisconsin. Clearinghouse. **Fetal Alcohol Syndrome Bibliography**. Madison, 1979. 2pp. $0.15.
Fetal alcohol syndrome is the second most important cause of mental retardation and learning disabilities. Recommended print and nonprint materials are found in this reading list of over one hundred citations. Both technical and nontechnical literature are included.

991.   Wisconsin. Clearinghouse. **Lesbians, Gay Men, and Their Alcohol and Other Drug Use**. Madison, 1980. 16pp. $0.35.
Ample annotations are provided for this selective listing of print and film resources on alcohol and drug abuse among homosexuals.

992.   Wisconsin. Clearinghouse. **Resource Reviews: Alcohol and Other Drugs 1979-1983**. Madison, 1983. 1 vol. $10.00.
This is an evaluative bibliography to over 140 recent films, pamphlets, and books on drugs for teachers and youth workers. Information on price, access, and recommended uses is supplied.

993.   Wisconsin. Clearinghouse. **Resource Reviews: Youth and Families 1979-1983**. Madison, 1983. 1 vol. $8.00.
Here are over 150 sources on drugs, related youth development, sexuality, sex roles, and other family issues. Books, films, and pamphlets are cited. Access, prices, and recommended uses are provided.

ECONOMY/ECONOMICS

994.   Wisconsin. University, Madison. Social Systems Research Institute. **Biennial Report, 1981-1983; Publications Index, 1981-1983**. Madison, 1983. 66pp. Free.
This report serves as a bibliography to over seventy-five studies on various aspects of the social sciences. International trade, business cycles, and general monetary problems are emphasized. There is an index according to author.

995.   Wisconsin. University, Madison. Bureau of Business Research and Service. **Equipment Replacement Aspects of Capital Budgeting: A Bibliography**. (By Barry Shore) Madison, 1969? 39*l*. LC card No. 74-633402. Wisconsin Project Reports Volume 3, No. 5.
The two hundred citations in this report would be useful for state budget offices and purchasing departments.

EDUCATION AND TRAINING

996.   Wisconsin. University, Madison. Center for Cognitive Learning. **Bibliography of Publications**. Madison, 1970- . Annual. Free.
Each annual edition of this bibliography reports on approximately 150 citations of books, technical reports, theoretical papers, and practical and working papers

produced by the center staff. Each is simply annotated. There are author indexes. These publication lists/bibliographies present current educational research on individualized instruction, administration, language teaching, reading, and other subject areas.

997.   Wisconsin. University, Madison. School of Education. Center for Educa-
       tion Research. **Bibliography of Publications, 1982 Supplement**. Madison,
       1982. 60pp. Free.
Ninety-five of the center's latest publications—books, technical reports, theoretical papers, and working papers—are reviewed in depth in this collection. The emphasis is on reports concerning student diversity. There is an author index.

998.   Wisconsin. University, Madison. Center for Cognitive Learning. **Concept
       Learning: A Bibliography**. (By Herbert J. Klausmeier et al.) Madison,
       1970. 36pp. Free. Technical Report No. 120.
This bibliography from the Project on Situational Variables and Efficiency of Concept Learning offers over two hundred citations.

999.   Wisconsin. University, Madison. Center for Cognitive Learning. **Goal
       Setting: Review of the Literature and Implications for Future Research**.
       (By John P. Gaa) Madison, 1970. 29pp. Free. Working Paper No. 47.
The twenty-five citations in this collection are reviewed according to variables of goal setting: knowledge, explicitness, originators, and monetary incentives.

1000. Wisconsin. University, Madison. Center for Cognitive Learning. **Individ-
       ual Differences, Learning and Instruction: A Selected Bibliography**.
       (By Frank H. Farley) Madison, 1972. 54pp. Available from ERIC. Work-
       ing Paper No. 92.
This eight-hundred-item bibliography, while developed for use by researchers, might also be useful for practicing teachers. Part I has general references; part II reports methodological references; part III includes reports on aptitude; and part IV treats individual differences and learning.

1001. Wisconsin. University, Madison. Center for Cognitive Learning. **Learning
       by Discovery: A Review of the Research Methodology**. (By Joseph A.
       Scott and Dorothy A. Frayer) Madison, 1970. 31pp. Free. Working Paper
       No. 64.
The thirty-six citations in this review are related to concept learning and the development of cognitive skills. The annotations are in depth.

1002. Wisconsin. University, Madison. Center for Cognitive Learning. **Materials
       for Teaching Adults to Read**. (By Wayne Otto and David Ford) Madison,
       1966. 46pp. Free. Working Paper No. 2.
Designed for those working with illiterate adults, this bibliography includes over five hundred citations; most are annotated. Government publications are included.

EMPLOYMENT

1003.   Wisconsin. University, Madison. Wisconsin Vocational Studies Center. **Job Seeking and Job Keeping: An Annotated Bibliography.** (By Carol Kowle and Deborah Trout) Madison, 1977. 18pp. Free.

This bibliography is the first product of a project on systems approach to assessment and evaluation for postsecondary education planning. Approximately ninety titles are reviewed, with a range from low literate to postsecondary. Most titles are available from the ERIC System or from individual publishers.

ENERGY

1004.   Wisconsin. Department of Energy. **Bibliography on Solar Access.** Madison, 1983. 16pp. Free. DSE/RR No. 519.

This bibliography emphasizes both solar access rights and general studies for the nonspecialist. This is a Division of State Energy Research Report.

ENVIRONMENT

1005.   Wisconsin. Department of Natural Resources. **Bibliography of Freshwater Wetlands Ecology and Management.** (By Linda C. Hall) Madison, 1968. 222pp. Free. Report No. 33.

This is a collection of over eight hundred citations on all aspects of wetlands.

1006.   Wisconsin. University, Green Bay. Library. **International Environmental Policy, an Annotated Bibliography.** (Compiled by John Dinsmore) Green Bay, 1972. 20*l.* Free. UWGB Library Occasional Intercompilation No. 2.

"The purpose of this bibliography is to provide access to a sampling of thought on formulation of international environmental policy as of early 1972." There are 113 citations from periodicals and documents, including citations from the *Congressional Record*. Arrangement is alphabetical by author.

1007.   Wisconsin. University, Madison. Sea Grant Institute. **A Select Bibliography of Public Information Materials about Polychlorinated Biphenyls (PCBs).** (Linda Weimer, project coordinator) Madison, 1981. 12pp. Free. Public Information Report No. 137.

This select bibliography on PCBs presents full bibliographic information and brief summaries for over sixty public information reports and brochures and in-depth background reports. Most are government publications with some periodical articles. Addresses for acquisition are provided.

HEALTH

1008.   Wisconsin. Department of Health and Social Services. Division of Community Services. **Bibliography on Autism from the Collection at the Central Wisconsin Center Library.** Madison, 1980. 4pp. Free.

This is a current reading list of over fifty citations on books and periodicals relating to autism.

1009.   Wisconsin. Department of Health and Social Services. Division of Community Services. Bureau of Mental Health. **Directory, Resources in Mental Health for Nursing Homes: An Annotated Bibliography.** (Compiled by Janet Merle and Jeanette Conrad Nelson) Madison, 1980. 314pp. Price on application.

This is an important bibliography on general mental health services in Wisconsin, mental health education, and the psychology of nursing home patients.

1010.   Wisconsin. Clearinghouse. **Resource Reviews: Wellness and Mental Health, 1979-1983.** Madison, 1983. 1 vol. $7.00.

This bibliography of evaluations on recent noteworthy films, pamphlets, and books related to drug use would be helpful in making selections. Price, access, and recommended uses are discussed.

RECREATION/TOURISM

1011.   Wisconsin. University, Madison. Sea Grant Program. **Annotated Bibliography of the Effects of Water on the Design and Management of Lake and River Marinas.** (By Lon C. Ruedisili) Madison, 1974. 65pp. Free. Sea Grant Advisory Report No. 7.

This bibliography contains 191 references on the effects of water on the design and management of lake and river marinas. Each reference is listed alphabetically by author for the following topics: water quality, flushing-mixing-circulation, harbor improvement, and shoreline modification.

SOCIAL CONDITIONS

1012.   Wisconsin. University, Madison. Department of Rural Sociology. **Annotated Bibliography on Community Development.** (By Helen L. Poppe) Madison, 1968. 35l. Free.

Decision making, the police, and sociology are some of the highlighted studies in this collection of 150 books, bulletins, and articles on community development. Government publications figure prominently. Most of the entries are extensively annotated.

1013.   Wisconsin. University, Madison. Department of Rural Sociology. **Dissertations in Demography, 1933-1963.** (By Glenn V. Fuguitt) Madison, 1964. 72pp.

The first section of this bibliography is a listing by general subject within the field of population. The second section is a classification of entries by author. There are 539 citations in sixteen separate categories. Race, ethnic groups, and internal migration are highlighted topics.

1014.   Wisconsin. University, Madison. Department of Rural Sociology. **Rural Poverty: Annotated and References Bibliography.** Madison, 1970? 48*l*. Free.

Demography and poverty, education, youth, communications and adoption practices, social structure, values, and economic aspects are some of the topics addressed in this study of the literature of rural poverty. There is a special section on regional rural poverty. There are almost 250 annotated entries cited.

1015.   Wisconsin. University, Madison. Institute for Research on Poverty. **Subject Guide to Publications.** Madison, 1979. 107pp. Free.

This reference is a bibliographic description of reprints, discussion papers, and special reports from the Institute for Research on Poverty.

1016.   Wisconsin. University, Milwaukee. Center for Advanced Studies in Human Services. **Working Bibliography on Single Parents and Their Children.** (By Karen Steele) Milwaukee, 1977. 1 vol. $3.00. Working Bibliography No. 6.

Included here are approximately sixty annotated citations—mostly of journal articles—on the single parent related to coping and the adjustment of children to the single-parent family.

WILDLIFE

1017.   Wisconsin. Department of Natural Resources. **Bibliography of Beaver, Trout, Wildlife, and Forest Relationships.** (By Ed. L. Avery) Madison, 1983. 23pp. Free. Technical Bulletin No. 137.

Included in this bulletin are 440 citations with special references to beaver and trout. There is a special annotated section of the most significant reports on beaver-trout relationships. There is a short subject index.

1018.   Wisconsin. Department of Wildlife Ecology. Cooperative Extension Programs. **Bibliography of Cooperative Extension Service Literature on Wildlife, Fish, and Forest Resources.** (By Robert L. Ruff) Madison, 1982. 42pp. Free.

The over two hundred studies in this bibliographic publication list furnish a well-balanced beginning for researching Wisconsin natural resources.

WOMEN

1019.   Wisconsin. Clearinghouse. **All about Women.** Madison, 1980. 8pp. $0.50.

This is a bibliography of recommended print materials on women, chemical use, and awareness. A resource list of organizations, publishers, and film distributors is supplied.

1020.   Wisconsin. Historical Society. **Women's History: Resources at the State Historical Society of Wisconsin.** (By James P. Danky) Madison, 1979. 77pp. $3.95.

This is a fourth edition, revised and enlarged, of an excellent bibliography. It includes over five hundred annotations on all aspects of women, with emphasis on Wisconsin.

AGRICULTURE

1021.   Wyoming. Agricultural Experiment Station. **Wyoming Sugar Beet Research 1978: Progress Report.** (By Harold J. Tuma) Laramie, 1979. 127pp. Free. Research Journal No. 133.

Forty recent studies on the sugar beet are found in this state-of-the-art bibliography. There are six categories, including weed control and pest management. Detailed summaries of the findings are presented.

EDUCATION AND TRAINING

1022.   Wyoming. Department of Education. Vocational-Technical Education Division. **Adult Basic Education: A Bibliography of Materials.** Cheyenne, 1966. 164pp. Out-of-Print.

This is a bibliography to over twelve hundred citations on adult education divided into thirty-seven categories. Curricular materials, machines for learning, and equipment available to assist adult learners are highlighted.

GEOLOGY

1023.   Wyoming. Geological Survey. **Bibliography and Index of Wyoming Geology, 1950-1959.** (By Helen L. Nace) Laramie, 1979. 1 vol. $3.50. Bulletin No. 57.

This is a record of writings on all categories of Wyoming geology. There were companion studies for the periods 1917-1945 and 1945-1949.

1024.   Wyoming. Geological Survey. **Bibliography of Graduate Theses and Dissertations on the Geology of Wyoming through August 1973.** (By Sally L. Petersen) Laramie, 1974. 56pp. Free.

This is an in-depth bibliography to 569 citations on Wyoming geology. It updates Richard Monckton's 1970 bibliography of dissertations. Important college and university geology departments were contacted as part of the compilation. There are subject and area indexes.

1025.   Wyoming. Geological Survey. **Bibliography of Wyoming Geology, 1945-
        1949.** (By Jane M. Love) Laramie, 1973. 103pp. Free.
This supplement to the basic bibliography (No. 53) updates the collection to 1949
in over 850 citations. The primary arrangement is by author. There is a broad
subject index with emphasis on economic geology, mineralogy, and paleontology.

NATURAL RESOURCES

1026.   Wyoming. Geological Survey. **Bibliography and Index of Wyoming Uran-
        ium through 1973.** (By Charles E. Banks, David Copeland, and W. Dan
        Hausel) Laramie, 1981. 136pp. LC card No. 82-622529. Bulletin No. 61.
Over five hundred citations on the occurence and mining of uranium are presented
in this bibliography.

1027.   Wyoming. Geological Survey. **Bibliography of Wyoming Coal.** (By Gary
        B. Glas and Richard W. Jones) Laramie, 1974. 163pp. Free. Bulletin No.
        58.
The increasing coal mining activity in Wyoming means requests for information
about coal development are received by industry, government, and researchers.
This bibliography includes 1,223 references published through July 1973. Author
and subject indexes are supplied.

WILDLIFE

1028.   Wyoming. Agricultural Experiment Station. **Asilid Literature Update,
        1956-1976.** (By Robert A. Garver) Laramie, 1978. 134pp. Free. Science
        Monograph No. 36.
"Robber flies are a widely distributed group of predatory flies." Over three
thousand titles from *Biological Abstracts*, the Knutson Literature File, and other
related bibliographies are gathered here. Brief reviews of major subjects provide
overviews.

1029.   Wyoming. Agricultural Experiment Station. **A Bibliography on the Sage
        Grouse (*Centroercus urophasianus*).** (By Mark S. Boyce and James Tate,
        Jr.) Laramie, 1979. 12pp. Free. LC card No. 81-621766. Science Mono-
        graph No. 38.
This bibliography lists selected published literature on the sage grouse, Centrocercus
urophasianus (Bonaparte). The 250 citations will be useful for both biologists and
students. Unpublished Pittman-Robertson studies are included. Arrangement is
by author.

1030.   Wyoming. Department of Game and Fish. **A Partial Bibliography of the Mammals of Wyoming and Adjacent States with Special Reference to Density and Habitat Affinity.** (By Reginald Tothwell et al.) Cheyenne, 1978. 172pp. Free.

This bibliography was compiled under contract with the U.S. Bureau of Land Management. It is not intended to be exhaustive but places emphasis on Wyoming mammals. Sixty mammals are the subjects of the 681 citations. There are also summary reviews of literature categories and density charts.

1031.   Wyoming. Department of Game and Fish. **Wyoming Orinthology: A History and Bibliography with Species and Wyoming Area Indexes.** (By Jane Logan Dorn) Cheyenne, 1978. 369pp. Free.

The 1,956 citations in this collection emphasize density information relative to mining. Thirty-three categories of birds are included. Appendixes include historical account of research in Wyoming, literature summaries, and accounts of scientific expeditions.

APPENDIX
ACQUISITION GUIDE AND AGENCY ADDRESSES

Faced with the task of extracting from the unwieldy mass of state government publications the desired nuggets to meet the informational needs of users, the role of the reference librarian is an arduous one. The bibliographic apparatus at the national and regional level ... does not permit us to access state documentation easily and quickly.

These words of Dr. Joe Morehead in the introduction to *State Government Reference Publications: An Annotated Bibliography*, 2d ed. (Libraries Unlimited, 1981) summarize the continuing problem of acquiring state publications. Nevertheless, there are several sources from which one can generally acquire state publications. These are:

1. *State depository libraries*

   These comprise a system of complete and selective libraries who have contracted to receive, record, shelve, and preserve state publications and to give service to patrons. In 1981, the following states enacted depository systems:

1.	Alaska	20.	New Hampshire
2.	Arkansas	21.	New Jersey
3.	California	22.	New Mexico
4.	Connecticut	23.	New York
5.	Florida	24.	North Dakota
6.	Hawaii	25.	Ohio
7.	Idaho	26.	Oklahoma
8.	Illinois	27.	Oregon
9.	Indiana	28.	Pennsylvania
10.	Iowa	29.	South Dakota
11.	Kansas	30.	Tennessee
12.	Louisiana	31.	Texas
13.	Michigan	32.	Utah
14.	Minnesota	33.	Vermont
15.	Mississippi	34.	Virginia
16.	Missouri	35.	Washington
17.	Montana	36.	West Virginia
18.	Nebraska	37.	Wisconsin
19.	Nevada		

The scope of these depositories varies greatly from merely one or two libraries to a network of over twenty-five. The publications received also vary from any extra titles an agency may possess to a mandated number from each agency.

2. *Voluntary Acquisition from an Agency*

Many valuable state titles can be obtained in this way, either free of charge or as priced titles. Some agencies maintain mailing lists.

3. *Distribution Centers*

Several states have enacted central distribution centers where more popular publications can be purchased. Most sales are subject to payment in advance with the exception of public agencies of that particular state. Pennsylvania and Connecticut are two examples of states with this policy.

4. *Statutory Exchange Distribution to Out-of-State Libraries*

Principally of use with legislative and judicial materials, a state library commonly receives fifty to one hundred of each title to exchange with other state libraries on a regular basis.

5. *Educational Resources Information Center*

In recent years many state executive documents have been entered into the ERIC database. A sample of *Monthly Checklist of State Publications* from August, 1984 found eighty-six state publications from a total of 1,979. Many of these are noneducationally related.

6. *State Publications Not Available other Than through Interlibrary Loan*

As fewer of each state document are published, often a state library will acquire the only available copies. At times these limited copies are not available through interlibrary loan but an agreement can be made to copy them with a charge for each page. Most libraries would proceed through interlibrary loan procedures.

In order to facilitate the acquisition of items listed in this bibliography, a state-by-state address directory for all agencies or departments given in each bibliographic description is provided. Where no address is listed in the appendix the reader may assume that the item is only available through interlibrary loan.

ALABAMA

Development Office
3734 Atlanta Highway
Montgomery, 36130

Geological Survey
University of Alabama
University, 35468

Marine Resources Laboratory
Publications
Dauphin Island, 36528

State Department of Education
State Office Building
Montgomery, 36130

University of Alabama
Library
University, 35486

ALASKA

Department of Community and
    Regional Affairs
Capitol, Pouch B
Juneau, 99811

Department of Education
Pouch F
Juneau, 99811

Department of Fish and Game
Subport Building
Juneau, 99801

Division of Geological and
    Geophysical Surveys
College, 99701

Division of Geological Survey
see Division of Geological and
    Geophysical Surveys

Division of Mines and Geology
see Division of Geological and
    Geophysical Surveys

Historical Commission
3321 Providence Drive
Anchorage, 99504

State Library
Department of Education
Pouch G
Juneau, 99811

University of Alaska, Anchorage
Arctic Environmental Information
    and Data Center
707-A Street
Anchorage, 99501

University of Alaska, College Institute
    of Social, Economic, and Government
    Research
College, 99701

University of Alaska, Fairbanks
Fairbanks, 99701

ARIZONA

Arizona State University
Laboratory of Climatology
Tempe, 85281

Department of Game and Fish
2222 West Greenaway Road
Phoenix, 85007

University of Arizona, Tucson
Institute of Government Research
Publications
Tucson, 85721

University of Arizona, Tucson
Office of Arid Land Studies
Tucson, 85721

Water Commission
222 North Central Avenue
Phoenix, 85004

ARKANSAS

Division of Community Affairs
No. 1 Capitol Mall
Little Rock, 72201

Geological Commission
3815 West Roosevelt Road
Little Rock, 72204

Industrial Development Commission
No. Capitol Mall
Little Rock, 72201

Rehabilitation Research and Training
    Center
Publications
Hot Springs, 71901

CALIFORNIA

Air Resources Board
1025 P Street
Sacramento, 95814

Biological Control Services Program
see Giannini Foundation

California State College,
    San Fernando Valley
see California State University,
    Northridge

California State University,
    Los Angeles
Latin American Studies Center
Los Angeles, 90032

California State University,
    Northridge
Northridge, 91324

Department of Consumer Affairs
Room 409
1120 N Street
Sacramento, 95814

Department of Motor Vehicles
2570 24th Street
Sacramento, 95818

Department of Parks and Recreation
P. O. Box 2390
Sacramento, 95811

Giannini Foundation of Agricultural
    Economics
Publications
University of California
Berkeley, 94720

Health and Welfare Agency
Capitol
Sacramento, 95814

Office of Alcoholism
111 Capitol Mall
Sacramento, 95814

State Department of Education
Publications, Room 721
Capitol Mall
Sacramento, 95814

State Library
920 Capitol Mall
Sacramento, 95809

University of California, Berkeley
Department of Anthropology
Publications
Berkeley, 94720

University of California, Berkeley
Institute of Governmental Studies
109 Moses Hall
Berkeley, 94720

University of California, Berkeley
Institute of Transportation Studies
(available from:)
California Bibliographies
P. O. Box 229
Monticello, Illinois 61586

University of California, Davis
Water Resources Center
Davis, 95616

University of California, San Diego
Malcome A. Love Library
San Diego, 92115

University of California, Santa Cruz
Coastal Research Laboratory
1156 High Street
Santa Cruz, 95064

Youth Authority
714 P Street
Sacramento, 95814

COLORADO

Colorado Division of Wildlife
6060 Broadway
Denver, 80216

Cooperative Extension Service
Colorado State University
Fort Collins, 80523

Department of Game, Fish, and
    Parks
see Colorado Division of Wildlife

University of Colorado, Boulder
Graduate School of Business
    Administration
Business Research Division
Boulder, 80309

University of Denver
Center for Social Research and
    Development
Graduate School of Social Work
Denver, 80208

CONNECTICUT

Agricultural Experiment Station
Publications
Storrs, 02068

Department of Children and Youth
    Services
345 Main Street
Hartford, 06115

Department of Corrections
340 Capitol Avenue
Hartford, 06115

Department of Environmental
    Protection
Natural Resource Center
State Office Building
Hartford, 06115

Public Fire Education Committee
100 Washington Street
Meriden, 06450

State Department of Education
165 Capitol Avenue
Hartford, 06115

University of Connecticut, Storrs
Center for Real Estate and Urban
    Economic Studies
Publications
Storrs, 06268

University of Connecticut, Storrs
Library
Storrs, 06268

University of Connecticut, Storrs
Institute of Water Resources
Publications
Storrs, 06268

DELAWARE

Department of Labor
Office of Planning, Research, and
    Evaluation
Publications
801 West Street
Wilmington, 19801

State Planning Office
Publications
Governor's Office
Townsend Building
Route 13
Dover, 19901

University of Delaware, Newark
College of Marine Studies
Newark, 19801

University of Delaware, Newark
Department of Anthropology
Newark, 19801

FLORIDA

Atlantic University, Boca Raton
Sea Grant College
Publications
Boca Raton, 33334

Department of Education
The Capitol
Tallahassee, 32304

Department of Health and
    Rehabilitative Services
1323 Winewood Boulevard
Tallahassee, 32301

Department of Natural Resources
Marine Research Laboratory
St. Petersburg, 33731

Division of Vocational, Technical, and
    Adult Education
1323 Winewood Boulevard
Tallahassee, 32301

Game and Fresh Water Fish Commission
620 Meridian Street
Talahassee, 32301

State Library
The Capitol
Tallahassee, 32301

University of Florida, Gainesville
Sea Grant Marine Advisory Program
Gainesville, 32611

GEORGIA

Department of Natural Resources
Georgia Geologic Survey
King Drive, Room 400
Agricultural Building
Atlanta, 30334

Georgia State University, Atlanta
Department of Geography
Atlanta, 30332

Office of Planning and Budget
611 Trinity-Washington Building
270 Washington Street, S.W.
Atlanta, 30334

University of Georgia, Athens
College of Agriculture
Experiment Stations
Publications
Athens, 30602

University of Georgia, Athens
College of Education
Rehabilitation Counselor Training
    Program
Athens, 30602

University of Georgia, Athens
Institute of Government
Publications
Athens, 30602

University of Georgia, Athens
Libraries
Athens, 30602

HAWAII

Agricultural Experiment Station
University of Hawaii
Honolulu, 96822

Department of Education
Publications
1270 Queen Emma Street
Room 1201
Honolulu, 96813

Department of Planning and
    Economic Development
7th Floor, Kamamalu Building
250 South King Street
Honolulu, 96804

State Library
Office of Library Services
State Library Branch
478 South King Street
Honolulu, 96813

University of Hawaii, Honolulu
Hawaii Institute of Geophysics
Honolulu, 96813

University of Hawaii, Honolulu
Hawaii Institute of Marine Biology
Honolulu, 96813

University of Hawaii, Honolulu
Library
Honolulu, 96813

University of Hawaii, Honolulu
Sea Grant College
Honolulu, 96813

University of Hawaii, Honolulu
Social Sciences and Linguistics Institute
Publications
Honolulu, 96813

University of Hawaii, Honolulu
Water Resources Research Center
2540 Dole Street, Holmes Hall 283
Honolulu, 96812

University of Hawaii, Manoa
Social Science Research Institute
Honolulu, 96822

University of Hawaii, Manoa
College of Tropical Agriculture and Human Resources
2500 Campus Road
Honolulu, 96822

IDAHO

Bureau of Mines and Geology
University of Idaho
Moscow, 83843

Fish and Game Department
600 South Walnut Street
Boise, 83707

University of Idaho, Moscow
Bureau of Public Affairs Research
Moscow, 83843

University of Idaho, Moscow
Forest, Wildlife, and Range Experiment
  Station
Moscow, 83843

University of Idaho, Moscow
Library
Moscow, 83843

ILLINOIS

Department of Commerce and
  Community Affairs
222 South College
Springfield, 62706

Department of Education
Publications
100 North First Street
Springfield, 62706

Commission on Human Relations
160 North LaSalle Street
Chicago, 60601

Department of Mental Health
160 North LaSalle Street
Chicago, 60601
and
Publications
Springfield, 62706

Illinois-Chicago Project for Inter-Ethnic
  Dimensions in Education
see Department of Education

Legislative Council
State Capitol
  Room 107, Stratton Building
Springfield, 62706

Natural History Survey
602 Stratton Building
Urbana, 61801

Northern Illinois University
Center for Governmental Studies
Publications
De Kalb, 60115

Office of the Superintendent of
    Public Instruction
see Department of Education

Sangamon State University
Vocational Curriculum Center
Publications
Springfield, 62708

Secretary of State
State Capitol
Springfield, 62706

State Board of Education
see Department of Education

Southern Illinois University
Center for the Study of Crime,
    Delinquency, and Corrections
Carbondale, 62901

State Geological Survey Division
Peabody Drive at Sixth Avenue
Urbana, 61801

State Council on Nutrition
524 South 2nd Street
Springfield, 62706

State Library
Centennial Building
Springfield, 62756

University of Illinois, Urbana-Champaign
Department of Agricultural Economics
305 Mumford Hall
Urbana, 61801

University of Illinois, Urbana-Champaign
Water Resources Center
Urbana, 61801

Western Illinois University
Curriculum Publications Clearinghouse
Macomb, 61455

INDIANA

Indiana State University
Cunningham Memorial Library
Terre Haute, 47809

Indiana University
Chicano-Riquèno Studies
Bloomington, 47405

Indiana University
Department of Spanish and Portuguese
Bloomington, 47405

Purdue University
Krannert Graduate School of
    Management
West Lafayette, 47907

State Board of Health
A-405 Health Building
Indianapolis, 46204

IOWA

Department of Public Instruction
Grimes Building
Des Moines, 50319

Geological Survey
123 North Capitol Street
Iowa City, 52242

Iowa State University, Ames
Center for Agricultural and Rural
   Development
578 East Hall
Ames, 50010

Iowa State University, Ames
Gerontology Center Project
Ames, 50011

KANSAS

Agricultural Experiment Station
Publications
Manhattan, 66506

Emporia State University
School of Library Science
1200 Commercial Street
Emporia, 66801

Kansas State University, Manhattan
Food and Feed Grain Institute
Manhattan, 66506

Kansas State University, Manhattan
Institute for Systems Design and
   Optimization
Publications
Manhattan, 66506

University of Kansas, Lawrence
Libraries
Lawrence, 66045

KENTUCKY

Geological Survey
311 Breckinridge Hall
University, Lexington
Lexington, 40506

Department of Justice
State Law Library
State Office Building, Room 103
High Street
Frankfort, 40601

Department of Libraries and Archives
Division of Records and Archives
851 East Main Street
Frankfort, 40601

University of Kentucky, Lexington
Institute for Mining and Mineral Research
Publications
Lexington, 40506

University of Kentucky, Lexington
Libraries
Lexington, 40506

LOUISIANA

Department of Conservation
Geological Survey
Louisiana State University
P. O. Box G
Baton Rouge, 70893

Department of Education
Publications
P. O. Box 70804
Baton Rouge, 70804

Department of Natural Resources
Office of Energy
P. O. Box 44156
Baton Rouge, 70804

Louisiana State University and
    A and M College, Baton Rouge
Coastal Studies Institute
Publications
Baton Rouge, 70804

Louisiana State University and
    A and M College, Baton Rouge
College of Business Administration
Division of Research
Publications
Baton Rouge, 70804

Louisiana State University and
    A and M College, Eunice
LeDoux Library
P. O. Box 1129
Eunice, 70535

Secretary of State
P. O. Box 44125
Baton Rouge, 70803

University of New Orleans
School of Urban and Regional Studies
Earl K. Long Library
Lake Front
New Orleans, 70122

University of Southwestern Louisiana
Office of Institutional Research
Publications
Lafayette, 70501

MAINE

Department of Conservation
Bureau of Parks and Recreation
Community Recreation Division
Publications
State Office Building
Augusta, 04333

Department of Educational and
    Cultural Services
Education Building
Augusta, 04333

State Library Bureau
Cultural Building
Augusta, 04333

State Planning Office
184 State Street
Augusta, 04333

University of Maine, Orono
Department of Oceanography
Migratory Fish Institute
Orono, 04469

University of Maine, Orono
Fogler Library
Orono, 04469

University of Maine, Orono
Marine Advisory Program
Publications
Orono, 04469

University of Maine, Orono
New England-Atlantic Provinces-
    Quebec Center
Orono, 04469

MARYLAND

Department of Natural Resources
Tawes State Building
Annapolis, 21401

State Department of Education
P. O. Box 8717
Baltimore-Washington International
    Airport
Baltimore, 21240

State Law Library
Courts of Appeal Building
Annapolis, 21401

University of Maryland, College Park
College of Library and Information
    Services
College Park, 20742

MASSACHUSETTS

Agricultural Experiment Station
Publications
Amherst, 01003

Amherst College
Center for Urban Education
Publications
Amherst, 01003

Amherst College
Institute for Man and Environment
Amherst, 01003

Department of Education
Bureau of Educational Information
    Services
Publications
One Ashburton Place
Boston, 02108

Holyoke Community College
Library
303 Homestead Avenue
Holyoke, 01040

Rehabilitation Commission
Library
296 Boylston Street
Boston, 02116

Solar Action Office
Room 700
73 Tremont Street
Boston, 02108

MICHIGAN

Agricultural Experiment Station
Bulletin Office
Box 231
East Lansing, 48823

Department of Education
Office for Sex Equity in Education
735 East Michigan Avenue
Lansing, 48913

Department of Education
State Library Services
735 East Michigan Avenue
Lansing, 48913

Department of Natural Resources
7th Floor
Mason Building
P. O. Box 30028
Lansing, 48909

Eastern Michigan University
Library
Ypsilanti, 48197

Michigan State University
Department of Agricultural
   Economics
Publications
East Lansing, 48824

Michigan State University,
   East Lansing
Institute for International Studies
   in Education
Non-Formal Education Information
   Center
Publications
East Lansing, 48824

Michigan State University, East Lansing
Soil Science Department
East Lansing, 48824

University of Michigan, Ann Arbor
College of Engineering
Department of Naval Architecture
Publications
Ann Arbor, 48109

University of Michigan, Ann Arbor
Medical School
Office of Educational Resources and
   Research
Ann Arbor, 48109

MINNESOTA

Agricultural Experiment Station
Publications
St. Paul, 55108

Department of Education
350 Cedar Street
St. Paul, 55101

University of Minnesota, Minneapolis
Center for Population Studies
Publications
Minneapolis, 55455

University of Minnesota, Minneapolis
Immigration History Research Center
Publications
Minneapolis, 55455

University of Minnesota, Minneapolis
Industrial Relations Center
Publications
Minneapolis, 55455

University of Minnesota, Minneapolis
Institute of Agriculture, Forestry, and
   Home Economics
Publications
Minneapolis, 55455

University of Minnesota, Minneapolis
Training Center for Community Programs
Publications
Minneapolis, 55455

MISSISSIPPI

University of Mississippi, University
Bureau of Business and Economic
   Research
Publications
University, 38677

University of Mississippi, University
Research Institute of Pharmaceutical
   Sciences
School of Pharmacy
Publications
University, 38677

MISSOURI

Department of Conservation
2901 North Ten Mile Drive
Jefferson City, 65101

Department of Education
Division of Career and Adult
    Education
Jefferson State Office Building
Jefferson City, 65101

Division of Commerce and Industrial
    Development
Jefferson State Office Building
Jefferson City, 65102

University of Missouri, Columbia
Museum of Anthropology
Publications
Columbia, 65201

University of Missouri, Columbia
Public Information
Columbia, 65201

University of Missouri, Columbia
School of Library and Information
    Science
Columbia, 65201

MONTANA

State Library
930 East Lyndale
Helena, 59601

Superintendent of Public Instruction
Room 106
State Capitol
Helena, 59601

NEBRASKA

Agricultural Experiment Station
Publications
Lincoln, 68509

Department of Agriculture
301 Centennial Mall South
Lincoln, 68509

Department of Education
P. O. Box 94987
Lincoln, 68509

Library Commission
1420 P. Street
Lincoln, 68508

State Historical Society
1500 R. Street
Lincoln, 68508

University of Nebraska, Lincoln
Lincoln, 68588

University of Nebraska, Lincoln
Bureau of Business Research
Business Development Center
Publications
Lincoln, 68588

University of Nebraska, Lincoln
Department of Agricultural Economics
Lincoln, 68588

University of Nebraska, Lincoln
Political Science Department
Government Research Institute
Publications
Lincoln, 68588

University of Nebraska, Lincoln
Water Resources Center
Lincoln, 68588

NEVADA

Agricultural Experiment Station
Publications
Reno, 89557

University of Nevada, Reno
Western Research Center
Reno, 89557

University of Nevada, Reno
Desert Ranch Institute
Reno, 89557

NEW JERSEY

Department of Community Affairs
363 West State Street
Trenton, 08625

Montclair State College
Library
Upper Montclair, 07043

Department of Environmental
   Protection
P. O. Box 1390
Trenton, 08625

Office of Equal Educational Opportunity
225 West State Street
Trenton, 08625

Historical Commission
113 West State Street
Trenton, 08625

State Library
185 West State Street
Trenton, 08625

Library for the Blind and
   Handicapped
185 West State Street
Trenton, 08625

State Museum
Capitol
State Street
Trenton, 08625

NEW MEXICO

Agricultural Experiment Station
New Mexico State University
Publications
Las Cruces, 88003

Energy Research and Development
   Institute
P. O. Box 3EI
Las Cruces, 88003

Cooperative Extension Service
Range Improvement Task Force
Las Cruces, 88003

New Mexico State University
Water Resources Research Institute
Publications
Las Cruces, 88003

State Bureau of Mines and Mineral
  Resources
Campus Station
Socorro, 87801

University of New Mexico,
  Albuquerque
Division of Government Research
Publications
Albuquerque, 87131

University of New Mexico, Albuquerque
Institute for Social Research and
  Development
Publications
Albuquerque, 87131

NEW YORK

Agricultural Experiment Station
Bulletin Office
Ithaca, 14853

American Revolution Bicentennial
  Commission
Publications
Governor's Office
Albany, 12224

Cornell University
College of Agriculture and Life
  Sciences
Publications
Ithaca, 14850

Cornell University
School of Industrial and Labor
  Relations
Publications
Ithaca, 14853

Department of Commerce
112 State Street
Albany, 12207

Department of State
162 Washington Avenue
Albany, 12231

Division of the Budget
State Capitol
Albany, 13224

Division of Human Rights
(order Albany and NYC imprints
  from:)
Two World Trade Center
Room 5356
New York, N.Y. 10047

Narcotic Addiction Control
  Commission
Stuyvesant Plaza
Albany, 12203

Port Authority
World Trade Center
New York, N.Y. 10047

State Education Department
(all divisions)
Education Building
Albany, 12234

State History Office
Education Building
Albany, 12234

State Library
Cultural Education Building
Albany, 12231

State University of New York, Albany
Institute for Traffic Safety Management
  and Research
Albany, 12222

State University of New York,
     Buffalo
Department of Education
Buffalo, 14260

State University of New York,
     Geneseo
Geneseo, 14454

Syracuse University
School of Forestry
Syracuse, 13210

Temporary State Commission on Tug Hill
317 Washington Street
Watertown, 13601

NORTH DAKOTA

Agricultural Experiment Station
Publications
Fargo, 58105

Geological Survey
University of North Dakota
Grand Forks, 58202

Governor
Office of Energy Management and
     Conservation
State Capitol
Bismarck, 58505

Legislative Council
Publications
Bismarck, 58505

State Board for Vocational Education
900 East Boulevard
Bismarck, 58505

State Library Commission
Randall Building
Highway 83, North
Bismarck, 58707

OHIO

Agricultural Research
     and Development Center
Publications
Wooster, 44691

Biological Survey
State Capitol
Columbus, 43215

Department of Energy
34th Floor
30 East Broad Street
Columbus, 43215

Historical Society
State Capitol
Columbus, 43215

Kent State University
College of Business Administration
Kent, 44242

State Library
65 South Front Street
Columbus, 43215

The Ohio State University
Department of Agricultural Economics
     and Rural Sociology
Publications
Columbus, 43210

University of Toledo
Business Research Center
Publications
2801 West Bancroft
Toledo, 43606

OKLAHOMA

Department of Libraries
200 N.E. 18th Street
Oklahoma City, 73105

Geological Survey
University of Oklahoma
Norman, 73069

Oklahoma State University
Edmond Low Library
Stillwater, 74074

State Department of Education
Oliver Hodge Building
Oklahoma City, 73105

University of Oklahoma, Norman
Bureau of Government Research
Publications
Norman, 73069

OREGON

Agricultural Experiment Station
Publications
Corvallis, 97331

Department of Geology and Mineral
    Resources
(available from:)
Geological Survey
1069 State Office Building
Portland, 97201

Legislative Research
S-420
State Capitol
Salem, 97310

Oregon State University, Corvallis
Corvallis, 97331

Oregon State University, Corvallis
Sea Grant Program
Corvallis, 97331

Southern Oregon State College, Ashland
Library
1250 Siskiyou Boulevard
Ashland, 97520

State Department of Fish and Wildlife
Research and Development Section
1400 S.W. 5th Street
Portland, 97201

State Library
Salem, 97310

University of Oregon, Eugene
Municipal Research and Services Bureau
Publications
Eugene, 97403

University of Oregon, Eugene
School of Education
Publications
Eugene, 97403

PENNSYLVANIA

Department of Community Affairs
Old Museum Building
Harrisburg, 17120

Department of Education
533 Market Street
Harrisburg, 17120

Governor's Commission on Three
    Mile Island
State Capitol
Harrisburg, 17120

Historical and Museum Commission
William Penn Memorial Museum
    and Archives Building
Box 1026
Harrisburg, 17120

Office of Mental Health
Research Division
308 Health and Welfare Building
Harrisburg, 17120

State Library
Room 118, Education Building
Harrisburg, 17120

PUERTO RICO

Bureau of the Budget
Office of the Governor
Box 3228
254 De La Cruz Street
San Juan, 00904

Office of the Commonwealth
LaFortaleza
San Juan, 00901

SOUTH CAROLINA

Agricultural Experiment Station
Publications
Clemson, 29631

Commission on Alcohol and Drug
    Abuse
3700 Forest Drive
Columbia, 29204

Clemson University
College of Forest and Recreation
    Resources
201 Sikes Hall
Clemson, 29631

Department of Education
1429 Senate Street
Columbia, 29201

Sea Grant Consortium
Publications
Charleston, 29408

State Library
1500 Senate Street
P. O. Box 11469
Columbia, 29211

Tricentennial Commission
Office of the Governor
State House
Columbia, 29211

SOUTH DAKOTA

Agricultural Experiment Station
Publications
Brookings, 57006

Commission on the Status of Women
Kneip Building
Pierre, 57501

Cooperative Wildlife Research Unit
Anderson Building
Brookings, 57006

Legislative Research Council
Publications
Pierre, 57501

State Library Commission
State Library Building
Pierre, 57501

State Planning Agency
Office of Policy Information
Department of Executive Management
State Capitol
Pierre, 57501

University of South Dakota, Vermillion
McKusick Law Library
Publications
Vermillion, 57069

TENNESSEE

Division of Geology
Department of Conservation
G-5 State Office Building
Nashville, 57069

Memphis State University
J. W. Brister Library
Publications
Memphis, 38152

State Library and Archives
403 Seventh Avenue
Nashville, 37219

University of Tennesse, Knoxville
Institute for Public Service
Municipal Technical Advisory Service
Publications
Knoxville, 37916

TEXAS

Agricultural Experiment Station
Texas A and M University
College Station, 77843

Department of Community Affairs
Children and Youth Services
    Division
Box 13166
Capitol Station
Austin, 78711

Department of Education
201 East Eleventh Street
Austin, 78701

Department of Highways and Public
    Transporation
P. O. Box 5064
Austin, 78763

Department of Parks and Wildlife
4200 Smith School Road
Austin, 78744

East Texas State College
Gee Library
Commerce, 75428

Legislature
Legislative Reference Library
State Capitol
Austin, 78711

Texas A and M University
Sea Grant Program
College Station, 77843

Texas A and M University
Transportation Institute
College Station, 77843

Texas Tech University
International Center for Arid
   and Semi-Arid Land Studies
Lubbock, 79409

Texas Tech University
Library
Lubbock, 79409

University of Texas, Austin
Bureau of Business Research
P. O. Box 7459
Austin, 78712

University of Texas, Austin
Bureau of Economic Geology
Publications
Austin, 78712

University of Texas, Austin
Center for Research in Water
   Resources
Publications
Austin, 78712

University of Texas, Austin
School of Social Work
Center for Social Work Research
Austin, 78712

University of Texas, Austin
General Libraries
Austin, 78711

University of Texas, Austin
Institute for Constructive Capitalism
Austin, 78712

University of Texas, Austin
Institute of Latin American Studies
Austin, 78712

University of Texas, Austin
Tarleton Law Library
Publications
Austin, 78711

University of Texas, Austin
Texas Memorial Museum
Austin, 78711

UTAH

Agricultural Experiment Station
Logan, 84321

Department of Employment
   Security
P. O. Box 11249
Salt Lake City, 84147

Geological Survey
606 Blackhawk Drive
Salt Lake City, 84108

University of Utah, Salt Lake City
American West Center
Publications
Salt Lake City, 84112

University of Utah, Salt Lake City
Libraries
Salt Lake City, 84112

Utah State University, Logan
College of Engineering
Utah Water Research Laboratory
Logan, 84322

VERMONT

Historical Society
109 State Street
Montpelier, 05602

VIRGIN ISLANDS

Bureau of Libraries, Museums, and Archaeological Services
49 South King Street
Charlotte-Amalie, 00820

VIRGINIA

Division of Mineral Resources
P. O. Box 3367
Charlottesville, 22903

Virginia Polytechnic Institute and State
  University
Publications
Blacksburg, 24061

WASHINGTON

Department of Ecology
Olympia, 98504

Department of Game
600 North Capitol Way
Olympia, 98504

Department of Natural Resources
Public Lands Building
Olympia, 98504

State Library
Commission Building
Olympia, 98504

Superintendent of Public Instruction
Publications
Old Capitol Building
Olympia, 98504

University of Washington, Seattle
Department of Oceanography
Seattle, 98122

WEST VIRGINIA

Cooperative Extension Service
West Virginia University
Publications
Morgantown, 26506

West Virginia University, Morgantown
Library
Morgantown, 26506

WISCONSIN

Clearinghouse
1954 East Washington Avenue
Madison, 53704

Department of Health and Social
  Services
Wilson State Office Building
Madison, 53702

Department of Natural Resources
Publications
Madison, 53701

Department of Wildlife Ecology
see Department of Natural Resources

Division of Energy
Department of Administration
1 West Wilson Street
Madison, 53702

Historical Society
816 State Street
Madison, 53706

University of Wisconsin, Green Bay
Library
Green Bay, 54302

University of Wisconsin, Madison
Bureau of Business Research and
    Service
301 Commerce Building
Madison, 53702

University of Wisconsin, Madison
Center for Cognitive Learning
Publications
Madison, 53702

University of Wisconsin, Madison
College of Agriculture and Life
    Sciences
Madison, 53702

University of Wisconsin, Madison
Institute for Research on Poverty
3412 Social Science Building
Madison, 53706

University of Wisconsin, Madison
School of Education
Madison, 53706

University of Wisconsin, Madison
Sea Grant Institute
1225 West Dayton
Madison, 53706

University of Wisconsin, Madison
Social Systems Research Institute
1180 Observatory Drive
Madison, 53706

University of Wisconsin, Madison
Land Tenure Center
1525 Observatory Hall
Madison, 53706

University of Wisconsin, Milwaukee
Center for Advanced Studies in
    Human Services
P. O. Box 413
Milwaukee, 53201

WYOMING

Agricultural Experiment Station
University of Wyoming
Publications
Laramie, 82071

Department of Game and Fish
5400 Bishop Road
Cheyenne, 82002

Geological Survey
Box 3008
Laramie, 82071

TITLE INDEX

References are to entry number.

SUBJECT INDEX

References are to entry number.